BREAK-OUT

BREAK-OUT

Life Beyond the Corporation

Sara Williams

HAMISH HAMILTON · LONDON

HAMISH HAMILTON LTD

Published by the Penguin Group
Penguin Books Ltd, 27 Wrights Lane, London W8 5TZ, England
Penguin Books USA Inc., 375 Hudson Street, New York, New York 10014, USA
Penguin Books Australia Ltd, Ringwood, Victoria, Australia
Penguin Books Canada Ltd, 10 Alcorn Avenue, Toronto, Ontario, Canada M4V 3B2
Penguin Books (NZ) Ltd, 182–190 Wairau Road, Auckland 10, New Zealand

Penguin Books Ltd, Registered Offices: Harmondsworth, Middlesex, England

First published 1993
10 9 8 7 6 5 4 3 2 1

Copyright © Sara Williams, 1993
The moral right of the author has been asserted

Printed in England by Clays Ltd, St Ives plc

A CIP catalogue record for this book is available from the British Library
ISBN 0–241–12947–8

Contents

Preface

Some ten years ago, my husband Peter and I gave up careers within large organizations (Granada and Consumers' Association) to try our hands at creating our own businesses, first self-employment and subsequently founding a company backed by venture capital. We have been elated by our successes and wept at our near failure, thrilled by exciting prospects dancing tantalizingly on the horizon and disappointed when they have slipped away. We have cursed ourselves for choosing the wrong industry, market, product and congratulated ourselves for making the right choice! We have been humbled by the many people who have worked long hours and made personal and financial sacrifices to help the business flourish. And we have been exasperated by the failure of some to support us. But not once have we ever wished to return to working in a larger-company environment; not once have we cast a glance backwards.

An earlier book of mine, *Lloyds Bank Small Business Guide*, has sold remarkably well (300,000 copies in print) and has, I hope, helped many businesses. I have written this current book, *Break-Out: Life Beyond the Corporation*, to encourage managers and executives in their wish to run their own business, whether by management buy-outs, buy-ins or start-ups, with the backing of venture capital. Many, many entrepreneurs, coming from a large-company background, have contributed tips, advice and quite remarkable stories: they make fascinating reading for anyone interested in business. Some of them are friends, others I hope will become so, for there is always a high degree of support and interest towards others who have taken the same steps to independence and freedom.

I am exceedingly grateful to all those who have allowed themselves to be quoted and their stories to be told. Whether successful or not, my respect for them remains the same, because like the poppies in the field they have stood up tall and straight.

This book is very much a personal view, looking through eyes blinkered by the independent business owner's point of view. There are other books, by advisers, venture capitalists or non-executive directors, that are written from their own perspective, not mine, and I apologize in advance if in my views I have appeared to be unfair to them. As in any profession, there are those who are excellent and those who are not.

As well as those quoted in the book, many others have helped in the research. Several venture-capital organizations have contributed ideas. Foremost among them is 3i; through the pen of Elaine Williams, they have provided some case material. Various members of staff, but particularly Patrick Dunne and Matthew Kearney have encouraged and advised. Other help from the financial world has come from Martin Briggs of Welsh Development Agency, David Currie, Jeremy Dawson of Rothschild Ventures, Kathryn Dunn (formerly of NEDO Corporate Venturing), David Gregson (formerly of Globe Management), Gus Guest of Prudential Venture Managers, Catherine Lewis (formerly of CINVen), Chantal Ligertwood (formerly of APAX and Partners), Donald Patience (formerly of Scottish Development Agency), Laurie Rostrom of Alta Berkeley, Frank Thaxton of Thames Valley Partners, Chris Ward of Touche Ross, Peter Woodrow of Johnson Fry, and David Wyeth (formerly of Baronsmead). There are also other business people who spent time discussing their ideas, even though these may not have been attributed in the text. These include Alan Finden-Crofts, Nuala Hawthorne, Kevin Lomax and Geoff North.

Various organizations have been more than generous in allowing me to quote their statistics, data or survey findings. These include Arthur Andersen, Graham Bannock, British Venture Capital Association, Centre for Management Buy-Out Research, David Clutterbuck, Coopers & Lybrand, KPMG Peat Marwick, London Business School, Stoy Hayward, Touche Ross, Venture Economics and Warwick Business School.

On the production and marketing side, the book has benefited from the expertise of Karen Geary, Peter Phillips, and Keith Taylor. And, as always, my agent Brigid Avison has made a welcome input.

That the book has been written at all is a tribute to three people. First, Andrew Franklin at Hamish Hamilton has not uttered a word of reproach, despite the length of time it has taken to complete the manuscript. Second, the debt to my husband, Peter Williams, is obvious to all. And finally, Gail Croston (formerly of 3i) has persisted in enthusiastically providing ideas, discussing the structure, finding material, commenting on the text and coming up with lots of marketing initiatives: and all this despite so many false starts.

My thanks to all concerned.

I
MAKING THE BREAK

Money is a powerful motivator. It frees you to do what you want – and allows you to avoid what you dislike. You can make your own decisions, follow your own path, keep your own counsel. But take another's instructions? Money gives you the option to say no. In short, money gives you freedom.

In the eighties, many entrepreneurs found out how pleasant it is to have money – money they gained by buying or starting a company. But money is not the only, nor even the major, cause of satisfaction from building a business. Many have found that greater satisfaction has been derived in other ways.

Tim Hely Hutchinson has built up Headline Book Publishing from scratch, starting the company in 1986. He says: 'I like seeing the whole thing work. I like seeing a good array of my books when I pass through Bangkok Airport. I like making some unknown authors successful.'

Similar satisfaction is expressed by Peter Gibson, who founded Corin Medical, a manufacturer of artificial implants: 'I get an enormous kick coming to work and walking through reception. I love going to exhibitions and I love to see the name and the product – and Corin being shown at its very best.'

It's not just starting a business from scratch which can impart this intense personal satisfaction. Neill Bell bought out a company called Porth, which makes Christmas decorations. He describes how he feels about his achievements by saying: 'I've done it – me. I can see the results and know that I did it without interference or outside help. That is the most satisfying of all.'

And how admirable is the achievement of Brian Box, who at the age of fifty-eight, together with his wife Christine, sold his house to invest the proceeds in buying out Middle Aston House, a conference centre, from his previous employers. For him the most satisfying aspect is quite simple – freedom.

Is it possible to derive similar emotions and feelings about your role as an executive or manager in a large company, no matter how senior your position? Perhaps, for some, but by no means all. Those of you who can cope with the risks of going it alone, and who succeed, will be rewarded not just by money, but by the knowledge of personal achievement.

1

The Entrepreneur – Is It You?

Are you an entrepreneur? Or are you a manager? Entrepreneurs versus managers – the relationship between the two is like a pair of overlapping circles. Some managers will never be entrepreneurs; some entrepreneurs can never be managers. And some can be successful in either role. But how is this achieved? Are entrepreneurs born with particular skills and characteristics? If not, can these be acquired through a learning process?

Asked to name well-known entrepreneurs, most people would focus on folk-heroes (or former folk-heroes) such as Richard Branson, Anita Roddick, Sophie Mirman, Rupert Murdoch, Jim Slater or Freddie Laker. Folk-heroes such as these start their enterprises with a few hundred pounds and build them up to multi-million-pound empires – and, in some cases, lose it all some way down the track. Few of them, if any, had extensive management experience before they set out along the path of creating and building apparently successful businesses.

Over the past fifteen years, entrepreneurs have also emerged from a different background – from within the corporate field, acquiring extensive experience and operating at senior manager or executive level. They have been coming forward in increasing numbers to start or buy a business, with backing from venture capital. Their great strength is that if they have the pzazz needed to create the enterprise, they also have all the skills and abilities of their management experience to keep it afloat during the difficult first three years and beyond. They can provide the strategy needed in their entrepreneurial role to launch a business and plot the way forward, coupled with the tactical ability which their management experience provides. Strategy can't succeed without tactics.

The combination of entrepreneurial ability and managerial skill can prove immensely powerful. The traditional image of a start-up, for example, is that it will go through three phases. In the first phase, the entrepreneur will do almost every job going. In the second phase, the company grows and the entrepreneur employs other people to carry out some functions. And, in the third phase, the entrepreneur has to work through other people, two or more layers. Similarly, the information upwards is filtered through those same two or more layers. It would be an exceptional talent for any one person to be able to build the company through all three phases. More likely, the third phase would need to be carried out by someone else for the company to reach its full potential.

The entrepreneur with managerial skills does not set up a business as in the traditional first phase. Instead, he or she raises venture capital and, for example, buys a company, a business already past the first stage, one which can be transformed by application of management experience and talent, freed from the requirements of a parent company. Or the leader raises money to build a management team from the word 'go' to start a business. Because of their existing managerial and executive ability and experience, the team, with the entrepreneur as leader, can build up the business through phases two and three.

Entrepreneurs are simply people who behave in a certain way. Many managers can develop their latent entrepreneurial skills or even acquire some of them. But starting out with a certain character and set of abilities gives a greater likelihood of success.

Personality Traits

Entrepreneurs need style – a manner of doing and speaking which sets them apart. What kind of style is less important than its very existence. Style is important because it sets the tone for the whole organization. The personality and manner of the entrepreneur permeates the business in a far more comprehensive way than that of the chief executive of a larger company. The style of the entrepreneur sets the parameters for the corporate culture.

While the type of personality is not important, most entrepreneurs can usually convince others that they and their business can succeed against all the odds – sales ability on a grand scale. As successful entrepreneurs tend to speak with conviction, or even some passion, their selling ability is natural rather than acquired or trained. An entrepreneur who communicates with conviction will be far more successful than the average manager at motivating others and leading the business to success. Since success can usually only be achieved by the superhuman efforts of employees, as well as by the leader and the management team, inspirational ability is important for any entrepreneur.

Another characteristic which will differentiate a successful manager-turned-entrepreneur from a conventional manager is an unusual level of survival skills. No matter how tight the corner or how hemmed in with problems, the entrepreneur needs to be able to think of a way out of it. This occurs partly because of the ability to think originally and creatively and partly because such entrepreneurs won't give up or admit defeat. Until the very last moment, the entrepreneur will be searching for a solution and will 'never say die'. This attribute may emerge because the entrepreneur places little trust in the hand of fortune. If you consider you could be an entrepreneur, one character requirement is that you believe that the success or failure of your enterprise depends on your work and abilities. You know that with imagination and doggedness, a mountain can be moved by a teaspoon. Blaming other people or outside influences when events are in disarray will not give you that crucial edge.

Another entrepreneurial characteristic is the dislike of rigid or formal structures within an organization. An entrepreneurial business will be more flexible and employees who like building their own bureaucratic fortresses would find themselves uncomfortable in such an environment.

Entrepreneurs don't fear change and disruption; many employees do. Thus, an entrepreneur will also tend to choose like-minded people: people who can be trusted, who have also committed themselves to the business and who fit into the style created by the leader. Such people will be accommodated within the organization and jobs will be adapted to fit the individuals, rather than the other way round. Of course, this philosophy can only succeed in the early years of an organization. Once it has grown to a sufficient size, the emphasis will probably change to one of clearly defined responsibilities. People will be employed to fill that clear role. There will be less adaptation to the individual because the entrepreneur feels a sense of responsibility to that employee.

An entrepreneur needs to be brave – and daring. Entrepreneurs will face decisions in situations in which you feel as if you are stranded on the top of a high wall. You follow the maxim 'Look before you leap', but looking either side of the wall, you can see nothing. But you don't wait to be rescued. You jump. Bravery is also required to face the prospect of failure. Especially in our society, failure is sometimes regarded as a terrible blight – and you need self-courage to face this.

Nevertheless, while an entrepreneur is a risk-taker, this is not the same as being a gambler. It does mean that an entrepreneur will examine the proposition and calculate the odds of success and failure and will adopt those propositions with the strongest likelihood of success.

The most successful entrepreneurs will be those who show the right level of caution and look at how the risk can be minimized. With hindsight, it's obvious that some of those well-known entrepreneurs who went under in the recession between 1990 and 1993 failed to be cautious enough.

If you are brave and a risk-taker, this also implies that you won't automatically adopt the conventional, middle-of-the-road solutions to problems. As Aneurin Bevan said: 'We know what happens to people who stay in the middle of the road. They get run over.' Choosing the obvious route may mean being outmanoeuvred by the competition and other antagonists.

As you further develop your entrepreneurial talent, you will discover what many business founders have discovered before you: THERE ARE NO RULES. There are no conventions or accepted business 'rules' that you need to stick to when searching for the answer to a business question. Think of the off-the-wall solution to any problem rather than the obvious. Research it, assess it and follow it, if the odds look right. Once you've made your choice of route, plan it in meticulous detail - this way the risks are reduced even more and the odds swing further in your favour. While there are no business 'rules' or conventions which require adherence, there are laws and statutory regulations – and these are quite a different matter. And you will want to work out what your own code of conduct is – and this will become the code for your business, enshrined in the company culture.

Another characteristic which shines in many entrepreneurs is their liking for problem-solving. They carry this out by marshalling the best available resources and an array of skills which they focus on the particular problem. Frequently, the focus transforms a problem into a project; the impossible is transmogrified into the possible; the 'can't do' is converted to the 'can do'.

Considerable research has been carried out for 3i, the investment bankers, to examine what distinguishes a manager from an entrepreneur. The research was based on a test which could identify some entrepreneurs, but not all – because entrepreneurs are above all individuals who do not conform to a particular set pattern of behaviour or a particular character.

However, the research showed that an entrepreneur is 'passionate, personally identified with the company, trusting of people whose limitations he or she understands, loyal to members of the firm and demanding loyalty of them, intuitive more than rational in choosing people, liable to ignore formal reporting lines and fanatical about checking every detail of the product'. Managers don't have these qualities to such a high degree – or at all. By way of contrast, Abe Zaleznick of Harvard Business School identifies these characteristics for managers: group-orientated, pragmatic, logical, organized and preferring reason and persuasion to get results.

Entrepreneurs themselves have a clear idea of what differentiates them from the 'average Joe'. For example, Gerry Meredith Smith, who led the buy-out of Mohawk Computers in 1987, regards one of the key characteristics required by an entrepreneur as being: 'A good man manager who can motivate the team and make it fly.'

Malcolm Parkinson co-founded The Retail Corporation. He doubts whether all managers can become entrepreneurs: 'People who have lived on tramlines all their lives can't get off them. Ninety-nine per cent of people want to be led or restricted by some sort of box which limits their vision. People aren't born with entrepreneurial vision. It's absorbed at some stage in business. The strongest characteristic of entrepreneurs is probably ignorance, because entrepreneurs are so optimistic.' He clearly includes himself in this description, calling himself 'very much a half-full rather than half-empty person'.

Allen Jones, founder of A J's Family Restaurants, describes yet another quality required by entrepreneurs: 'I fully accept that anything that happens is my responsibility. I think that I am a persistent devil. When things go wrong, I generally go harder; I try not to be beaten and find another way to solve the problem. I have a mania for the smaller things (which irritates everybody else), such as when someone said that something would be done and it wasn't. And, for example, I make sure the pictures hang straight – if you get the small detail done, everything else will be OK.'

Tim Waterstone, who set up Waterstone's the bookshops, now in a joint venture with W. H. Smith, picks up on some other entrepreneurial characteristics, in describing himself: 'I do have two or three gifts. I have the gift of simplicity, of understanding how simple business is, a very simple strategic view. I can lift out the only things which really matter. You also need to have the gift of persuasion and leadership, to have courage and tenacity – and to have a slight contempt for money.'

2

Why Break Out – and How?

General manager, marketing director, vice-president – why should
people who have reached this level of decision-making within a large
or medium-sized corporation decide to jump ship, to abandon the
supertanker for a dinghy? And yet, the entrepreneurs who have helped
with this book (over thirty-five of them) had all risen to senior managerial or executive level before choosing to sever the corporate apron
strings and start or buy a business. For example, Malcolm Parkinson of
The Retail Corporation (garden centres) was a director of B & Q and
chief executive of Woolworth's; Allen Jones of A J's Family
Restaurants ran the Happy Eater chain; Peter Gibson of Corin Medical
was previously vice-president of Zimmer International; Peter Williams
of Vamp Health (a medical data management company) was a general
manager with Unilever and Granada; Roger McKechnie co-founded
Derwent Valley Foods ('Phileas Fogg' snacks), having previously
been general manager of a company in the food industry; Colin Guy
who bought into Agripac was responsible for the industrial packaging
group at Bowater; David Langston who started Blue Ridge had been
the vice-president of Riegel Textile in the USA; and Tim Hely
Hutchinson of Headline Book Publishing was the managing director of
Macdonald & Co. (Publishers).

Why Break Out?

Some of the entrepreneurs made the move because the opportunity was
thrust upon them. If the business you work for is to be closed down or
sold or your job is to disappear in a reorganization, your instant
response might be to seek another job as an executive or manager
within an established business. But an entrepreneurial reaction is to try
to buy the business yourself, buy another business or set up on your
own.

For example, Tina Tietjen and Maggie Tree (now managing director and chairman of Video Arts) were on the board when the other directors, who held 98 per cent of the shares, decided that the time had come to sell out. It was an automatic reaction on their part to stage a management buy-out.

Tony Leach wasn't trying to escape from the shackles of corporate life – he was quite happy with his position as marketing director of a new computer subsidiary of a medium-sized engineering company. He was forced to reconsider his future when the holding company was put into liquidation. The news of the insolvency was so sudden that staff had only half an hour's notice to leave the company's premises.

So in October 1981, he found himself out of a job. Tony says: 'I had made a lot of money for other people so I felt that I would like to make some for me. In future, if anyone was going to go bust, it would be me.' Tony also wanted a stable environment for his children. As an ex-employee of American multinationals like IBM and ITT, he knew that if he had gone back to working for a large computer organization, he would be moving around every two years. So Tony decided to start a business from scratch: Daton Systems, a software and systems house specializing in the government sector.

Paul Bates also faced a similar jolt when the US parent company announced that they were going either to close down or sell a business which Paul had set up for them only six months before. He had brought a loyal team with him from his previous employer and all would be faced with redundancy if the business closed. Rather than tell them his bad news, Paul set about buying the assets and establishing Straightset, a company selling garage and workshop equipment.

While Tina, Maggie, Tony and Paul responded to their imposed dilemmas by deciding that they could make it on their own, many managers-turned-entrepreneurs take the same positive steps without external jolts or threats.

For some managers or executives the turning point between climbing the corporate ladder further and striking out on their own pivots on a growing dissatisfaction with their careers. Robert Wright decided to leave British Airways because after flying for several years he still didn't have a command. Eventually, he realized that the hierarchy was such that he wouldn't get a command until the year 2017, which was ten years after his retirement date! (Robert happened to have been caught up during the period when the airlines had trained too many pilots and promotion was strictly by seniority.) To give himself time to think he took a year's sabbatical and studied for an MBA at Cranfield, identifying his potential business during that period. From this Connectair was born: a small airline business feeding passengers to the big boys.

The realization that he spent far too much time in airports and airplanes, some 60 per cent of his life, was one factor in Peter Gibson's decision to set up Corin Medical. And another factor was that although Peter had risen to be vice president in Zimmer International, owned by Bristol-Myers, he considered that his role as vice president didn't use his strengths. His appointment had coincided with a restructuring and the development of a centralist policy of marketing. Consequently, he was feeling mildly frustrated when the opportunity came up to cooperate with a leading orthopaedic surgeon and market some artificial implants.

Derwent Valley Foods was also born because of the founders' dissatisfaction with their business lifestyle. The idea germinated in a meeting at Easter 1981 between two friends: Roger McKechnie and Ray McGhee. Ray's job was based in Frankfurt with a lot of international travel and little time to enjoy watching his young family grow up. He wanted to return to the north of England. Equally, Roger was worried that his next promotion would take him away from his northern roots. He also felt that the recession in UK industry in the early eighties had demolished any sense of corporate responsibility for personnel, so senior executives could no longer be certain of job security. If he stayed where he was, he thought he might be on the scrap heap by the time he was fifty.

Undoubtedly, the shake-out in UK industry in the early eighties caused many managers to reassess the relative riskiness of staying within a large corporation or breaking out on their own. 'The higher you are, the more vulnerable you become. Politics come into it. You become a major threat to your boss. A large company is a political minefield, a battleground. You're spending 85 per cent of the time protecting your back and 15 per cent running the business.' This was Terry Weston's rather depressing assessment of his future within a large organization – and was one of the reasons why he decided to look for a company to buy, eventually carrying out a joint buy-in, with Bert Ramsden, of CEC-Time, a company which provided the specialized services of inspection engineering.

What else might prompt you to break out from your corporate mould and turn entrepreneur? Peter Williams of Vamp Health cites the desire for independence as a key factor in his decision and also sees the same riskiness in large companies since the early eighties as Roger McKechnie. 'I had set as my goal to be a main board director of a £500-million company this side of forty. But as I got closer to reaching it, I realized that perhaps my old plan wasn't so great. I was going to work my socks off, for what? To be given £100,000 and told to clear off at fifty?'

Les Hunt bought into Metalline with Glyn Davies in 1988. The company manufactures airfield lighting systems and electronics equipment for the aviation industry. He gives two main reasons for his decision to step outside the large corporate world. 'I think one of the reasons is that we both wanted to make a lot of money. I've noticed quite clearly how much cash I've been able to make for other people I work for and what little contribution they've made towards its accumulation. And it just seemed very sensible that if I could do it for them, I could probably do it for myself. The other equally important thing for me is the fact that it is yours and you make the decisions; if it's a bad decision you're stuck with it and if it's a good one you're stuck with it. I suppose you can have that working for a company, but it's never quite the same, it's a far more intense feeling. I think that just doing it for yourself turns on the gas and you get going through the peaks and troughs, which are far steeper.' How true.

Ed Hunter bought out Penman Engineering, manufacturer of safety cabs for construction equipment and specialist vehicle bodywork. His reasons were a mixture of business motives and a personal one, too: 'I had a strong desire to have an equity stake or accumulate capital because I could see that wandering through life working for A.N.Other, I would end up with a salary and a half-baked pension.'

Finally, it's probably true to say that managers-turned-entrepreneurs have several reasons for their final decision in breaking the corporate mould. In 1985 Stephen Hinton was employed by British Rail as the deputy works director at Doncaster, part of British Rail Engineering. It was planned to close the Doncaster site and Stephen, with three other colleagues, decided to try and stage a management buy-out of the 'Wagon Works' – which they achieved and turned into RFS Industries. In answer to the question why, he says: 'My job had gone; the career structure didn't look clever; I wasn't getting on too well with the directors of British Rail Engineering; I could see an opportunity; I could see I might make some money for myself.'

How to Break Out

How do you choose between starting a business, buying out the business you work for or buying into another business? Your choice hinges on four main factors:

– opportunity;

– risk;

– aptitude and personal circumstances;

– reward.

Some managers who want to turn entrepreneurs may suddenly find that an opportunity presents itself. It's there, it's available, you've researched it and it looks good. There's probably not a lot of mileage in starting to agonize about whether it's the perfect form of a business venture. For example, many of those completing management buy-outs (MBOs) have suddenly found that the opportunity was there, because the shareholders want to sell or because the holding company of the group goes into liquidation, say, and they have had to decide pretty quickly what their reaction is to be. Similarly, start-ups have arisen because time-specific opportunities have emerged and the managers have turned entrepreneurs to exploit them.

Where no particular opportunity is obviously present, it becomes a question of creating one. If this is the situation facing you, it could be worth spending some time considering whether a buy-out, buy-in or start-up is the most appropriate.

Despite the failures of some buy-outs occurring during 1989–92, this remains the least risky of the three forms, provided that the terms of the purchase and the financial structure are reasonably conservative. This level of risk is lower because the business, its infrastructure and the management team are in situ.

In the past, management buy-outs have provided very handsome rewards after a fairly short period of time for successful management teams. For example, nine directors at Premier Brands shared some £150 million, when it sold itself to Hillsdown Holdings in May 1989, three years after the buy-out from Cadbury Schweppes. And Istel, the computer services company, was bought out from Rover for £35 million, but sold to AT&T in 1989, two years later, for £180 million. In summary, the management buy-out has come top of the risk/reward league in the past.

Buy-ins have become popular more recently than buy-outs. Initially, they were considered to be close in the risk/return league to an MBO, but subsequent problems have shown that in this respect they resemble a start-up, rather than a buy-out. There are some serious dangers to watch out for. Assessing an organization and its infrastructure from the outside is complex and inherently risky. And introducing a totally new management team is a very delicate operation which can totally fail if misjudged. As management buy-ins (MBIs) were a relatively new phenomenon of the late 1980s, few have reached fruition, in terms of providing reward for the management team, so giving a guide to the sort of reward which might be possible is problematic.

There is also a mixed category, known as a BIMBO, that is buying in and buying out at the same time. In these cases, a leader from outside is added to the existing management team, which is thought to be sound, but not inspirational. Such an arrangement can mitigate the risk of a buy-in; the drawback is that you may not pick the right members of the team if you know little about them beforehand.

Finally, some believe that the riskiest form of venture is the start-up – although others would argue that this is not so. The real danger period is the first three years – and it is expected that start-ups take relatively longer than buy-outs to be established and so reach their full potential in terms of monetary reward for the entrepreneurs.

A further consideration is your own personal aptitude and circumstances. For example, start-ups require more mercurial ability than buy-outs, say. You need greater flexibility and fleetness of foot. And someone in the team needs to have the 'barrow-boy' instinct – the ability to add up the figures on the back of a fag packet and know whether it makes a profit or not. On the other hand, if you have these talents, you should find that start-ups will be more responsive to your decision-making, certainly in the early days. A management buy-in requires great all-round management experience, the ability to manage change and the wisdom to move towards a management objective at a measured pace. Finally, to succeed in a management buy-out, you would need a more professional, considered and organized management style which enables you to see the opportunity to pare the business without cutting into the quick.

There is also the question of time-scale. A few years ago it was thought that a start-up takes longer to reach its full potential than either a buy-in or a buy-out. This was certainly the reason that Terry Weston chose to buy into CEC-Time: 'It takes too long with a start-up to get credibility and hit the market; it can take five to ten years to get established, plus a further five years to expand it. I would be an old man. We see five years as the target for us.' However, more recently the sort of time-scale to achieve an exit from a buy-in is now considered to be much the same as a start-up. Patrick Dunne of 3i, which has financed more than 200 buy-ins, guesstimates that the average period from purchase to exit is around eight years.

The lack of an obvious choice of business to start up was mentioned by Les Hunt of Metalline as one of the reasons for a buy-in: 'I'm sure a lot of people sit at work and do a particular task and then think "God, I ought to be doing this for myself" and go out and set up a business doing exactly that. We weren't in that situation, so the best option seemed to be to look for something that was already up and running.'

In conclusion, go with the best opportunity regardless of whether it's a buy-out, start-up or buy-in. If the deal is done on the right terms, a buy-out potentially has the least risk and a relatively short time-scale.

Buy-ins and start-ups are riskier and have a longer time-scale to exit. Your final choice should take into account your own personal abilities and circumstances.

3

Second Thoughts

The large, established corporation and the smaller, entrepreneurial environment are chalk and cheese. Undoubtedly, some managers will find it too tough to operate at their optimum ability in a start-up, smaller buy-out or buy-in. The whole atmosphere is markedly different from a well-structured large company with its well-defined roles. This freer-form existence, with its loss of all creature comforts, may be too stark a contrast for some managers to make the successful leap into the role of entrepreneur or part of the management team.

Even if you raise substantial venture capital to start a business with a management team and an infrastructure, there will still be many detailed jobs to be carried out and no one else available but you. In a start-up, for example, the chief executive is also often the office boy. Buying into or buying out a company may superficially be closer to the operating style you are used to, but with both you need to make them more profitable and this means stripping away layers of bureaucracy. Hence, you will probably find yourself more likely to do your own photocopying, get your own tea, organize your own office, answer the telephone and so on. Another small difference you will find is that you can no longer meet colleagues or associates over lunch, which is normal business practice with big companies. With small companies, you have neither the time nor the money.

Malcolm Parkinson of The Retail Corporation expresses the difference between the two environments succinctly by saying: 'With a small company your security blanket is taken away – there is not a smart office, not a secretary bringing you coffee, not a big smart car. You've got to recognize that you're suddenly going to go back to being a skivvy.'

Running a small company can be incredibly frustrating. It is not always an intellectual exercise. As well as keeping to a long-term plan for growth, the management of it consists of carrying out a lot of boring, commonsense actions, consistently and well. You find that you have to check that the staff are doing what you want. You have to dot the i's and cross the t's. Of course, checking all the details should be carried out in large companies, just the same as small ones. But, somehow, it's less urgent, because the large company won't go bust in the short term if you don't dot and cross, whereas a small company might. And in a large company with well-defined responsibilities, there will be layers of managers and employees to carry out that detailed checking task for you. In a small company, ultimately it's your responsibility, because you care more than anyone else.

Ed Hunter of Penman Engineering pinpoints another difference: 'In a large group, you normally have financial and technical departments and decisions can be passed on to the specialists. You can't do this in a small company.' Even though you will be starting off with a management team, whether a buy-out, buy-in or start-up, nevertheless you no longer have the use of all the detailed specialist services – on many occasions, you have to become a jack or jill of all trades yourself, because using outside professional advice for every problem will be too expensive. So you will spend some part of your working time involved in work which you are not very good at and which you certainly don't enjoy.

Another substantive difference between larger companies and the smaller, entrepreneurial ones is the way that decisions are made and carried out. Decisions are considered and made at board level and they can be communicated much more quickly. As a result you can be much more effective. This is also Stephen Hinton's view: 'Your relations with people are much easier and it's easier to get the message across. The results of your actions have a bigger effect on the business as a whole.'

A final difference you would find outside the corporate mould is that the responsibility will be fairly and squarely in your hands – and the stress level can rocket. Stephen Hinton again: 'Everyone has entrepreneurial terror... the waking up at three o'clock in the morning and wondering if you've made the right decision. You do this when you're working for a big company, but it's at a trivial level, not the destiny-making level. It's "Are you going to get a bollocking from your boss? Are you going to get the promotion you want?" With a small company the question can often be "Are you going to survive?"'

The title of this chapter is 'Second thoughts' – and this is essential. You must think before you leap. You may find the prospect of turning entrepreneur exciting and potentially fulfilling, you may regard operating within a large company environment as bureaucratic and cumbersome, you may be convinced that you can cope with the extra work and stress and the changed working environment, but there are still some potential problems which you may not have assimilated in your assessment so far of the risks and returns.

Strain for the Family

The first potential hazard you should consider is the loss of status and how it will affect your family. Of course, if losing status bothers *you*, you shouldn't even be considering breaking out from your present comfortable existence. But how your family will react is another matter.

The support of your partner and family strengthens the prospects of your successfully raising sufficient finance and launching your business. You can use your family as a potential resource for solving problems and providing another pair of committed hands. However, you should also consider what effect your changing role will have on your family's lifestyle. While the loss of status is not as dramatic now as it was ten or fifteen years ago, because enterprise seems more socially acceptable, you may have to give up your big car, move to a smaller house and cut back on your living standards. Malcolm Parkinson of The Retail Corporation emphasizes that you must recognize how your plans will touch your family: 'Families often live in reflected glory. If you step out and do your own thing, you're getting fun out of it, but your family are getting little of that. Involve your partner as much as you can in what's going on. Try to use him or her as a sounding board, saying "This is what I've done today, what do you think?" You will be surprised how often an interested but uninvolved person's comments help to clarify the situation or enhance the decision.'

Relocating your home while buying into a business or starting one adds to the stresses and strains. Moving home is a major cause of stress on its own; it also tends to lead to more DIY in the house and greater personal financial commitments. While relocating you will be travelling greater distances between home and work. The conclusion must be to look to buy into a local business or start one near your existing home. If you are relocating, take the opportunity to lower your financial commitments and select a dwelling with low maintenance needs and low running costs.

Pressure on Personal Finance

A severe practical hurdle for you to overcome could be the lack of sufficient personal finance which you can provide. It can be daunting to work out how to raise the money, but one comfort may be that it is not necessarily the amount which you have to invest which is important. Instead, the venture capitalist may focus on the relative size of your financial commitment in terms of your own personal wealth. One obvious source of money for your equity stake, apart from savings or redundancy money, is a loan secured on your house. The interest on a loan raised to invest in a close company (which your venture may be) can be deducted from your income before working out your tax bill.

Typical amounts expected to be invested by you and the rest of the management team would be in the £30,000 to £100,000 range. The venture capitalist will be able to structure the deal so that you will end up with a greater share of the equity than your investment would justify, when compared to the venture capitalist's investment.

However, you must examine other financial considerations before you decide to raise a loan on your house. You're probably unlikely to be able to carry on with the same salary level as in your existing job, although you may be able to justify it. Certainly, always negotiate with your potential investors. Thus you have two possible squeezes on your lifestyle – less salary and more interest to pay. You must involve your family in a close examination of your finances and how you can withstand the cold draught of cutting back your lifestyle now for what you hope will be a sizeable capital gain in the future.

Another problem which you should pay some attention to is what effect breaking out from your corporate role will have on your pension. Few small companies, funded well by venture capital or not, have the resources to put in pension schemes – and certainly not with the sort of provisions which the schemes of some large companies can provide. You should take professional advice on pensions.

While not falling within the grouping of problems, you may want to consider whether it would be beneficial for you to take personal tax advice, for example, to help you mitigate the effects of tax on a future capital gain. It may be that a tax consultant could come up with some tax-efficient scheme for you. Of course, when you're struggling to pull together funds to provide your share of the equity for your venture, it's difficult to justify spending a couple of thousand or so trying to protect some gain which may, or may not, occur.

Facing the Prospect of Failure

It also makes sense for you to examine the scenario of failure. Produce a plan for what will be the outcome if your business venture fails, because you should never forget that for some, IT FAILS. How would you survive financially? And would you be able to come to terms with failure itself? In the United States, attitudes to failure are far more robust – they are often regarded as learning experiences from which you can draw the appropriate lessons. The UK is less open-hearted, and in some social circles failure still has a stigma attached to it.

The research for this book has been carried out over a three-to-four-year period, spanning the recession in 1990-93. A few of the entrepreneurs who have contributed to this book have foundered during that period, along with many other ventures. Raising adequate finance to fund a venture is no guarantee of survival.

Dealing with Your Present Employer

There is one potential problem area, which if not approached sensibly can result in your plans being scuppered at the first step. Your dealings with your present employer, and how your plans fit in with your contract of employment, are crucial. One obvious, and feared, source of conflict is your employer's reaction if you voice the idea of a management buy-out.

You may be forced out. John Cavill of Logical Networks (see Chapter 15) tried to buy the division of the company he worked for. At first, it seemed as if the buy-out would occur. But, eventually his employer had a change of heart and ultimately John was forced out. However, he didn't shed many tears – and this reversal simply gave him the impetus to start his own business.

It is not only trying to buy out your employer which causes controversy. Colin Guy, formerly of Bowater, completed a management buy-in of a business called Agripac. He found out the hard way that an employment contract with existing employers can handicap potential ventures. He was accused of breaching his fiduciary duty to his employer, although he maintains that he did not do so. Their management buy-in was finalized, but only after some protracted negotiations which cost the business a lot of money. At the end of this chapter, you can read the full story of what went wrong and what were the consequences.

Problems can also occur if you plan to start up a business which would be in competition with your existing employer. Some employers react with equanimity. For example, Tim Hely Hutchinson found a sympathetic response from Robert Maxwell, when he told him he wanted to leave Macdonalds, the publishers, to start a new publishing house. But many other employers could, in this situation, seek to prevent you establishing yourself successfully. One way to do this is to allege a breach of its intellectual property rights, confidential information or trade secrets. To seek information to support its case in the court, it can apply for an Anton Piller Order. This would give your former employer's representatives the right to enter your premises (including the directors' homes) to examine your records and search for documents and other items which you might have taken or copied from your employment.

Such an order can be very damaging to your business prospects and effectively halt the business in its tracks. Such bully-boy tactics were used on Andrew Lock, managing director of Safeline. Lawyers, acting for his previous employer and showing a court order, arrived to search his house at dawn on a cold winter day. Not only was Andrew's house searched, but the houses of two fellow colleagues and the business premises. While Andrew happily has been able to establish their innocence of the accusations, they have only been able to recover part of their costs and have not received any damages as yet for the unfounded accusation. Furthermore, the action delayed the development of their new business and consumed a great deal of management time.

The obvious precautions to take are to be aware of its possibility, to take it very seriously and to try not to allow yourself to fall into any potential trap. Seeking legal advice or advice from your venture capital backers at a very early stage is compulsory if you are to have any chance of fighting it successfully.

Finally, the *Financial Times* reported a case where a company bought out another imposing restrictions on competition by the selling shareholders. One of those shareholders was no longer an employee but had acquired his shares as part of his original remuneration package. He intended to start up a business in competition to the purchaser. But the purchasing company successfully argued that the non-competition clause applied to all shareholders, not just employees.

In conclusion, leaving your existing employment to found or buy a business poses numerous problems as well as advantages. These range through the emotional issues of loss of status and detrimental effect on the family, personal financial issues and issues of duty to your existing employer. All these problems need to be considered carefully and a plan to mitigate their effect needs to be carried out.

In the case of problems with your employer, ask yourself always whether you are taking the high moral and legal ground in your dealings with your boss. Be on the look-out for conflicting duties and take early legal advice. Employees have real and binding commitments to their employers. These obligations are important.

Colin Guy and the Purchase of Agripac

In December 1988, Colin Guy and two colleagues completed the negotiations to buy a company called Agripac, a manufacturer of woven fabric and flexible intermediate bulk containers (enormous plastic bags for holding materials like fertilizers). Colin's previous career was with Bowater, where he was responsible for the industrial packaging group, which comprised three businesses in the UK and one in the USA. However, in many ways a lot of the fun had gone out of the work. 'Instead of being able directly to develop the business which I was good at and got my charge out of, I spent my life manipulating people. I was being promoted but I felt more restricted,' Colin explained. The crunch time came for Colin in August 1988 when the Bowater management asked him to build up the packaging business in the USA. 'Quite frankly I don't want to live in the US. I spent a week a month in the US in 1988. I like Americans as individuals but I can't say I like their way of life.'

Colin realized that the time had come to leave Bowater, but he decided: 'If I am going to leave Bowater, I want to do something on my own.' The opportunity came sooner than he thought when Bowater was offered, but turned down, the chance to buy a competitor in the flexible intermediate bulk container business called Agripac (at that time a loss-maker). It was at this point that Colin felt he was free to make an offer for Agripac himself. He asked two of his staff at Bowater, a technical manager and production manager, to join him in the venture. With this team, Colin felt he could turn Agripac round. Financing was arranged with 3i, a sale and purchase contract prepared and agreed and due diligence on the company carried out by KPMG Peat Marwick .

On 23 December 1988, the papers were signed in the lawyers' office. At one point in the proceedings, there was a break so that the three Bowater men could fax their resignations. This done, the deal was completed.

Early in January, Colin was requested to be at the Bowater headquarters in London the following day. There he was greeted by the Bowater lawyers who told Colin that he had been acting in breach of his fiduciary duties in buying Agripac. 'They told me that I was not acting on my own behalf but on Bowater's and they wanted me to sign my shareholding over to Bowater.'

This was something of a bombshell. Legal opinion prior to the conclusion of the buy-in was that the fiduciary duty question was unlikely to be a major problem. A few days later, Colin and his colleagues received a letter of suspension and a letter outlining the legal case against them. Colin consulted with his lawyers who thought that Bowater did not have much of a case. Counsel was taken and the advice given was that if he chose to contest this accusation, there was a good chance that he would succeed. However, the threat of the court action, the delay and the cost, meant that he could not fight but had to negotiate a settlement with his former employer. But Colin admits: 'If I had been Bowater, I would have acted in exactly the same way.'

Bowater's view was that Colin had been instrumental in forming the decision not to purchase Agripac as a going concern. The company believes that it should have been informed of his intention and that he was not permitted to use his fiduciary position to acquire a secret investment opportunity, particularly since Agripac was a competitor which would be run by senior Bowater employees with an intimate knowledge of Bowater's view. This opinion was supported by their lawyers and counsel.

After three or four meetings with Bowater, where each side tried to barter, an agreement was finally made on 28 March. The equity base was enlarged and Bowater settled for a 15 per cent stake in the company. The 3i shareholding was diluted to 34 per cent from the previously agreed 40 per cent and the three colleagues ended up holding 51 per cent (against the planned 60 per cent).

But there were other conditions – Bowater could call on the advice of the team for one year and Agripac was subject to certain constraints in dealing with established Bowater customers. In addition, Bowater is entitled to a place on the Agripac board. Clearly, the emotional wrangling that went on unsettled the three colleagues and, in the short term, altered their view of the deal. Nevertheless, they still look to have made a good purchase, having acquired 51 per cent of the shares while putting up only one-sixth of the purchase price.

You can read more about the story of Agripac in Chapter 17, 'Unlocking the Cupboard'.

4

The Right Time, the Right Place

In the sixties, there was great anxiety about the numbers and importance of small businesses in the economy. The Bolton report, published in 1971, found that the numbers of small businesses and their share of output and employment in Britain had declined up to the middle 1960s. What the statistics now show was that the decline was reversed in the mid sixties. From that point, there has been a rise, albeit fluctuating, in the number of people becoming self-employed and forming new companies. This period of increase culminated in the eighties – the decade when making a million was never easier, the decade of the so-called enterprise culture. Starting or buying a business became a macho sign. Will these changes in enterprise continue through the nineties? The decade began with appalling economic news, as also occurred at the start of the eighties: a high number of insolvencies, very tight cash conditions, major redundancies. But the statistics for 1991 and 1992 show that the number of new businesses incorporated had still increased, although not by as much as during the eighties boom.

Will the rest of this century see more entrepreneurial activity? And how do you pick the right moment in an economic cycle? Is it better to launch an enterprise in a depression or a boom?

The Changing Entrepreneurial Climate

The evidence of an increase in enterprise since the mid sixties ranges from personal and anecdotal observations to economic statistics. Undoubtedly, it became more socially acceptable to leave the protective fold of the large established company and develop your own entrepreneurial skills. Most of you reading this book will know one or more friends or colleagues who have done just that. This would not apply to readers of a book like this published ten or fifteen years ago.

Another piece of evidence is that from 1975 onwards, for the next twelve years, there was an increase in the number of business books and business magazines aimed at those becoming self-employed. And business schools, universities and colleges also rushed to incorporate courses in entrepreneurship and small-business management.

Another sign of the increase in activity in the formation of businesses was the burgeoning competition among the clearing banks, who vied with each other to offer more elaborate services for their customers, including specialist small business centres, small business advisers and the application of less stringent conditions for loans and overdrafts. Some of the banks have since retrenched from this competitive activity as a response to their losses in the small business sector.

The government too played a part in increasing awareness of the opportunities, first by offering advice services and consultancy and second by devising some financial schemes, such as the Business Expansion scheme (winding up in 1993), the Enterprise Allowance scheme (now administered by the Training and Enterprise Councils) and the Loan Guarantee scheme.

So much for supplementary evidence – what about hard facts? Since 1979, the number of new businesses has grown significantly. From 10 per cent of the male and 5 per cent of the female workforce, the proportions rose until 16 per cent of men and 7½ per cent of women were self-employed in 1990 (in total, 3.3 million). However, the numbers have fallen slightly in 1991 and 1992, to just under 3 million. During the eleven years to 1991, a total of 356,000 additional businesses registered for VAT.

From any budding entrepreneur's point of view, the most encouraging statistic of the past is the increase in the availability and types of finance. In particular, the decade saw a phenomenal growth in

Table 1: Fund Management Groups, Members of BVCA, 1983–92

1983	1986	1988	1990	1992
35	77	107	121	114

Source: British Venture Capital Association.

the venture capital industry: in 1979, there were around twenty companies supplying venture capital; by 1983, when the British Venture Capital Association was formed, it had thirty-five full members; by 1990 the number had rocketed to 121, falling slightly to 114 members by September 1992 (see Table 1 on previous page). The bulk of the venture capital on offer consists of funds from institutions, such as pension funds, either providing funds direct or investing in funds run by independent venture-capital organizations, which in turn invest in start-ups, management buy-outs and management buy-ins.

In the last eight years, the venture-capital organizations have provided an impressive amount of money to invest in a healthy number of deals (Table 2 below). The inescapable conclusion is that the amount of venture capital available and the number of companies funded both increased significantly to a peak in the late eighties, but fell back in the early nineties.

Towards the end of the eighties, venture-capital organizations were showing more international awareness: some US groups had established themselves in the UK or were investing in UK companies and

Table 2: Venture-capital Investments (UK), 1984–91

	Number of companies	Total amount (£million)	Average investment (£000)
1984	350*	139*	397
1985	517*	278*	538
1986	600*	384*	640
1987	1,174	934	796
1988	1,326	1,298	979
1989	1,302	1,420	1,091
1990	1,221	1,106	906
1991	1,196	989	827
* Did not include 3i.			

Source: British Venture Capital Association.

some of the UK venture-capital organizations were extending their interest to Europe. A survey of venture-capital organizations showed that more emphasis is likely to be placed on Europe. This, coupled with an expected reduction in the number of organizations, suggests a reduced future availability of venture capital in the UK both in terms of the number of deals and the average size of the investment, although not returning to the levels experienced at the start of the eighties.

As well as dramatic improvements in the availability of venture capital, there has also been much innovation in the type and form of capital. Mezzanine finance, placed between loan and equity in the risk/return spectrum, was not especially common at the start of the decade, but by the end most entrepreneurs and would-be entrepreneurs had heard of this strange structure. This was largely due to the development of management buy-outs, as mezzanine finance is an integral part of most large packages.

So what is the forecast for enterprise in the rest of the nineties and beyond? It's obviously impossible to give an accurate prediction. There may be less venture capital available than at the end of the eighties, but intuitively one feels that there are likely to be as many, if not more, opportunities for entrepreneurs in the turbulence of the nineties. Changes in socio-political systems, technological advances, rapid expansion of information technology, inability of the corporate dinosaurs to adjust speedily and their subsequent break-up into smaller units, swings in consumer expectations, changes in employee attitudes – these are all sources of tumult. And where there is tumult, there are openings for the adventurous.

Changing Opportunities

In any period, there are changing opportunities; industry, the economy and politics never stand still. The constant shuffling and adjustment are bound to throw up new opportunities all the time. For entrepreneurs in the eighties, one of the important changes was that large companies and organizations developed a far more relaxed attitude to contracting out some of their activities to smaller concerns. The sixties and seventies had been periods when large organizations wanted to supply their own services in-house. The change in emphasis allowed many new businesses to flourish with large organizations as their customers.

During a recession a different adjustment occurs: large companies retreat to core businesses. This may mean opportunities arise for buying out or buying into businesses which larger companies wish to shed. And where businesses have gone into liquidation, many of the subsidiaries, healthy if underinvested, may be the subject of buy-ins and buy-outs. There is also a surfeit of restructuring and redundancies during a recession – implying opportunity and availability.

Another change which emerged during the eighties was the privatization of many government or local government activities. Once again this threw up possibilities waiting to be seized by managers with entrepreneurial vision.

Better to Break Out in a Boom or a Recession?

The nineties started in much the same way as the previous decade – rising numbers of redundancies, insolvencies and bankruptcies. But if you had started a business in 1980/81, and survived that recession, many of you would have been sitting pretty by 1989. Of course, who can tell what will happen over the next few years? The inference to be drawn is that recessions in themselves do not necessarily doom the launch of a successful growth business.

Different opportunities will emerge because there is a recession. Some businesses are recession-proof; other businesses are counter-cyclical and flourish most in a recession. Still other businesses will be much more successful in an expanding economy than a declining one, but can be planned and established during a recession to be able to take maximum advantage of the upturn when it comes. You may also find an industry in which existing potential competitors will be so weakened by the efforts of staying afloat in a recession that a fresh new venture with strong management and adequate funding can become a major player.

Management buy-ins, in particular, can flourish in a recession. A determining factor in the success of an MBI is the price paid – the realization expectations of vendors plummet in a recession, enabling

MBI teams to snap up targets at more realistic prices. There can be golden opportunities for buy-outs, too, to pick up a plum from the receiver if a holding company goes into liquidation or a parent company is selling a business because it is strapped for cash. Finally, as the economic cycle picks up, the advantages for start-ups emerge: weak competitors, low cost structure but increasing demand.

The Right Place?

The location of your business hinges on many factors. Your personal preferences, the geographical spread of your intended business, and the availability of skilled labour are just a few of the considerations you need to assess before making your decision. But a financial consideration can be very important. Some businesses have been partially funded at the outset by taking maximum advantage of the availability of government grants. Quite a range exists – regional development grants, urban development grants and so on.

Roger McKechnie of Derwent Valley Foods explains how he found the money to start the firm. 'It took us six months to raise the money. We had no real equity ourselves. We needed half a million in capital but could raise only £50,000 between us.' No one organization was prepared to fund the lot. 3i provided the venture capital and Barclays Bank came in as a traditional clearing bank with a business start-up loan. Despite this there was still a funding gap. Luckily, the government provided a regional selective assistance grant of £108,000. Roger believes that the grant from the Department of Trade and Industry (DTI) would not have been forthcoming had they not set up in Consett, which had suffered the devastating closure of the steel mill. More funds and advice were also forthcoming from the major employer in the area, British Steel, which was desperate to replace some 4,000 jobs. Conveniently, Consett was also only ten miles from where the four founders all lived.

'If we hadn't been in the North East, we wouldn't have had a cat in hell's chance. It was difficult convincing them that we weren't con men,' recalls McKechnie – the recent fiasco of the DeLorean affair in Northern Ireland had made many financiers and government officials nervous. 'After all, we were selling them this idea. We had got this great idea of making snacks for adults,' said Roger, but that was all.

With a total of around £150,000 of 'up-front' money, as McKechnie puts it, the bank was reassured and came in with its contribution. So the final funding package was rather a mixed bag which included a £30,000 British Steel loan, £150,000 of public sector grants, £85,000 from the bank plus the 25 per cent equity stake from 3i and the founders' own investment.

The four founders had approached Derwentside Industrial Development Agency for help in raising the money and this provided high-level contacts. For example, at the DTI the four founders spoke to the case leader who dealt with really large company start-ups, including the Nissan factory in the north-east. With this contact, the four learnt how to get the most out of government grants.

After six months, when the four felt they had been going round in circles most of the time, the final stage was a letter from the government agreeing its grant. The letter arrived three days before Christmas and the team had only three weeks to accept it.

5

The Team

It's an old, old cliché: the four ingredients for a successful business are management, management, management and a good market. But cliché or not, the assertion remains a valid one. If you need to raise venture capital to start or buy a business, above all else the venture capitalist will focus on the perceived strength or weakness of yourself and the rest of the management team. The composition and cohesiveness of the team and the abilities of the individual members will be scrutinized. This policy is pursued because past experience has shown that it is the management team above all else which holds the key to successful business creation. A skilled management team with commitment, motivation and enthusiasm which is working towards a common goal can build a highly profitable business in a mediocre market. Equally, it can take a company which looks like it's going nowhere in particular (one of the 'living dead') and transform it into a growing, buzzing business.

If you are unable to summon a complete team, or any part of it, before the funding, you will still be able to progress your plan for starting or buying a business if you meet the criteria of the financiers and make clear to them that you understand the gaps which need filling. In the case of management buy-ins, it is the quality of the individual manager, above all else, which is the major factor determining success or failure. The support of other managers before the buy-in is generally irrelevant to its success. Being a lone manager is not a disadvantage.

With a start-up or buy-out, an individual may be able to get a venture off the ground, but will need to work hard to convince the venture capitalist that he or she can build the right team. Venture capitalists will use the following phrases to describe management teams that they are going to back: 'Management is strong', 'Management is sound', 'Management impresses' and so on. So how do you build a management team which will receive the venture capitalists' stamp of approval and improve your chance of succeeding? There are particular constituents which a team requires: a mix of skills, personalities and abilities plus the required resolve and tenacity to work together and catapult a start-up to the established stage – or the living dead to the fast-growth track.

Selecting the team members and sorting out their roles and share-holdings are the fundamental steps in moving from wishful thinking to cutting your corporate apron strings. It's difficult to emphasize how crucial this is to the likely future success or failure of a management buy-out and start-up. Almost all entrepreneurs will find that one or more of the team does not make the transition from manager; the breakdown of the management team can also be the precursor to disaster. It's very difficult to be building or turning around a company if one of the team is not pulling his or her weight or if there are disagreements about strategy or roles.

A Clear Leader

Every team needs a focal point – an entrepreneur with style in whom the rest of the team have tremendous faith. For example, Peter Gibson of Corin Medical is such a leader. He says: 'Privately, I'm amazed at how much confidence other people seem to have in me; it's more blind faith. If they could see the real me!'

Without an obvious leader, management will be by committee – and likely to be indecisive, long-winded and over-cautious. An entrepre-neurial company needs an involved management with clear vision which is prepared to take calculated risks. To be successful in the sort of ventures you are considering, you have to be daring. A leaderless team may be unable to respond in this way. Instead, the team may be full of independent forceful individuals each wanting their opinions to hold sway. Failure to focus around one individual with leadership qualities may lead to bickering and disintegration.

The leader will take the lion's share of responsibility for the success or failure of the enterprise. Often, the team and the employees want a leader who will take the ultimate responsibility.

How does the leader emerge? Usually, it will be obvious that one individual can generate greater confidence among the rest of the team and so the choice will be a natural one. Derrick Bumpsteed bought out part of STC in 1986; this became Exacta, a manufacturer of printed circuit boards for electronic equipment. He had been with that part of STC for only one month, but nevertheless emerged as the leader. 'I'd been brought up here as the general manager to run the place. I think they had thought about a buy-out in the past; it had gone through some people's minds, but it had never really come to anything – but I pushed it. Without being modest, I would be the natural leader to do it.' Derrick considered this to be due both to his position and his personality. 'It has to be a bit of both. Obviously, if you're the general manager and you want to do this, you automatically take the lead, but they came round and said yes we'll do it and we'll go with you. It has to be a part of the personality, I suppose.' Seniority is definitely not the crucial factor.

The Alter Ego

Some leaders find they operate more effectively if there is another person, a sort of partner, with complementary skills. The Retail Corporation was started by Malcolm Parkinson and John Kennedy, who were two of the six original managers of B&Q, subsequently sold to Woolworth's. Malcolm explains: 'No one person is going to have all the facets to create a big business. One person can create a small one. I'm very much the marketing and leadership element – the persuasive character. My partner is the plumber. Without him, I couldn't succeed; without me, he couldn't.'

The need for an alter ego, a partner with complementary skills, is particularly strong for start-ups. Peter Williams started Vamp Health in 1984, raising venture capital at the start of 1985. The management team was cohesive but missing a strong financial element. One of the first tasks after raising capital was to employ a financial controller, with the idea that the appointee might progress to become financial director. Unfortunately, this did not occur and eventually he left. Finally, James Loch joined as financial director. James contributed

more than strong financial experience; he also provided the organiza-
tional skills to complement Peter's marketing ability and strategic
thinking. James had extensive management experience, having previously worked as financial director for multinational companies, as well
as smaller ones. He says: 'Typically, you find a nucleus of young and
very committed people, inspired by the entrepreneurial leader, but
under tremendous stress, fighting in the trenches. I had the advantage
of being able to introduce change swiftly, because experience brings
the ability to see the battle plan very quickly, to guide the troops
tactically and most importantly to turn the hand to anything and
everything that needs doing that no one else can do. With Vamp
Health, it was the operational and control functions of the business
which needed strengthening.'

Another interesting example of two people complementing each
other's skills and working well together as a partnership is Glyn
Davies and Les Hunt, who bought into Metalline Holdings. Les is
Glyn's son-in-law of eighteen years – so superficially this partnership
as a business relationship might ring alarm bells. However, he says:
'We know each other quite well and whilst we've never worked
together before the buy-in, we've obviously taken an interest in what
each other was doing. And I think that we've always thought that our
skills complemented each other. Glyn has a great deal of experience in
running companies as chief executive and my expertise lies in sales
and marketing so the two elements work well together.'

A Lone Manager

So far this chapter has mainly looked at the individual who is the
leader and who builds a team. With management buy-ins, the scenario
may be very different. The success or failure is heavily dependent on
the individual manager. The most successful are those who are
experienced, have already been outstandingly successful in their
careers, have taken over a company before and have been used to
managing change. Other characteristics displayed by the most
successful managers include being financially prudent, having good
negotiating skills and being adept at strict cost control.

A brilliant curriculum vitae, in terms of school, university or social status, is not relevant to the likely future success of the manager – nor is age or existing wealth. Far more crucial is previous experience in management. A survey by the Centre for Management Buy-out Research into buy-ins found that the buy-in manager is indeed likely to have had extensive general management experience, obtained principally in a large company.

The Right Mix for the Team

If you are a leader who is looking to stage a buy-out or effect a start-up, there are four important points to bear in mind while team building:

– balanced skills;

– strong financial presence;

– relevant experience;

– common value system.

First, you need *a balanced team* covering the major skills which would be needed in your type of business. Tony Davies has experience of start-ups. The first business he was associated with was formed when a group of engineers from a research laboratory with the Plessey group split off to form a company. They made the classic mistake that all the partners had the same disciplines, so although strong in engineering skills, they lacked financial, sales and management know-how. This was a mistake which Tony didn't repeat, although he encountered other difficulties with building a management team (see page 41).

The team you should assemble needs to cover skills in sales and marketing, finance, technical know-how, general management and organization. But this leads on to the second point: *strong financial expertise* is very important. Not only is this needed when it comes to planning the business and raising the venture capital, but after the business is afloat the crucial task of cash management and detailed budgeting and financial reporting needs to be in a very safe pair of hands. If you are unable to include an accountant in your team at the outset, it must be set out as a priority after raising your venture capital. The survey by CMBOR into buy-ins certainly confirmed this. Virtually a third of buy-in chief executives recognized that there was a gap in the financial expertise and skills of the original team. And the case study at the end of this chapter shows the problems which one start-up faced because the team didn't include a strong financial presence from the outset.

The third important point about your management team is that it is more likely to be successful if the team has *experience in the industry* you're entering. For example, Malcolm Parkinson and John Kennedy had gained all the experience they needed to start The Retail Corporation from their activities at B&Q. And Brian Gilda, who started his company Peoples by buying a Ford dealership, has sold cars in North America, as well as running a couple of garages over here.

Tim Waterstone's view is that: 'Investors look for relevant and direct experience in the entrepreneur, rather than experience of loose relevance and a general nature. Funds for a fish-farm venture may be available to a trained fish-farmer, who now wants to build his own business, but very difficult to secure for a marketing director who has spent a lifetime marketing paint, say.'

Finally, the team needs to be cohesive and to share *a common value system*. Around this value system, you will build the company culture – its style, beliefs and manner of conduct. Generally, such cohesiveness is more likely to occur where the members of the team know each other well and, in particular, already have experience of working with each other. They may have already built up the mutual trust and respect which is necessary for the team to function as a whole. A team which has divisions or doubts about any of its members will struggle to make the leap from managers to the more entrepreneurial exercise of starting or buying a company.

The team must lead the company and its employees. In-fighting or conflict will negate the effectiveness of the team in this objective. A survey by David Clutterbuck of teams that successfully negotiated buy-outs found that they rated their leadership qualities as far more important than their entrepreneurial qualities in the success of the buy-out (see list of recommended books).

Many entrepreneurs find the most straightforward and successful way of building the team is to join up with current or former colleagues. For example, Tim Hely Hutchinson of Headline Book Publishing had been managing director of Macdonalds (Publishing). When he started Headline he did so with two colleagues from there: Sue Fletcher, the publishing director, and Sian Thomas, the head of sales and publicity.

Another successful example of colleagues joining together is A J's Family Restaurants, where the team which had previously run Happy Eater set up a new chain of restaurants. Allen Jones says: 'We were a management team that was known and had a past record. The institutions took the view that it was less risk.'

The alternative to bringing a team of colleagues that have worked together is to build one from scratch and this is a much more difficult proposition. When Tony Davies left his first venture (the group of engineers mentioned on page 39 above) he decided to set up on his own and assemble a well-balanced team combining all the necessary skills. However, he failed to realize that while you can recruit people to form a team, you can't make them work as a team. That mysterious component of personal chemistry can make all the difference. Assembling a team from a group of people you know well means you have a fair idea of their abilities, likes, dislikes and idiosyncrasies. He says that anyone setting up a business would be totally 'imprudent to presume that you'll have the same team after two years. You have to rework the team.'

One management buy-in team found out the hard way that it is important to know each other well before teaming up to buy into a company. Terry Weston and Bert Ramsden were both looking to buy into a company and both investigating CEC-Time as their target. Rather than compete against each other they decided to team up, as they had complementary skills. However, gradually over two years they realized that it just wasn't going to work as a team and finally Terry Weston left the company. He has subsequently bought another company and his team includes his son and his wife.

One phenomenon you have to watch out for with a start-up, buy-out or buy-in is the 'hangers-on' syndrome. Starting or buying a business is very exciting and, before you know what is happening, you can find quite a number of people who are keen to join the team with the hope of making a lot of money. Above all else, look carefully at the required skills; consider the composition and unity of the team and if you have any doubts about a potential team member, take tough decisions before you start on your venture. It's better to fall out in the planning stage than after you've set up or bought the business. The consequences of falling out later on can be far more serious.

Inheriting a Team

A dilemma you face if you are attempting a management buy-out is whether to retain the existing team in its entirety or to be very selective and plan to fill the gaps once the buy-out is successful. Part of the dilemma stems from the uncertainty of the venture capitalists' reaction. For example, Ed Hunter of Penman Engineering says: 'With a management buy-out, you're stuck with the team you've got when the opportunity arises. The team wasn't perfect and not the one we wanted. But we thought that if we tinkered with the team, it would worry the banks and financial institutions. Instead, we got through the first year and then put in the team for the next ten years.'

Neill Bell of the Porth Group expresses similar worries. He held the theory that in order to appeal to the institutions he needed to keep the same people, but realizes with hindsight that he could have got away with introducing someone else into the team. 'When you are doing a management buy-out, perhaps what you don't do is think "What is it going to be like eighteen months ahead?" "Are these people going to grow with us?"'

Picking the best management team is an intuitive task, but one which must be faced up to before you go ahead with the buy-out. Essentially, the leader will have to come to some conclusion about the abilities and personalities of those members of the management who want to form part of the team. Some will be unwanted members – it's a hard task to face, telling a colleague that he or she is not good enough to be part of the buy-out team. But if you can't face this difficult task now, your chances of making the buy-out fly are remote.

There is also the problem that the venture capitalists will instantly probe the weak areas of the team – you should carry out that tough analysis first, otherwise the institutions may not believe in you and back you. Apart from the opinion of the venture capitalists, firm action at the outset can bring greater dynamism to the business, as Stephen Riley recommends as a result of the buy-out of Denby Pottery. You can read more about this buy-out in Chapter 13, 'Finance for a Buy-out'.

Your Family as Part of the Team

Quite a few entrepreneurs who start a business from scratch, whether raising substantial venture capital or not, involve one or more members of their family as part of the team. Siblings and spouses are the commonest. Peter Gibson of Corin Medical includes his wife as part of the team: 'My wife works for the company and acts as a sweeper, in the football sense.' And spouses were involved in the founding of Connectair (see Chapter 16) and Middle Aston House (Chapter 18).

I was one of the co-founders of Vamp Health with my husband Peter Williams. In the early years, I took time out from my own business to undertake any job that needed filling: receptionist, operations manager, helpline operator, saboteur of competition and so on. Nine years on, I remain a shareholder and sounding board while having returned full-time to my own activities.

The advantages of involving your family are that you all know each other well, your weaknesses as well as your strengths, and feel loyal to each other. You are also very committed to the success of the business. The disadvantages are that too much of the family fortune is tied up in one venture, thereby increasing the risk. There is also the problem that work differences can spill over into home differences and destabilize the family.

Sorting Out the Shareholdings

Who gets what amount of the shares? What is the fairest way of allocating them? Frankly, fairness doesn't necessarily come into it.

Equal shareholdings to make everyone feel better may lead to inertia and deadlock in a couple of years, if views diverge over the proposed development of the business. Decisiveness is much improved if the leader of the business also holds the clear majority of the management's portion of the shares. Neill Bell's approach to dividing up the shareholdings when the team was discussing the buy-out of Porth Holdings is rather appealing. 'Sorting out the share stakes was very amicable because I started out by saying that I wanted 51 per cent of our share, in other words of the management share. I wanted to be able to outvote everyone, and as far as I was concerned that was it. They agreed immediately.'

One company which later on had problems about how it should grow was founded by the former chairman, Alex Smith (not his real name). Here the shareholdings were divided up in the following proportion: chief executive officer 25 per cent, chairman 20 per cent and technical director 15 per cent. This left none of them with a decisive majority, a decision which Alex now regrets. 'I suggested the split of shareholdings. The split is fair but a mistake.'

Clearly, the share stakes should tally with the amount of capital each invests, so this implies that the leader must be prepared to put up the lion's share of the management equity.

Case Study 1: Choosing the Team for a Management Buy-out

STC had bought Exacta, a manufacturer of printed circuit boards, some time in the seventies. The bulk of Exacta's output went to STC, but during the eighties this fell, until by 1985 quite a small proportion was used within the group. At this time, STC embarked on a policy of selling off non-core businesses and Exacta was identified as one of these. The idea of a buy-out had been floating about when Derrick Bumpsteed was sent up to manage the company. He'd only been in that seat one month when it became clear that a buy-out was a real possibility. Derrick Bumpsteed and the rest of the management got the Edinburgh office of Arthur Andersen in to advise them.

One of the first tasks was to work out who would be in the management team. It wasn't an automatic choice because there were potentially seven or eight in the first line and this was ultimately reduced to four. Derrick explains: 'I went for the people I wanted as directors, to run the company independently rather than as part of the group. For instance, the financial controller had to go, because his experience was all on the management accounting side and he did not have the experience to run a company with all its own banking and all its own investment arrangements. That decision had to be made. There was another guy who'd been here a long while and was very good, but I think his personality would have caused clashes. We had to have a team with the essentials that could work well together – and that was just the four of us. A month after the buy-out, we took on somebody else and he became part of the team, but at the time of the buy-out four of us went ahead and did it. I had to bite the bullet and tell people that they weren't going to be part of the team. Two left and one stayed as a senior manager who reports to me, but not on the board.

'It's pretty crucial to sort the team out, because you've got to work together. It has also got to be a team that's acceptable to the investors – if you don't do it, they'll do it for you. They're much more supportive if they see that you're willing to take the decisions and get the right people.

'Since the buy-out, we've had the obvious ups and downs, but basically the team has hung together and we're still driving in the same direction. It was a team that had two people who'd been in the company for twenty years or so and there were two of us who had been round and about. Although I'd been in STC a long while, I'd been in about six or seven jobs. Another of the guys had been in companies like Cummings, Fisher Price and had good experience there. I think they have good balance. We had two experts and two with broader experience.'

Case Study 2: Building a Team for a Management Start-up

Derwent Valley Foods started with two old friends reaching the barrier of their fortieth birthdays and wondering what they should be doing with the rest of their lives. Roger McKechnie was general manager of a company in the food industry and Ray McGhee was a senior manager with an American advertising agency – and spending too much time travelling about the world. The idea of building a company in the snack market was born. While Ray returned to his job, Roger interested two younger men, both aged thirty, in his idea of setting up a new venture. Keith Gill and John Pike both worked with Roger and felt that they were willing to risk two years of their careers following the challenge of building a business of their own. With Ray, this formed the nucleus of the team.

While Roger and Ray were both strong in marketing strategy and personnel management, they lacked financial and production experience. John Pike was the production man with the right sort of experience and personal chemistry to work well within the team. Keith Gill, who was working for Roger, was a good detail man and a very quick learner. He had a background in accounting systems and personnel before becoming a marketing man. The team did recognize that there was some weakness in the financial side which they hoped to redress by appointing a suitably qualified accountant when the business developed.

Keith, with his enthusiasm, wit and strong personality, proved to be an important catalyst in the team. Both he and Roger stand out as the front men. They find public speaking easy and have a charm and easy manner which makes them approachable and able to convince others to invest in their ideas.

However, John and Ray are equally important to the team. Keith said that it was the differences between them, coupled with the obvious personal liking they have for each other, that made the team work so well. An important point, too, is that all seem happy with Roger taking the spokesman role with the company.

But the lack of a strong financial expert in the team caused a subsequent crisis. Demand for their product was racing away and to meet this demand they moved into a bigger factory, doubling both production space and the workforce. 'We just let it rip,' said McKechnie.

At this point, the first real crisis hit Derwent. The computer carrying the company accounts broke down and the team believed that they were in the region of £100,000 better off than they actually were. They spent £150,000 on a television advertising campaign for the Phileas Fogg brand names.

When the bank manager found out the truth of their situation, 'he went white', recalls McKechnie, 'and threatened to close us down'. While they were fighting to save the business, Prince Charles arrived to open the new part of the factory. Legend has it that the bank manager had the documents to put the company into liquidation nestling in his pocket during the opening ceremony. The company managed to get a three-month stay of execution. The team visited the suppliers to explain their situation and ask them to accept part payment for their goods until the problem had been solved. All were understanding.

But this had taught the team an important lesson. They had to plan growth in a controlled manner and they had to do something about the weakness in finance they had identified from the beginning. They brought in experts. 'We intend to pay well and get good people. We've got real professionals. They are young. We let them have their head and reward them well.'

6

The Board

There may seem to be more pressing problems during this planning stage than developing the composition and nature of the board of directors. But a little foresight can prevent entrenched problems later on during the development of your business. Boardroom rows may lead to the downfall of any business. A business developing nicely according to its business plan can be completely thrown off target by emotions and resentments aroused by disagreements at board level.

One entrepreneur found this to be the case, albeit some five years after he founded the business: 'We had raised some development capital and the new shareholders wanted to have a representative on the board. We were so relieved to have funded the next stage of our development that we weren't sufficiently stringent in examining the suitability of their representative. The culture clash was too deep. We soldiered on for a year or so, but finally the board, including the other non-executive director, the shareholders and the venture-capital organization he represented, wanted this director to go. He wouldn't. The next three months were locked in personal and business threats and legal wrangles. He threatened my job, the company and my family. It seemed like an episode from Dallas. We succeeded in the end, but it was at a great cost. At a crucial stage of very rapid growth in sales and the sales team, the boardroom rows and fighting took our eye off the ball. The expansion of the sales team wasn't carried out with our usual ruthless attention to detail and the sales growth was slower than it should have been. Selecting a non-executive director who didn't fit the company was a costly mistake for us.'

Another entrepreneur, Alex Smith, saw the company he co-founded split by boardroom rows. Disagreements about how the company should grow were one of the reasons why the company was sold. Says Smith: 'No one wanted to double or treble the company, except me. With hindsight, I would have kept more executive authority.'

These two examples illustrate perfectly why the composition of the board and who should represent the shareholders and the venture capitalists is a decision which should be considered at the outset of your planning. You need to start with a board which is appropriate, with the right expertise for you in the early stages, but one which you should make clear will evolve as the company grows and changes. Companies can outgrow the abilities and range of experience of its directors and that should be taken account of in your long-range plans. No-one is guaranteed a job for life.

When you are gathering a team together to start a business, for example, beware of confusing members of the team with the skills you need with those members who will be able to recruit and develop their own team beneath them and contribute to the development of the business. The former are employees; the latter are potential directors.

You should recognize the possible boardroom problems which can lie ahead and perceive how damaging these can be. Think clearly about the format of the board, the number of executive and non-executive directors. Don't be frightened of reaching conclusions during the planning stage about who will make it as a director and who won't. Equally, if you find that the board is not functioning in the way you think it should, take clear decisions to adjust it; but bear in mind that this is more problematic once the business is established and growing.

What is the Board's Job?

Broadly speaking, the board should manage the business but not on a day-to-day basis; it must restrain itself from trying to be managing director or marketing director. It cannot operate effectively unless it is presented with the up-to-date monthly trading and budget figures and a management report; it is the management's responsibility to ensure this is prepared and given to the board members in advance of the meeting.

Strategic moves, key trading decisions and board appointments should be discussed and thrashed out at the board. The board should also review and monitor the performance of the business and the management and employees (but not at an individual level, apart from the managing director or chief executive).

Who Should be on the Board?

The need for the board to evolve as the company grows implies that membership of the team which puts together a proposal to start a company or buy a company, for example, does not give automatic entry to the board of directors. It is quite feasible for some founding members to have an equity stake, but not to be on the board. The leader of the team has to make the decision: if you consider that a team member won't make the transition from a small company, as it will be as a start-up, to a fast-growing company, which is your plan for two or three years' time, you should not make that team member a director. To a certain extent this is what happened in the case of the business co-founded by Alex Smith. In his view, he left too much executive power with the chief executive and 'the perfect manager of a small company built a team to manage a small company'.

In the case of a management buy-out, your need is to select directors who will be able to execute the necessary decisions for a much smaller company than most of you will be used to. This also implies that the members of the team who carry out the buy-out may not necessarily be on the board. The buy-out of RFS Industries was carried out by Stephen Hinton, now its chief executive, and three others, who called themselves the Gang of Four. But the day before the buy-out was completed, Stephen took the decision that two of the four should not be directors – a very unpopular move, but not one he regrets. He has subsequently brought in two directors from outside whom he considered gave the board the range of expertise it needed. It left the company in the rather odd position of having two major shareholders outside the board of directors.

In buy-outs, it is not unusual for one or more of the original directors to find it difficult to adjust to the different nature of business life after the buy-out.

There is no set size for a board of directors. However, beware of allowing it to grow like Topsy – four executive directors and two non-executive directors seems the maximum number for an efficient board which can take real decisions. Allow the board to grow too extensive and a secret board may develop: two or three key movers make the real decisions away from the boardroom and stage-manage the board meetings. While this may work in the short run as a means of managing the business, it cannot in the long run develop the potential of the business.

A curious fact, not always readily appreciated before launching into a venture, is that power on the board is related closely to numbers on the board, rather than to shareholdings. While there will be a shareholder representative on any company funded with venture capital, and while that representative may have greater influence than any other member of the board, nevertheless power rests with the majority of hands. In the case of Alex Smith's company, he considers that the majority of the shareholders backed the fast-growth option which was his preference, but there were too many hands on the board from other directors, without shares, who preferred to keep it like a family business. And essentially, except in very rare cases where the business looks like it might founder, the shareholders will back the management team, even though they control the equity.

The balance of power can shift from the shareholders to the management if the venture capital comes from more than one source, even if there is more than one shareholder representative. In this case, it is possible for the management on the board to retain even greater power. As Tim Waterstone says: 'If you have more than one institution financing you, it is possible to divide and rule. You can't do this if there is just one major backer.'

Who Should be Chairman?

Should you combine the role of chairman and chief executive or not? Peter Williams of Vamp Health chose to combine the roles during the first six years of the company's existence. His reasoning was as follows: 'I thought that if Vamp was successful, there would come a moment in time when I wasn't necessarily the best person to carry out the operational management of the business. I would want to bring in a managing director. What role would there be for me? So I had to hang on to the chairman's position so that I could kick myself upstairs at the right time and retain control of the strategy. If I had bought in a chairman earlier, even a non-executive, I would have been tempted to hang on to the managing director's role long after I should have passed it on.'

Combining the roles of chairman and chief executive is obviously attractive to other entrepreneurs, as this is the choice made by many companies quoted on the Unlisted Securities Market. Entrepreneurs seem to ignore the conventional wisdom that the two roles should be separate to provide the necessary checks and balances in the board and to prevent too much power accumulating in the hands of one person. Checks and balances sound like a luxury which start-ups, smaller-scale buy-outs and buy-ins can't afford.

However, some entrepreneurs starting businesses have appointed a non-executive chairman from day one. Allen Jones of A J's Family Restaurants says of his non-executive chairman: 'His experience and overall wisdom is an asset, as we are "operators". We see him as a neutral player between us as users of the money and the institutions as suppliers of the money.'

While Allen Jones has been successful in his choice of non-executive chairman, finding an experienced and sensible business person who is prepared to join a start-up as non-executive chairman can be a demanding task. A start-up or small buy-out or buy-in doesn't have a lot to offer – little status and reward and potentially onerous responsibilities.

So what are the pros and cons of being both chairman and chief executive for you as the entrepreneur? The advantages include a decisive board, clearer leadership, potentially greater thrust for growth and space at the top for introducing new senior management from outside as the company grows.

The disadvantages include the absence of an experienced sounding board (but this function can be fulfilled by non-executive directors) and the doubled workload that comes from being both chairman and managing director (which is more than people realize). Institutions may put pressure on you to appoint a chairman during your fund-raising, especially following the various upsets which have occurred where the business has been run by a lone entrepreneur, acting as both chairman and chief executive. However, for new, small, fast-growing businesses, you can feel confident that it is not essential and should be more a matter of choice for you and the management team, not a requirement of the venture capitalist.

Do You Need Non-executive Directors?

The theory behind the adoption of non-executive directors on the board is that they can stand back from the hurly-burly of the business. They won't be submerged in the day-to-day problems and thus can adopt a more rational, more strategic approach to the business which will be of benefit in the long term. A non-executive director should be able to give independent advice on all issues and act as a sounding board for the managing director. The independent director should also be able to indicate how the external world views the company. Finally, a non-executive director should keep an eye on the company to see that it is acting in the best interests of all the shareholders and the employees.

A non-executive director sounds completely essential for any business and yet opinion differs on how crucial the role is for early business ventures. For example, Tim Waterstone considers that non-executive directors are not essential for a small business and it is more important that backers should understand the business and support it.

Malcolm Parkinson set up The Retail Corporation with £10 million of venture capital to build a chain of garden centres. He obviously has some mixed views on the value of non-executive directors. He says: 'Non-executive directors come in two types. The first, and most annoying, is because they want their name on the letterhead – and they are just a nuisance. The second type is someone who has expertise in an area you know little about – but you mustn't let him become a dictator in that area. A non-executive director is not necessarily a great sounding board. They are invariably sitting there judging you, so you can't always tell them the unvarnished truth.'

High-tech and leading-edge companies experience particular difficulties in finding non-executive directors with the knowledge and expertise to enable them to offer sound advice. The managing director of one such company comments: 'We have non-executive directors who are financially experienced, but don't know the business and so can't make a contribution. I have to spend a lot of time educating non-executive directors. There is one industry expert nominated by a venture capitalist and he is very supportive and helpful.'

But other entrepreneurs have so far encountered mainly good help and advice. Tim Hely Hutchinson of Headline says of his non-executive directors, who were originally representatives of investors: 'They have seen a great many business situations and give general commercial advice.'

Lyn Davies is an experienced non-executive director for a number of small firms. His view is that 'Non-executive directors always bring another dimension to the problem. They are essential to the logical thought process of any business. A business needs good outside people to identify real issues and, if necessary, change direction.'

Finally, Neill Bell's view comes smack in the middle of this range. He says: 'The point is that non-executive directors can be very helpful or they can be a pain in the arse. They can put you in touch with people. The problem is sometimes that one or two non-execs would like to be executives and I think that is where you run into real problems. And I think you've got to make it clear from day one, who runs the company. Because if you don't and you try and be nice and helpful, you'll suddenly find them walking all over you.'

The Representatives of Venture Capitalists

Broadly speaking, venture capitalists fall into one of two groups: 'hands-on' and 'hands-off'. Hands-off venture capitalists may suggest that you could benefit from appointing a director in a particular area, perhaps where the board lacks expertise. The non-executive director is not on the board to represent the investor, but simply to provide independent advice and impartial guidance which the management team may find helpful. The hands-off venture capitalist may help you to find a non-executive director to compensate for the identified weakness.

Hands-on venture capitalists will insist as part of the shareholder agreement that you will sign on raising venture capital that you appoint a non-executive director whom they nominate. Very often this is an employee of the venture capitalist or an associate. Such non-executive directors, compared to those suggested by hands-off venture capitalists, will regard themselves as having an extended role.

First, there are the normal duties of a non-executive director: giving independent advice, acting as a sounding board, adopting a more strategic view and so on. Second, there is a monitoring role for the shareholder the director represents. To carry this out, the director needs to be presented with timely and accurate information. To this end, monthly board meetings will be required at which you will need to present proper monthly management accounts, updated budgets and cash flows, discussion of monthly performance and key issues which the board should decide. No doubt this would be what was planned by any serious entrepreneur with strong management experience, but if it is not, it could be insisted on. It is also probably the minimum which every non-executive director would require, whoever suggested the appointment – hands-on, hands-off or your own personal idea. But the hands-on venture capitalist may go further and want to be involved in defining the prescribed format for the information or to specify that more detailed information be presented in certain key areas. For example, you may be presented with a request to show the non-executive director stock figures or cash statements. Even closer involvement might be required: weekly meetings with the management team, more detailed reporting requirements, meetings with suppliers and customers and possibly even a part-time executive role.

Finally, the hands-on venture capitalist imagines that this closer involvement, coupled with some industry knowledge, will be able to add value to the business. The argument runs along these lines: a non-executive director nominated by a hands-on venture capitalist will be prepared to spend more time in the business, is more committed and has great experience of companies at the early stage of development and those in the fast-growth stage and so will be able to offer particularly apt advice.

However, a survey by London Business School for the British Venture Capital Association found that the 'promise of on-going help' from the venture capitalist was not a high priority when raising money. Only 22 per cent of entrepreneurs interviewed said this influenced their choice of venture-capital investor positively. Indeed, 61 per cent stated they were originally seeking 'funding with a passive hands-off relationship'.

There are examples of entrepreneurs who have wholeheartedly embraced the concept of the more active non-executive director and have regarded the appointee as an extra valuable resource. The survey above found that, at the end of the day, it was the non-financial contributions made by venture capitalists that were most important. In particular, the entrepreneurs valued venture-capital directors for their general business advice and finance skills, for providing a good 'sounding board' and challenging executive managers with different points of view and for helping with corporate strategy and direction.

There are also examples of entrepreneurs who find the additional control imposed by this role stifling and who resent their inability to manage without an investor nominee overseeing their every action. Indeed, a cynic might say that the hands-on venture capitalists see the role of the non-executive director as a way of rewarding their own employees with income, and, in some cases, capital gain from options on the shares. In other words, the benefit accrues mostly to the venture-capital organization and not to the company in which it has invested.

In conclusion, a director nominated by a hands-on venture capitalist could add value, but the person needs to be sensitive to the feelings of the management team, as well as in possession of deep knowledge of the industry and broad financial experience of developing companies. Perhaps such individuals are rarer than the hands-on venture capitalist would imply. Certainly the greatest benefit from such organizations would apply to those entrepreneurs with the least management experience.

Choosing a Non-executive Director

Great attention should be given to the choice of non-executive directors and to the terms on which they are appointed. There is a natural inclination to be so grateful to the source of finance for raising the money to start or fund your venture that your normal ability to discriminate between appropriate and inappropriate personnel goes flying out of the window when the venture capitalist nominates a non-executive director. Whether hands-on or hands-off, you should insist on interviewing and applying the normal criteria for selection. Brian Gilda runs Peoples, Ford main dealers. He says: 'Our venture capitalist wanted to put someone on the board. We had lunch and said "No way" – he was hopeless, at least twenty years behind the times in our industry. Subsequently, we did agree to a non-executive director who was much more in keeping with our aspirations.'

Once you have followed the normal selection pattern, you should still try to include some let-out terms, for example notifying in advance that the nature and composition of the board will change as the company grows. And you could try using a potential non-executive director as a consultant for some project of value to the business, before agreeing to him or her joining the board.

Dispensing with a Non-executive Director

Faced with a personality conflict or clash of management styles, it is possible to change a non-executive director. If the company is growing well and the management team feels in a strong position, that is the time to strike. The shareholders will generally back you rather than the non-executive director, no matter who nominated the director or what the background. Of course, if the business is in difficulties, you are unlikely to be able to shift an unwanted NXD – and may find that it is you who is outmanoeuvred instead. Not all the entrepreneurs interviewed for this book had needed to change a non-executive director, but those who had set out to do so had achieved their objective.

The example of the bitter dispute at the start of this chapter wasn't typical of other entrepreneurs. For example, Tim Waterstone over the years had asked three non-executive directors to resign: 'I took them aside and said it wasn't really working. I've remained friends with them all.' Malcolm Parkinson of The Retail Corporation recommends: 'Be totally and completely open with the investor. Give seven reasons, none of them that you don't like the man personally.'

The best approach is to the director first, rather than to the nominating investor. Try to persuade the director that his or her own personal interest is best served by resigning rather than having it brought out into the open that the arrangement is not working well. Most rational people will see the sense in that; the problem occurs if the director is not particularly rational, or has become over-committed to the company, linking its future success to his or her own personal success.

What are a Director's Responsibilities?

This book can give only general guidelines and you should take legal advice on this, but there have been a number of changes in recent years in what directors must do and how they should behave. You may have the impression that a director's personal responsibilities and potential liabilities have become very onerous. In practice, they amount to responsible business behaviour. A director has to act in good faith in the interests of the business and should not carry on the business of the company with intent to defraud creditors or for any fraudulent purpose. The directors should not knowingly allow the company to trade while insolvent ('wrongful trading'). If they do, they may have to pay the debts incurred while insolvent. A director must not deceive shareholders and must have a regard for the interests of the employees in general. Directors must comply with the requirements of the Companies Act, by providing what is needed in accounting records or filing accounts for example.

If the company becomes insolvent and the directors have failed in their duties and obligations, they could be declared 'unfit' and disqualified from becoming a director of any other company for up to fifteen years. In 1990/91, 254 directors were disqualified, mostly for periods of between two and five years. Five were banned for the maximum fifteen years. A further ten directors were disqualified for wrongful trading. In 1989, for the first time, two directors were made to pay company debts incurred after they should have known the company was insolvent.

II

SPOTTING THE OPPPORTUNITY

'You will always find some Eskimos ready to instruct the Congolese on how to cope with heatwaves' (Stanislaw Lec, Polish poet and aphorist, *Unkempt Thoughts*). And you will always find some entrepreneurs prepared to stake their money, reputation and effort on some other equally unrealistic business idea which turns out to combine high risk with low return. After the importance of a strong management team, the other essential ingredient to make an enterprise fly is the choice of market you will enter.

One glaring mistake, which nevertheless all too frequently occurs, is choosing a product as your business idea rather than selecting a market. Despite this being an obvious pitfall, entrepreneurs may seize upon a product, because it is 'a major innovation', 'will save lives', or 'change society'. Failed entrepreneurs know with hindsight that the product may not achieve any of these worthy objectives if the market is not ready.

Tony Leach of Daton Systems has survived for over ten years, but it is only in the last four or five years that the business seems to have stabilized. In particular, the business has evolved through a number of marketing strategies. Tony's first business idea (pre-Daton) was to sell a suite of database software that had been launched in France. He started with a one-month exclusive licence to market it in the UK. However, it quickly became evident that distributing one computer program, however sophisticated, was not the basis of a long-lasting business. The general principle must be that you should first decide on a market to enter and subsequently seek the product – and this Tony has carried out in later plans.

Another glaring mistake to which you could fall prey is the knee-jerk reaction that might occur when the company you work for is put up for sale, threatened with closure or is in the hands of the receiver. A desire to save your employees' jobs, as well as your own, may be laudable – but foolish. Take a cool, detached look. Closure, for example, may well be the right destination.

7

Choosing a Market

Entrepreneurs who start successful new businesses are generally not gamblers – they may be risk-takers, but they should be able to assess and minimize the risks. Much of your effort should be directed towards lowering risk. There are many different types of risk – market, technological, financial for example.

One key element in risk minimization is spotting the right market opportunity to seize. With a strong management team, you can succeed if you choose a market opportunity which is not ideal, but you may find yourself struggling to survive through lack of sales. The problem for other entrepreneurs, on the other hand, could be coping with too much demand. No entrepreneur would prefer the former problem to the latter.

Your task with the venture capitalist must be to explain the risks and to help it to see where the risks are in your venture and what you are doing to counter them. It is a more substantial task to persuade a venture capitalist to fund a high-risk venture than one it regards as low-risk. Where the venture capitalist perceives a higher risk, it will look for a higher profit potential to counteract the risk. If it cannot see higher profits, the venture capitalist will want to be compensated by higher equity.

Of course, what to one person is a sure-fire certainty may to another be too hot to handle. Whatever your venture, you need to be able to demonstrate solid evidence and plans to support your proposal that this is the market to enter. A significant part of this support should consist of your assessment of the risk and how to lay it off. With start-ups, it's all about lowering risks and demonstrating this ability in your business plan will encourage venture-capital investors.

How You Can Minimize Risk by Your Market Choice

A risk-minimization strategy is to aim to shorten the struggle for survival in the crucial start-up phase. There are five key factors to consider in your selection.

Choose a market opportunity:

– in which you have experience;

– which has a regular flow of sales of small unit value;

– with a lower break-even point;

– which builds a customer base for further sales or sales of other products;

– and plan in detail before the launch and exercise control after it.

Undoubtedly, a key factor in those new businesses which have met or exceeded expectations in the first couple of years has been entering a market in which the founders already have extensive experience and knowledge.

Headline reversed the general trend in start-ups by exceeding the forecasts in its business plan after eighteen months. It returned to its original investors, Rothschild Ventures, CINVen, County NatWest Ventures and 3i, and they put up a second tranche of £1 million to help it carry out 'the same plan but much bigger'.

Headline's founders – Tim Hely Hutchinson, Sue Fletcher and Sian Thomas – had spent the three years prior to the start-up managing a publishing company with a list aimed at a very similar section of the book-buying market, 'publishing books that people want to read – not an ivory-tower publisher'. Their extensive knowledge of that market segment garnered from their previous work must have been a considerable help in Headline's flying start.

The general conclusion which can be drawn is that the more you know about the industry and the market in which you are going to operate, the lower the risk of the business. A good starting point for any new business would be to select the industry in which you already have experience. The advantages this strategy gives you are fairly obvious: knowledge of suppliers, the distribution structure, perhaps a ready-prepared customer base. Venture capitalists are also much readier to back a management team that is proposing a venture in an area of their recent experience and expertise.

Another rule of thumb to bear in mind when selecting the right opportunity is that lumpy businesses can be nerve-racking. Choosing a business which gives a regular flow of sales with small unit values gives a greater chance of success because it eases the founding of the business. One such business which learned to conquer 'lumpiness' was Calidus, a company specializing in installing Distribution Centre Management Systems and associated consultancy and training. Initially, the intention was to ease into the industry and to make profits in the first couple of years by consultancy. However, early success came for them in a different way when they gained the rights to a leading software package. Says Brindley Reynaud, former chairman and co-founder: 'Suddenly, we had a major, major product. Each sale is easily £1 million, almost never less than £½ million and has been as high as £8 million. There is also a very long sales cycle. We didn't produce the tiny profits we had planned in early years; in fact, we produced large losses.'

Calidus had to return to their venture-capital backer, Baronsmead, for more funds to cover this period. This proved less of a problem than might have been imagined because the founders of Calidus had had the foresight to put this forward as a possibility when they raised funds initially and to secure the agreement of Baronsmead at the outset, should this possibility turn into a reality.

Nevertheless, the lesson that you can draw from Calidus's experience is that life would be more stable in the early years if you choose a market which you can sell to with a lower-value product, where you can look for a regular flow of sales. If, for other reasons, you choose a market where the products are very high-value and irregular, it is imperative that you plan properly at the outset to cope with the fluctuating sales and their effect on cash flow.

On a similar theme, the riskiness of a business start-up is also considerably reduced, the earlier your business can reach the break-even point and pass from cash consumption to cash generation. A consequence of entering some markets that are already established is that you need critical mass to succeed – and this can be unnerving and frightening. You cannot underestimate competitive reactions and to muscle in against well-established businesses your business must be of the right size and right stature. This is essential where your customers are major companies. Unless you can establish your credibility, you can't expect large companies to take you seriously.

Setting up this type of business is a little like launching a ship – on day one of the business, you have a massive vessel with nothing inside it, no customers and no production. As a consequence, your first major battle is to reach that magic cross-over point from cash negative to cash positive. So this type of business carries with it a significant level of risk compared to a business with a much lower break-even point.

The risk of successfully negotiating the minefields of the crucial early days, weeks, months and years of a start-up can also be lessened if you can demonstrate pre-launch orders or you collect deposits. It sounds a remote possibility to be able to achieve this – and yet some of the entrepreneurs interviewed for this book have carried out what less optimistic people might regard as impossible.

Tony Davies started up a business called Membrain, subsequently sold to a large company in the electronics industry. In the early years, Membrain managed to generate its own funds to develop products because it asked for large customer deposits. And Peter Gibson of Corin Medical recalls that he managed to obtain orders for his products very quickly – before the factory was set up, the machines bought, or the workforce employed.

Yet another way for you to increase the chances of a successful business launch is to select a market which would involve you in building a customer base to whom follow-up sales or sales of linked products can be made. A business which has a high proportion of sales revenue coming from its existing customers looks a high-quality proposition to financiers.

High-technology ventures used to be the darling of the venture-capital world, but because of high failure rates venture capitalists have been far more wary of them for a number of years. Currently, low-technology industries and markets are rated as having greater potential for the launching of successful ventures. This is not to imply that the business itself should use only low-technology methods; on the contrary, venture capitalists regard it as important that the business is run using the latest methods to provide superior efficiency and business information. The fact that venture capitalists have moved away from favouring high-technology ventures does not imply that you cannot start a business in this sector. Indeed, some venture-capital organizations still specialize in this type of venture and all venture-capital organizations will consider a sound, well-researched and well-prepared proposition.

However, a high-technology venture today would need to be a large-scale start-up to improve the probability of success. With the rapid pace of technological improvements, it is vital for such a venture to make a quick impact in the market-place to enable you to derive the required return on the investment provided by you and the venture capitalists. This is different from what could be achieved during the seventies. Tony Davies started Membrain in quite a low-key fashion, and built the company through the first two or three stages of its development to arrive at its eventual product range. He would not recommend this style of start-up in the nineties in the technology-business environment because the fast pace of technology development can so quickly make a product obsolete.

The final way in which you can minimize the risk of your business start-up is to indulge in detailed planning before the launch and strict control afterwards. Extensive research is the most obvious way you can satisfy yourself and the venture capitalists that your business proposition will succeed. David Langston of Blue Ridge Care, for example, had not previously operated in the disposable nappy market. Before he founded Blue Ridge, Langston had been vice-president of a US textile company, and had developed a package of technology and investment to enable the company to set up outside the USA. He worked long and hard getting enough operational and market knowledge before recommending a project for the UK. This gave him a close working knowledge of the business. Once the US company decided to pass up the opportunity, Langston, a US citizen himself, couldn't let it pass by, setting up the factory in the North East. 'It was a time-specific opportunity. The opportunity was in Britain; if it had been in Yugoslavia, I would have gone there.' As it was, the detailed research had forecast correctly; for the first couple of years after the launch, the disposable nappy industry was an emerging market and Blue Ridge Care caught it on the start of an up-wave. Unfortunately, the business foundered some six years on. During this period, one of its main competitors, Proctor & Gamble, increased its market share in the UK from around 20 per cent to about 70 per cent. Langston's opinion is: 'If a very big company decides there are too many players in what it wants for itself, you may as well go home.'

What Could Your Marketing Strategy be?

Very broadly, the marketing strategy for a successful start-up could be grouped in three ways:

– a niche strategy;

– a challenge strategy;

– a lead strategy.

First of all, you could plan *a niche strategy*, where you seek to enter a small or well-defined segment of a much bigger market. This probably carries with it the lowest level of risk and may be why there are a number of successful examples of venture-capital-backed enterprises who have made a niche their own. For example, this is what Robert Wright set out to achieve when he set up Connectair. He couldn't launch an airline to meet the big boys head on, but he saw an opportunity in the airline business for small companies feeding passengers to the bigger airlines. This business was too small for a large company to exploit but perfect for a new and emerging business to make its own and grow with it.

Vamp Health also selected a niche market as its target, the general-practitioner computer market. It became market leader, with over 30 per cent of the installed sites. However, it has proved to be a difficult market, despite being so well defined. It is very subject to political interference and hence this leads to very quick and sudden fluctuations in demand. Learning to cope with this variability has strengthened Vamp's position and today the barriers to entry for any new main player are very high.

A third example of a successful niche strategy is Derwent Valley Foods. The founders' experience was in the food industry, so they decided to concentrate on this. But they developed their concept further by selecting snacks for adults as an unexploited niche. This represented a very small sector, largely ignored by the major snack manufacturers, but the management team assessed it as having considerable potential. The team believed this to be a much-lower-risk proposition than that entailed in trying to wrest a share off the three big manufacturers who dominate 90 per cent of the snack market.

A *challenge strategy* is another possibility, but carries with it potentially higher levels of risk. A J's Family Restaurants is an example of this. Once Little Chef acquired the Happy Eater chain, this left no other main player in the family-restaurant market. Allen Jones set up A J's to challenge this monolith.

Finally, you could propose *a lead strategy* for a new company. This is likely to be based on a new or innovative product or service and increases the level of risk, even assuming that the market has been thoroughly researched and you are confident that it is ready for the innovation. Three years after its launch, Vamp Health decided to take the innovative step of accumulating anonymous patient data from some of its GP computer systems. This covers over four million patients and can be used for research into drug safety and health planning. Such a database would lead the world, would take time, more funding and great skill and expertise. The project is now successful and is steadily building profits and sales. However, the adoption of the project increased the level of risk of the business and made it more difficult to fund.

Some Specific Opportunities

The phrase 'window of opportunity' is familiar to all. It implies that there is only a short gap, which you must rush to exploit before the opportunity disappears. This may apply in a few cases, and some examples are given below of potential time-specific opportunities. But the window of opportunity is generally miles wide, not inches. Your business idea does not need to involve an innovative, unique or new product. Opportunities include offering a better product or service, operating more efficiently or simply developing a stronger marketing approach to an industry.

If there is turbulence, there will be some opportunities for you to exploit. Turbulence could imply substantial technological or regulatory changes or economic or political developments. But these opportunities *are* very time-specific. Fleetness of foot and mercurial ability are required to spot the opportunity, plan its exploitation and carry the development through successfully.

A more attractive opportunity may exist in an industry which is in the early high-growth stages of evolution. Where the market is growing, competitors can live side by side more easily and mistakes you might make are not penalized quite so heavily. The perfect point to enter such a market can be difficult to judge – and it may be impossible to achieve perfection. If you enter a market too early, even one which is going to grow substantially over the years, you may still find yourself struggling. It may be difficult to sell your product because its possibilities, and hence its advantages, are not yet established in the customer's mind. The only way to succeed could be to educate the market, and this can be like pouring time, money and effort down a black hole.

So the conventional wisdom on entering a new market is that market penetration needs to be in the order of 15 per cent for sales to be rising at the sort of rate needed to sustain a growing business. However, rules of thumb are there to be broken and this is no exception. Entering a market in its early stages, as long as you have funded for the early difficulties, can render many long-term advantages. As long as you survive, you can reap the advantages of establishing yourself as market leader and creating significant barriers of entry for later comers.

Exploiting an Opportunity with a Major Backer

There may be opportunities for linking in one way or another with major companies to seize particular market niches or developments that would be beyond your current resources. Large companies may be interested in backing your venture because they recognize that a more entrepreneurial approach is needed to achieve success in a new or rapidly developing field. Entrepreneurial attributes that may be valued are commitment, resourcefulness, leanness and flexibility of operation. New business development is sometimes considered to be dependent on entrepreneurial vision. Or it may simply be that the large companies don't want to take the risk of damaging their image by trying and failing. These market-led developments are simply a specialized form of corporate venturing, which is much more popular in the USA than in the UK. Corporate venturing is a term used to describe partnerships between established companies, generally of substantial size, and smaller, more innovative ones.

Corporate venturing can take many different forms. There are two simple versions. In version one, you make a licensing deal or similar arrangement. You hand over the rights to exploit your product to the larger company in exchange for payment, often royalties. In version two, you hand over nothing, but the corporate venturer invests in your shares similarly to the way a venture capitalist does, often handing over the monitoring of the investment to a venture-capital fund. This investment may be accompanied by certain rights over the disposal of your business, such as a pre-emption clause. This allows the corporate venturer to buy the business by matching any other offer to buy which an alternative purchaser makes. A pre-emption clause can have the effect of depressing the value of your business by frightening off other potential purchasers.

More complicated corporate-venturing arrangements involve some form of ongoing collaboration, including pooling of resources and use of certain skills and expertise provided by the larger company. Such arrangements imply a loss of independence for your business. It's a trade-off between independence and greater business muscle to help your product maximize its revenues for you.

An article in *The Economist* at the end of 1991 pointed out, however, that in the USA corporate venturing can be more attractive than raising venture capital. *Upside*, a technology magazine, recently calculated that entrepreneurs have to give away 10.8 per cent of their company for each $1 million raised in venture capital, but only 4.4 per cent for $1 million provided by a corporate venturer. A venture capitalist is only interested in the financial return, while a corporate venturer has a strategic interest, too.

While this may appear attractive, the corporate-venturing approach has disadvantages compared to the venture-capital approach. Frankly, some corporate venturers may be fickle – because this is only a sideline to their major interest. For the venture capitalist, investing in new and growing businesses is their only activity. Interest can wane for a number of reasons: changes of personnel, changes of ownership, changes in strategy.

There is no reliable list of companies which may be interested in corporate venturing. A company may make the commitment only once, or several times. Some companies known to have been involved in the past include Olivetti, British Gas, British Petroleum, Pearson. But you may be able to interest any large, well-established business in your industry if it can see the potential. Before its closure NEDO ran a Corporate Venture Register; it is now operated by Base Consultants and you may find it helpful to contact the register. You may find a potential backer. And you will certainly need advice on how to structure a corporate-venturing partnership so that most of the benefit does not accrue to the larger partner.

Pearson started a venture-capital fund in 1988, which made a few investments, although it has been inactive more recently. Mark Burrell of Pearson explained their interest: 'Pearson is coming out from being a diversified conglomerate to being more focused on publishing. We should be looking at a more electronic approach, rather than newspapers and books. We are seeking "crackfillers" to look for the growth prospects of the nineties.'

Olivetti has had a long history of corporate venturing. Elserino Piol in the book *Approaches to Venture Capital Investing* explained their reasoning. 'When planning for growth, we realized that Olivetti's R&D, however effective, could not economically supply the required amount of new products. Available time, funds and skills were simply not enough, and an alternative approach had to be found. We therefore turned to venture capital, so as to establish strong ties with small companies with exciting new products and to keep a "window" open on technologies.'

British Gas has become interested in corporate venturing more recently. Frank Corrigan of British Gas explains: 'It's a corporate programme, not a social policy or a pension-fund investment, but a business activity. We are looking to achieve a good financial return and have adopted a narrow focus of investing in companies which are innovative in our area. We are trying to find companies which we would like to see in our market.'

British Gas has created a separate fund, BG Ventures, managed by external advisers, Electra Innvotec. The aim of the £15 million fund is not to try to build an ever-increasing portfolio of small businesses, but to pump-prime and get some products to the market. Because of the use of an intermediary to manage the fund, the investment in the businesses is at arm's length, and they remain independent. Says Corrigan: 'Later on, we might look to develop closer relationships with the businesses, possibly joint ventures, using the expertise of British Gas. We see our role as a "facilitator".'

Finally, you may not need to seek outside sponsors and financiers – you may be able to spot a market opportunity in your own back yard. There may be potential to persuade your present employers that a more entrepreneurial approach would be successful in exploiting some development or opportunity and you may be able to negotiate a 'spin-out' or 'spin-off'. These could take the form of a joint venture or a very autonomous part of the large corporation.

Input to the Business Plan

The choice of market opportunity is so crucial to the success of a venture, especially in its early days, that it will come as no surprise that the market input to the business plan will be scrutinized closely by the venture capitalists. The more succinctly you can express where your venture will be positioned in the market and its competitive advantages and disadvantages, the more impressed will be the reader of the plan. While it may be stating the obvious, your plan will need to outline your best guess at the competitive reaction.

And a final thought: 'What a new business has to do is build brand image, brand awareness, market share. That gives a company its value. You must establish its brand identity. Profits will follow afterwards' (Tim Waterstone). Unless you're in the own-label business, the marketing section of your plan needs to show how you will achieve this.

8

Looking for a Company to Buy

If you want to avoid being a cuckoo in the nest, the company you buy into needs to be selected with great care and delicacy. A management buy-in carries with it a risk not present in start-ups or buy-outs – the risk that the chemistry between the management team and the company is explosive. With a buy-out, the team, or the major proportion of it, is already in situ; with a start-up, you build the team and the company in a style which is consistent with yours; but with a buy-in, your style and the company style are already firmly in place and the result of mixing the two together could be disastrous.

Of course, part of the attraction of buying a company is that a structure is already in place and an organization already operational – but this very attraction could also hold the seeds of its failure. Hence, without a doubt, the most complex aspect of a management buy-in is finding the right company to buy. Indeed, some managers spend a considerable length of time, years even, before they find a suitable target.

A survey of management buy-ins by the Centre for Management Buy-out Research found that over half the respondents took more than six months to find a target, followed by negotiations lasting on average five months.

What is a Buy-in?

In its structure and in some of its commercial aspects, a buy-in is similar to a buy-out. Management from outside the company achieves boardroom control and, with financial backers, control of the equity. In some buy-ins, the vendor will retain a percentage of the equity.

Over and above the amount of money put up to purchase shares, this probably will not be sufficient to buy the company or to develop it as in your plan. Extra funds will be needed to provide for working capital and capital expenditure. So, as with a buy-out, there will be bank loans and medium-term loans, which in turn implies that post-buy-in, the business will need to be able to generate sufficient cash flow to meet the interest payments.

The Growth of Management Buy-ins in the Eighties

At the beginning of the eighties, management buy-ins were relatively unknown, but in the latter half there was strong growth in the number and the value (see Table 3 on the right), although they remained much smaller in quantity than buy-outs. The main drive has been to buy into private companies, but there was also something of a flurry to buy into public companies – and, of course, these were some of the bigger deals (Table 4 on the right).

The figures show that there was a fall in the number of buy-ins during 1990, most dramatically of management buying into public companies. However, the numbers picked up again for purchases of private companies during 1991.

What Sort of Businesses Can You Buy Into?

There are various categories of businesses which may prove fertile ground for a successful buy-in. For any company to be a suitable vehicle for a management buy-in, it needs to be underperforming its potential, with scope for improvement (without necessarily being a loss-maker). This could apply equally to a publicly quoted company or a private company. The possibilities may include:

– family businesses with succession problems;

– owners looking to dispose of their businesses;

– start-ups which are ailing or which need an injection of different management skills to be able to expand;

– failed buy-outs.

Table 3: UK Management Buy-ins, 1980–91

Year	Number	Value (£ million)	Average value (£ million)
1980	0	0	0
1982	9	317	35.2
1984	6	5	0.8
1985	30	41	1.4
1986	51	316	6.2
1987	90	306	3.4
1988	113	1,216	10.8
1989	148	3,614	24.4
1990	110	654	5.9
1991	119	674	5.7

Source: Centre for Management Buy-out Research.

Table 4: UK Management Buy-ins, Private and Public Companies, 1985–91

	1985	1986	1987	1988	1989	1990	1991
Private							
Number	23	25	47	85	119	96	112
Total value (*£m*)	20	81	194	607	496	560	640
Average value (*£m*)	0.9	3.2	4.1	7.1	4.2	5.8	5.7
Public							
Number	7	26	43	28	29	14	7
Total value (*£m*)	20	236	112	609	3,118	94	34
Average value (*£m*)	2.9	9.1	2.6	21.8	107.5	6.7	4.8

Note: Total values rounded up to nearest million.

Source: Centre for Management Buy-out Research.

The statistics collected by the Centre for Management Buy-out Research give some indication of the source of buy-ins (Table 5 below). As the table shows, the major source of buy-in targets was in families who wished to divest for some reason. This is hardly surprising, as three quarters of all UK companies are family-owned and together they provide more than half of the UK's employment. A management buy-out is not the answer in many cases, as the leader is usually leaving.

Families can consider a buy-in to be more attractive as a way out for them than a trade sale, because if they choose the 'right' purchaser, they hope that the business might continue to be managed in the same traditions as they have followed, including the same social and moral code. With a trade sale, there is little chance that they may be able to dictate this.

A study of family-owned businesses was published by Stoy Hayward in 1989. In it they quoted some interesting facts about family businesses in the USA:

- more than 98 per cent of corporations in the United States are family owned;

- more than one third of the 'Fortune 500' companies are family owned or controlled;

- about 42 per cent of the largest companies in the United States are controlled by one person or family;

Table 5: Source of Buy-ins, 1989, 1990, 1991

Buy-in from:	1989 (%)	1990 (%)	1991 (%)
Receivership	1.7	6.3	19.3
UK parent	30.7	35.4	29.0
Foreign parent	5.3	3.1	3.6
Families	62.3	55.2	47.3

Source: Centre for Management Buy-out Research.

BUT

- the average life cycle of a family business is twenty-four years, which coincides with the average tenure of the founder;

- only 30 per cent of family businesses reach the second generation;

- fewer than two thirds of these survive through the second generation;

- only 13 per cent of family businesses survive through the third generation.

These facts tell a story: a business is started by an entrepreneur but, in many cases, the same business talent does not persist through to the second and third generations and the business goes into decline and even closes down – 'clogs to clogs in three generations'. Family businesses have inbuilt structural weaknesses which require planning, training and consultation to counteract; without this, failure may loom, certainly stagnation will.

When a business relies on family management, it often implies that the business will be starved of new ideas, because it is more than likely that sons and daughters will grow up in the shadow of the founder, learning his or her business methods. This may lead to an unwillingness and inability to respond to change.

A further problem is that the founder may have dynastic instincts, wanting to pass on the business to the next, and succeeding, generations and thus be unwilling to introduce outsiders into the management structure.

There may also be a continual inherent conflict between family goals and business goals. The family may wish to obtain status, pursue a caring philosophy or maintain a certain attitude towards its employees without letting the fresh air of sound commercial principles gain access. A final problem which can beset a family business is that there may be disagreements within the family which spill over and become disagreements within the business. All these factors tend to enhance the likelihood of a negative outcome for the continued growth and survival of a family business.

A successful management buy-in could reverse this downwards trend. But to succeed, the second and third generations of the family have to come to terms with the realization that they don't possess the necessary talent to drive the business forward. They have to take a hard decision – they may choose to sell out altogether or to remain shareholders and coexist amicably with the incoming management team and new shareholders. This negotiation is a task of great delicacy.

One entrepreneur who bought a family-owned company, described it as follows: 'There was a family that owned 80 per cent of the shares and the old managing director, who wasn't family, had 20 per cent. The chairman hadn't worked in the company for the last ten years. He'd sort of occasionally have a look at the books and draw his salary. His father started the company just after the First World War and he'd got some children, but one son was already in business in Cornwall, his other son had no aspirations to be in business and neither had his daughter. So they decided to sell the company.'

Another fruitful source for a potential buy-in occurs when the owners of the business want to dispose of it. This could include individuals selling or a parent company wishing to dispose of a business because it no longer fits into its strategy or needs an influx of good-quality management to enable it to perform. Individual owners, often the founders, may want to sell simply because they have reached the point where they no longer wish to commit all their time and energy to running the business, for example, because they wish to retire or are in ill-health or wish to move on to another venture.

Buying from a classic entrepreneurial owner is very dangerous and should be handled with care. The owner may be the glue which is holding the operation together. Change the ownership and the whole operation may fall apart. However, Stuart Swinden bought into EFM, a company founded by just such an entrepreneur and has succeeded so far in maintaining an equilibrium. You can read about this in Chapter 17, 'Unlocking the Cupboard'.

Opportunities may also emerge if a start-up is ailing – the original venture capitalist may be the catalyst for a buy-in, because it has become dissatisfied with the performance of the enterprise under its founding management team. The company may have become what venture capitalists term 'the living dead'. This could be at an early stage – or after a number of years when it becomes clear that if the business is to continue its expansion and growth it needs a different management style from that possessed by the original entrepreneur. Brendan Farrell was brought into Noctech, an Irish biotechnology diagnostics company, at the insistence of the venture capitalists; the original founder had been devoting himself only part-time to the business, which had struggled from 1980 to 1985, and the financiers wanted a new approach. While not a straightforward buy-in – Farrell did not invest any money – he had such extensive options that if he met the targets he would end up with more shares than the founder.

Finally, another legitimate target for a buy-in team could be a failed buy-out. Again, the moving force behind the decision to bring in fresh management may lie with the investors who put up the money for the original buy-out. They may feel that they have not received the sort of return they were expecting and take the decision to install new faces to return the investment to the profit pattern they were looking for.

Setting Your Own Criteria

The overriding criterion must be that the target company has potential which is not being exploited by the current management team. However, alongside that there may be other considerations which you wish to establish as the criteria for your choice. There should be little difference between your approach to the strategic evaluation of the industry and market positioning for a start-up or a buy-in.

The ultimate aim must be to select a company where the management task matches your own experience. A business will have a number of characteristics: sector, size, location, turn-round or not, type of people, complexity of task and so on. Choose a company with only one of these variables at odds with your previous experience and stress rises; change all these variables and pressure levels go through the roof.

Take location. The outcome of your MBI is likely to be more positive if you buy a company locally rather than at some distance, which involves your relocation. With a local business, you're more likely to know the company and its people, and so have greater insight before the purchase. In addition, relocation causes such stress in itself that you may perform at a lower level in your new management role.

Les Hunt explains the process which they set up when they decided to search for a business to buy into, rather than start one from scratch: 'We sat down and specified the business we were looking for from an ideal point of view; we laid down what parameters it ought to fit into. We would like it to be in the Midlands, but if it was the right business it wouldn't really matter where it was. One of the hardest aspects was finding worthwhile businesses to consider, so we wanted to cast our net as wide as possible, and wouldn't restrict our search to our local area.

'We thought about what sort of turnover it ought to be running and we specified something between £1 and £2 million. We also said it didn't need to be profitable: what it must have is the potential to make profit.'

Of course, the size of the business is important, but equally telling is the size of the management task, rather than the turnover level. A business with revenues of between £1 and £2 million could turn out to be very complex.

Terry Weston, formerly of CEC-Time, with a background in engineering and running inspection companies, emphasized a further crucial factor: 'I was looking for a vehicle to build an inspection group. I consider that if you're going to do anything, it must be something you understand. You should stay in an associated field. It also makes it easier to find a target; you must be aware of the companies in that field. By careful vetting, you can produce a short-list of targets. If you decide to target a business you don't know, you need a contact to furnish the information.'

How to Look for a Company

Quite the most dispiriting aspect of pursuing the ideas of a management buy-in is the search for a target company. Without doubt, finding a suitable candidate that meets the criteria set can be very time-consuming, and in some cases the search can last a number of years. Of course, finding a 'possible' business is only the first step in the process. The pool of suitable companies is undoubtedly smaller than the pool of management wanting to purchase – and there are other competitors, too, at every stage. It's worth bearing in mind a technical point: you may be interested in buying only the assets of the company, not the company itself. The choice of route will emerge when you have found your target, and you must take your own tax advice on this.

You may be tempted to resign your existing employment to carry out a full-time search, as this is undoubtedly an arduous undertaking. However, past experience has shown that the speed is unlikely to be any greater. Furthermore, leaving your current job produces a new pressure – the desire for a quick result may lead to an unwise decision.

Methods of identifying a possible object for your ambitions will vary, depending on your inclination, knowledge and the type of market. If you have experience in a small sector, you are likely to be aware of the existence of any underachieving businesses. This was Terry Weston's approach to the problem of finding a company in the inspection sector of engineering. Generally speaking, you need to adopt a structured approach to the search, although the truth is that, in many cases, your eventual success in finding a target is likely to be a matter of luck.

Other methods include:

- inquiries through individual contacts, such as through suppliers (likely to be the most successful source);

- desk research, studying well-known information sources such as Extel;

- following up businesses advertised for sale in the national newspapers, often by liquidators and receivers;

- advertising for potential businesses (on the whole, advertising or answering advertisements is not particularly fruitful);

- writing to businesses within your chosen sector;

- employing management consultants to carry out searches;

- contacting some of the venture-capital organizations that are interested in investing in buy-ins. Some of these maintain extensive databases of potential 'victim companies'. Indeed, some of them regard the marriage of management team with company as a contribution they can make;

– contacting some of the major firms of accountants which may maintain a source file of companies who wish to sell (or to buy).

The CMBOR survey found that three quarters of the target companies were in industrial sectors in which the manager had existing experience and had identified them through personal knowledge. Over half had special knowledge of the company (for example, from professional contact) and a fifth had previously been employed by the company. Certainly, some venture capitalists recommend working for the company before purchase as it minimizes the risk.

Les Hunt and Glyn Davies tried most of these avenues in their search for a company. 'We put an advertisement in the *Birmingham Post* – I can't remember whether that turned up anything or not. We also wrote to a lot of accountants and groups of companies which were acquisitive, on the assumption that they were also the groups which would be trying to dispose of the ones that didn't fit. We sent an awful lot of letters out. And we got in touch with companies which are a sort of broker – if you want to sell your company, they'll do it for you and if you want to buy, they'll help as well.'

Brokers and intermediaries permeate every level of the venture capital and enterprise scene. They can charge substantial fees for the work they carry out – nevertheless if it is the only possibility of achieving your objective, you may consider them a necessary evil. With most reputable intermediaries you should be able to negotiate that they work on a contingency basis. This may be, at the extreme, no success, no payment; more likely, you might find they offer you the choice at the outset of a set figure, regardless of success or failure, contrasted with a much higher figure which is only paid on success.

While many entrepreneurs carry out the search themselves, Alistair Jacks considers an intermediary to be essential in the whole process. Alistair already has a successful track record: he bought out a computer software company called BOS in 1983, selling it some six years later. After a period of gathering thoughts together, he was ready for the next challenge – buying into a company. This had to be a different industry, partly through inclination and partly because of a non-competition clause when he sold out. He uses an intermediary in his search for suitable targets. He explains: 'The masterstroke for me is finding someone to research sectors and industries. You need an intermediary to make initial contacts, so you don't need to reveal who you are. Buying a business is a threatening situation, that's why it's called a takeover. The combative element is dissolved with an intermediary, but he or she must be genuinely independent.' Another advantage in using an intermediary is that it increases the level of debate, which can be fruitful if it helps you to avoid a ghastly mistake.

Utilizing all their sources of information, the Metalline duo eventually came across their first prospective 'victim', a metal-bashing company, and they invested a considerable amount of time in trying to make this buy-in happen – only to find after six months that they were unable to summon the required backing from financiers. There followed a further four or five attempts to buy into a business, including a couple of occasions when they almost were at the stage of signing contracts, only to find the deal collapsing at the last moment. 'There was one business which was a metal-pressing business in Tamworth – the chap wanted to sell it and retire. It was a bit smaller than we wanted but it was good. We had got everything sorted out and were all off to sign the documents on Monday morning. On Sunday the chap phoned up and said he'd changed his mind and couldn't sell it after all. He'd been unable to sleep! We had been working on that particular deal for three months.'

The other deals fell through for a variety of reasons: liquidation, competition, lack of finance as well as the vacillation of owners. In the end, Metalline came to their attention by chance. The pair had been to see 3i about buying another company which was in project engineering and Lloyds Bank had drawn 3i's attention to Metalline. This deal was put through very quickly indeed, in the space of two to three weeks.

The ultimate responsibility for finding a business lies fairly and squarely on your own shoulders, but venture-capital companies can sometimes be helpful in looking for targets and Alistair Jacks has found this to be the case. 'There is no market or prospect list to help you find a business. There are just the usual sources. I've put myself about – and this is where the venture-capital companies come into their own. You can only process one or two situations in parallel. The hit rate of looking at situations is only about one in fifty. You could work for eighteen months to two years and still not have found one to have a crack at. The venture-capital company knows you and wants to back you, so puts you together with any suitable businesses.'

Simon Unger's experience was somewhat different (although this was back in 1988, so perhaps the organizations can provide more detailed help now). He began his search by contacting his accountant. Between them they drew up a list of venture-capital people; Simon approached them to explain his purpose and his thought pattern: 'What I found was that none of them were prepared to give me any help at all, except for one, in looking for targets.' Simon was working within the computer supplies and stationery industry at that time and didn't want to be identified as looking for a company. So he valued the help that the venture capitalists (a very small firm) would give him in carrying out company searches and making the initial approaches. 'They weren't going to charge me for the work, but the charge would be reflected in their introduction fee when a target company was found.'

Simon and the venture-capital team went about it in the following way: 'It was a sort of joint effort; we'd meet up every now and again and just have a chat and come up with a few targets and have a look into them. I'd drop some names to them and they would make contact. We'd both be scouring the *Financial Times* on Tuesday and the *Sunday Times* and the financiers would use their database and other contacts as well.'

At the time Simon was trawling for sound businesses, there was a lot of activity in the particular market he was interested in. It's a distribution industry and so there are significant economies of scale. There were two or three companies snapping up a lot of the smaller fry – so there was stiff competition for any good business, and silly premiums being paid. In all, Simon estimates that the team looked at around one hundred businesses and made bids on just three out of that total.

Nayyer Hussain and James Wooster bought into Martin Electrical Ltd, a sleepy company manufacturing resistance welding equipment in 1988; their principal method of searching was to utilize personal contacts. 'We hunted for nearly a year – it was a constant process of talking to individuals who might know a suitable business. This is the major problem for most MBI teams – finding a decent business to buy.'

A dilemma you will face is who should you approach first, the company or the venture capitalists. It would be wise to introduce yourself to a number of venture capitalists at an early stage – and long before you find your target company. As venture capitalists back management teams, you should devote some time and thought to persuading them that you are worthy of their backing, provided a suitable business for investment is found. Furthermore, your negotiations for a business may need to be conducted speedily, once you are at that stage, particularly if there is some competition about or if you are promoting the idea of buying a company from the receiver. Thus you may be under pressure to put the deal together with a financier. Any preparatory work you have carried out with the venture-capital groups can only enhance your position.

The venture-capital organization may assess your performance during the search and the negotiation. They will look at your past record, the way you approach the task of identifying a target, how you handle the negotiations to purchase the business, the firm direction and focus you give to accountants while conducting an investigation of the business on your behalf and the manner in which you ensure that professional costs are kept under control.

All these tasks are crucial to the likely success of your buy-in, so you must concentrate on them for your own benefit. Additionally, your performance in these tasks might affect the enthusiasm the venture capitalist has for providing the funding and the terms on which it is provided. Thus your stake in the business could be increased or decreased by the venture capitalist's view of your actions in the preliminary stage. Of course, other factors such as your previous experience and results will be determinants, too.

What Particular Problems Might You Face?

In view of the experiences related so far by those who have hunted and successfully bought into a company, it is clear that the major problem is finding the quarry. However, further difficulties emerge once the quarry has been spotted. Thus you may find that you bid for two, three or more companies before you achieve your objective.

Here are some of the developments of which you should beware before you can achieve success:

- competition from other predators;

- lack of information and data on which you can make an informed judgement;

- vacillation of sellers;

- speed which may be required to conduct a delicate tripartite negotiation;

- pension or tax problems.

Predators take all forms and Alistair Jacks has lost out one purchase to a surprise competitor. After many false dawns, he had finally lighted on a sound business with potential. He began the round of venture capitalists, trying to interest one or more of them in the deal. Generally, venture capitalists prefer not to have a majority of the equity and Alistair was putting together a deal that involved more than one venture capitalist to fund the purchase, known as syndication. Alistair says: 'The crisis of completion was approaching, when to my amazement, one of the venture capitalists kicked all the potential syndicated partners and myself out of the deal and did it on their own. They claimed they were entitled to do this. You should be aware that if you introduce a business idea to a venture capitalist, if they are of a mind to cut you out, they can do so. This is very surprising as the whole image of venture capitalists is that they are the embodiment of confidentiality. The unwritten rule is that they don't steal your proposal. Check your venture capital company carefully. The industry knows which venture capitalists are well known for dirty tricks.'

Undoubtedly, this is unexpected behaviour on the part of the venture-capital group, but predators abound everywhere: look out for them and expect them to appear. Silence on your part and confidentiality agreements imposed on others is not an overreaction, but is the manner in which you should conduct your search for a suitable company and any subsequent negotiations.

While competition exists in unlikely quarters, you must also assume that other more conventional competitors will emerge. Terry Weston and Bert Ramsden felt under great pressure during their negotiations to buy CEC-Time to avoid any hint of their proposed purchase reaching the ears of the major competitor in the inspection field. 'We had to maintain secrecy.'

The mania for merger and acquisition created severe difficulties for Simon Unger in his chosen market of computer-supplies distribution. He explains: 'There were loads of companies being snapped up at the time. Our biggest limiting factor in competing with two or three particular companies was that we didn't want to pay a premium for the company we were buying; we wanted to pay asset value or below.'

Not only was the competition pushing up prices, it also meant that there was little chance of any bid being successful: 'Any ad in the *Financial Times* to sell a computer-supplies company was receiving between sixty and one hundred replies. In the three companies that we bid for, there were five or six other bidders.' The intense competition may have led Simon and the venture capitalists to be tempted to buy into a company that with hindsight is seen to be a mistake (see Chapter 17). They first contacted the company in September and put in an offer in November, which they were told was too low. But no final decision was made and contact was maintained on an irregular basis. Finally, in March they were told that four other buyers had fallen out, that there was a fifth buyer interested but if that negotiation fizzled out, their bid would be considered – and that was the outcome.

Obtaining adequate information about a company remains a persistent problem; a trenchant approach is required to unearth the true figures about a company's performance. No matter how difficult it is to obtain particular figures or facts from the company, you must not be deterred. Simply refuse to take the deal any further unless you have free access to the information essential to evaluate the business. If you are putting up money, it is likely to be the only stake which you will be able to provide out of your own resources. Don't waste it on a pup. Of course, you can, and must, insist on warranties. But legal wording cannot cover every eventuality, particularly the less tangible circumstances.

The advice of the Hussain/Wooster duo is to concentrate on the management accounts and to remember that lack of information increases the risk. 'If you can't see into the business, make your estimates more conservative.'

A further complication which may emerge during your hunt for a business to buy is that sellers can always change their minds – right up to the moment when signatures are to be attached to the contract, as the Metalline pair discovered. In your contact with the vendor you need to tailor your approach according to the type of vendor: a private owner who wishes to sell the business to retire or to move on to fresh pastures may need to hear a different message from a public company or group disposing of a subsidiary. Be sensitive to these requirements. Les Hunt expands: 'I think you have to present yourself as a far more prudent character if you're approaching private shareholders. Both sides become a little too sensitive as to who they are and why they are selling. With a PLC, it's just part of the business on agenda. Funnily enough financial considerations are not always important to the PLC. For example, with the first company we looked at, I think the PLC selling it was more interested in arranging the sale so that it wouldn't create an embarrassing moment when the board went through the balance sheet. But they weren't looking to make any huge profits out of it.'

A sensible approach is to try to analyse the motives of the vendor and pitch your bid to give yourself the greatest chance of success, as well as the best return on the money you invest. Non-financial considerations can play an important subsidiary role in any deal.

The attitude of the existing or remaining management can influence the outcome of your bid. Offering shares or options can act as a stimulant to them in the revitalization of the business – and they may consider it their divine right. Of course, such an action is not always successful, if the existing team is not the right calibre.

Nevertheless, bringing the deal to the table is a difficulty. 'The target company needs a marked stimulus to make the move to sell. You must make sure that the stimulus is real, is accepted and is fully understood, otherwise it will disappear expensively in the heat of completion,' advises Jacks. Advisers are expensive and thousands of pounds are at risk in the final stage.

Sellers often try to force too speedy a process on you. The only answer is to resist this and to ensure that you are not induced to make mistakes by trying to push a deal through too quickly. Sometimes, of course, it is difficult to resist. While the vendor may wish to press for haste, the buy-in team may delay, hoping to negotiate the optimum deal possible. And hindsight will always encourage buyers to curse that they might have been able to negotiate a better price or share of the equity. Nayyer Hussain and James Wooster stress that this may be the case, but the 'important thing is to do the deal'.

Finally, the pension scheme and the tax liability may cause particular problems. The pair which bought into Martins found the suspicion over the pension scheme endangered their deal. 'There was a strong suspicion by the seller that we simply wanted to raid the pension scheme – and so we didn't get it.' You would be well advised to obtain specialist advice on these technical aspects.

9

Can You Buy the Company You Work For?

The story of any company is a dance to the music of time – the music stops, the company changes partners, it stops again, the company takes a rest. MBOs are all about timing; but with a few exceptions, there may be little you can do to influence the band. When the music next stops for the company you work for, where will you be sitting? Will you be able to seize the opportunity to buy your company if it becomes for sale for some reason?

Once a buy-out looks possible, the dance becomes less elegant. Musical chairs takes over. A number of interested parties may be scrambling for the last chair – your aim must be to ensure that you and your management team book that seat before any other competitors. But, just like musical chairs, there may well be an undignified scramble.

With a few MBOs, the opportunity has been carved out by the management team on their own initiative, by persuading the owners of the company that it is a better investment for them to sell all or part of it and allow the management a free rein. John Leighfield of Istel, now part of AT & T, achieved just this when he led a buy-out of the computer services division of British Leyland. He says: 'During 1984, the board of BL had as a top priority the privatization of BL. I realized in late 1984 or early 1985 that this posed either a threat or an opportunity. It dawned on me that perhaps we could privatize Istel separately and make it part of the IT industry, rather than being forced back into the motor industry. This idea initially caused scepticism within BL and there were grave doubts as to whether Istel could be separated.'

The doubts arose because during 1984 only 20 per cent of the company's turnover came from outside BL. 'People said that with that sort of profile Istel couldn't possibly be separate.' John spent most of 1985 trying to persuade BL of the contrary – against fairly constant opposition based on the belief that a buy-out wasn't feasible or that the management team wouldn't be able to achieve it. 'Either because of my stubbornness or my charm[!], the board of BL agreed to a management-led employee buy-out in 1985. And they said they wouldn't go outside for a sale provided the management team came up with a sensible bid. We put forward a proposal for the April 1986 board. The arrival of the proposal coincided with the arrival of Graham Day. He said there must be competition. BL didn't advertise Istel for sale but information went out to a large number of interested organizations. In the autumn of 1986 we put in a bid, along with other bidders. In December 1986, the board accepted Istel's bid. Even then, it took until June 1987 before the buy-out happened – a period of two and a half years in all.'

John Leighfield's example shows that you may have to plan for a number of years before you are successful. Even if you think it looks unlikely that you will ever be able to buy out your company, should the opportunity arise, some pre-planning and forethought could put you one foot ahead of your competitors in reaching that chair. But first, however the business comes to be for sale, you need to investigate and assess it closely to test the hypothesis that it is a suitable candidate to be bought out.

What Makes a Management Buy-out?

The mechanics of a buy-out are usually that the existing management of the business forms a new company. The management and the venture capitalists subscribe for shares in the new company. The new company purchases the shares (occasionally the assets) of the company being bought out. But together the amount subscribed for shares in the new business will not be sufficient to pay the whole purchase price. So, in addition, there will be bank loans and medium-term loans made to it to raise the full amount needed for the buy-out. Rarely can a buy-out be achieved with loans alone and without equity.

Technically, MBOs are horrendously difficult; it can be easy to be tripped up and carry out the wrong action, falling foul of the law or tax rules. It is essential to get good technical advice – and there is no substitute for previous experience. Make sure your advisers and venture capitalists have extensive experience of buy-outs. If this is the case, the chances are that they will have come across most odd technical points and know what the pitfalls and benefits are. Because of the combination of technical complexities, the three-way negotiation between vendor, purchaser and venture capitalist, and the need for you to carry on as full-time managers of the business, achieving a buy-out is generally a more exhausting process than finalizing a buy-in or a start-up.

These are the nuts and bolts of how an MBO works, but what are the characteristics of a successful buy-out? These are:

- ample cash flow in the business you want to buy;

- risk-taking: investing your own money;

- the introduction of gearing, which improves the return on the investment;

- incentives, which you should negotiate for yourself, but opinions on the value of ratchets, for example, vary;

- a strong management team, without which you won't get funding.

Without these five ingredients, purchasing the company you work for is unlikely to deliver the sort of return on your investment that you desire, although it's probably true to say that at the time of the buy-out this is not uppermost in your mind. It tends to become important to you later.

The most important ingredient is *cash flow*: a strong cash flow from the potential buy-out business is vital to its success. Generally speaking, it should look sufficient to provide an interest cover of two to three times. If the business is not already generating a positive cash flow, your plans must be able to show that it can do so within a short space of time. Generating a positive cash flow is crucial – you are taking on a lot of debt in buying the business. Without a good cash flow, how will you pay the interest and make the repayments due? It would be an added advantage if the business can show good security in assets for the debt, although technically you can't give security on the assets to purchase the shares.

The second essential feature of a management buy-out is *risk-taking*. The managers of the business must be prepared to invest a large bite of their own personal wealth in the shares of the company which has been formed to buy the target business. It's difficult to be precise – and rules are always there to be broken – but financiers are probably looking for a commitment of £100,000 to £150,000 from the management. They may look for even more if this would be a small proportion of your assets. If the buy-out is substantial, it is unlikely that the management will hold a majority of the ordinary shares of the company, but probable with smaller purchases.

A third feature is the investment of funds in the company by venture-capital organizations and other institutions in return for some shares and some debt. This gives the institutions a mixture of potential capital gain and income. The *gearing* provided by the debt will improve the return to the shareholders, provided of course that the business performs at or above target.

With a buy-out you will need two lots of money; the first buys the company; the second provides working capital for the business. Generally speaking, once you have bought the business you find that the banking facilities have stayed with the vendor. This further finance is usually provided by a bank term loan or overdraft.

Next, the financing structure may include additional *incentives* for the management, over and above the shares that the management have bought. So, for example, there may be share options and ratchets, which allow the management to increase their proportion of the equity, provided that certain agreed performance targets are met. These could include exit values or profit targets. But some entrepreneurs warn against ratchets. Finally, the condition vital to the success of all enterprises is just as important for an MBO – there must be *a strong management team.*

The result of this shuffling about of money should be that for a relatively small amount (maybe a large part of your personal wealth), you, the management team, should end up controlling a company.

MBOs, the Rolling Snowball of the Eighties

At the start of the eighties, the term 'buy-outs' was not as common in business as it is today. MBOs were around and did exist, but many of the potential entrepreneurs hidden in large corporations knew nothing about them. Instead, driven by the desire to break out, the most common reaction was to start up a business.

But MBOs were just like a snowball which you start rolling down a hill – tiny at first, but getting bigger and bigger as it reached the end of the eighties. The term 'MBOs' was on everyone's lips. It appeared that bigger and bigger buy-outs were being announced – and more of them. And it seemed, just as frequently, that those lucky entrepreneurs who had bought out in 1984–6 were coming to the stock market, either for a full listing or, more commonly, to be quoted on the Unlisted Securities Market. There were also examples of companies that had been bought out by the management subsequently being sold to another larger company. The day of the near-instant millionaire seemed to have arrived.

UK Paper (now part of Fletcher Challenge) is one of the outstanding examples of what was possible in those exciting times. In 1986, the management team bought out the company from Bowater UK Paper

Table 6: UK Management Buy-outs, 1979–91

Year	Number	Total Value (£ m)	Average Value (£ m)	Year	Number	Total Value (£ m)	Average Value (£ m)
1979	18	14	0.8	1985	263	1,142	4.3
1980	36	28	0.8	1986	315	1,175	3.7
1981	143	180	1.3	1987	344	3,215	9.3
1982	237	347	1.5	1988	375	3,712	9.9
1983	235	366	1.6	1989	373	3,887	10.4
1984	237	403	1.7	1990	484	2,456	5.1
				1991	446	2,155	4.8

Source: Centre for Management Buy-out Research.

for £38 million. Within eighteen months, it was floated on the stock market with a value of £108 million. Its offer for sale was oversub-scribed eleven times. At the end of 1989 it was bought by Fletcher for £299 million. So the value of the company had apparently increased by nearly eight times in three years. If the MBO was structured in a typical way, it's likely that the value of the management's investment would have increased by much more than that.

Table 6 (on the left) and Table 7 (below) show how strong was the growth in the number and in the size of management buy-outs during the eighties. The impression which closet entrepreneurs had was correct: they were getting bigger and more frequent, that is, until the start of the next decade. The year 1990 showed strong growth in the numbers of buy-outs but the average size fell and in 1991, the average size fell yet again, although the numbers of deals remained high.

The heady days are gone. The snowball has reached the bottom of the hill; it hasn't disintegrated, but it's shrinking in size. Conditions have changed for deals of £10 million and over, but at the lower end of the scale (under £10 million) there is still a lot of activity.

Finding the Opportunities

A major source of good candidates for buy-outs pops up during periods of corporate turbulence, when a large company reassesses its overall strategy and direction – or is forced to by some outside event or

Table 7: Size of UK Management Buy-outs (%): Selected Years

Value range	Pre-1982	1984	1987	1989	1990	1991
Less than £1 million	84.03	74.68	37.79	28.42	33.06	33.18
£1–£5 million	11.76	18.98	48.84	45.84	48.55	53.36
£5–£10 million	2.10	3.80	5.23	10.46	8.47	5.38
£10–£25 million	1.68	1.27	2.33	6.70	6.61	4.04
More than £25 million	0.43	1.27	5.81	8.58	3.31	4.04

Source: Centre for Management Buy-out Research.

person or other business. For example, at the start of the nineties many companies have found themselves with too much debt and under pressure, perhaps from their bankers, have to realize assets. The company may focus on activities which are outside the core business and don't fit logically or efficiently within that core. This is the commonest reason for the availability of a company to its managers. David Clutterbuck's survey of MBOs found that 37 per cent of respondents picked divestment of non-core activities as the reason for the company's sale. And Table 8 below confirms this is the major source of buy-outs. Some companies in 1991/92 have been particularly keen on divesting non-core activities – see Table 9 on the right.

Here are some examples of the sort of opportunity that you might be able to work in your favour:

– some products unessential to the business as a whole may be unprofitable or barely profitable or not meeting the required rate of return for the company;

– a stand-alone unit or business may be struggling to make profits;

– a business may be making satisfactory profits now, but its long-term future may be in doubt without the company devoting investments and resources to it;

Table 8: Sources of Management Buy-outs, 1982, 1987, 1990, 1991 (%)

Source	1982	1987	1990	1991
Receiver	14.3	0.7	12.9	19.6
UK parent	62.2	51.1	44.2	43.6
Foreign parent	10.2	10.7	7.8	9.1
Family ownership	9.2	25.8	28.5	24.0
Privatization	4.1	10.4	4.7	2.3
Going private	0.0	1.3	1.9	1.4

Source: Centre for Management Buy-out Research.

– the main company may be wanting to devote more resources to one of its activities and need to divest a business to fund it;

– the main company may simply need to reduce its own borrowings or loans and the business you work for is a discrete chunk which could be sold off without loss of efficiency to the main business;

– the business supplies services or products to the main company but it could be more profitable if it was independent and succeeded in grabbing a larger share of the whole market.

All these are examples of opportunities for you. If you work for a group or business which is currently reviewing its make-up, think laterally. Can you use this information to make a case for you and your management team to buy out your bit of the business? Of course, in all these examples, the first that you may know is that the group announces it is selling or closing your bit of the operations.

This is what happened when Derrick Bumpsteed and his team bought out Exacta from STC. 'By about 1985, only 10 per cent of what we made was going into STC. STC had problems and Arthur Walsh from GEC was bought in. The board started saying that it had to get back to core businesses and Exacta wasn't a core business. They more or less put the company up for sale.'

Table 9: Numbers of Multiple Buy-outs January 1991–June 1992

Enterprise	Number	Enterprise	Number
Lloyds/Abbey Life	6	Burns Anderson	4
Dalgety	4	Dean & Bowes	4
First Technology	4	Scottish Heritable Trust	4
Aitch	3	Berisford International	3
Courtaulds	3	Cray Electronics	3
Electron House	3	Faber Prest	3
Lex Service	3		

Source: Centre for Management Buy-out Research.

A more straightforward reason for a company wanting to dispose of a subsidiary or discrete business occurs when it faces its own financial problems and needs to dispose of assets to prop up its shaky finances. In 1987, in a much-publicized takeover, Combined English Stores, which was a highly diversified group, moved into the hands of the Next group. One of CES's subsidiaries was Eurocamp (upmarket self-drive tent and mobile-home package holidays).

The management team at Eurocamp realized that Next had a completely different management style to that of their former owners – more intrusive. The management team, headed by Richard Atkinson, also felt that their company would not sit well in the Next fashion empire. 'We thought that Next might sell us,' said Richard. 'So, we saw this as an opportunity for a management buy-out.' Unfortunately, Next said no.

However, within a year, Next was having severe cash-flow problems. The company had ousted George Davies, its chairman. The group was carrying out a major reorganization. Once again, the Eurocamp team offered a buy-out deal. When they went to the Next management with their proposals, they found out that the Rank group had already expressed an interest in buying Eurocamp. The team were given the chance to bid alongside Rank.

The team approached their accountants at the end of July 1988. They had previously produced a business plan when they first attempted to buy the business, so this was quickly updated. 'In early September, we went to Next,' recalls Richard. They were told their bid was too low, but Next indicated that if the team could match the Rank offer, the company would be theirs. They were given only forty-eight hours to raise the money for the deal.

Richard said that at one point they were in the ridiculous situation that Rank directors were visiting Eurocamp in the belief that they would buy the company while Next had already agreed the management team's buy-out.

So far this chapter has looked at opportunities which may emerge when a large or diversified group decides to shed itself of one of its businesses, or a product, or some of its assets. But there are other candidates for management buy-outs. One of the likely possibilities is a company which is owned by a private group of shareholders, possibly, but not exclusively, a family. A management buy-out may solve problems associated with retirement or differing objectives of the shareholders, for example. Video Arts was a company started up in 1972 by some now-famous shareholders – and by the late eighties they had simply come to the point when they wanted to realize their shareholdings and move on. At the time of the buy-out, which was led by Tina Tietjen and Maggie Tree, the founding shareholders held 98 per cent of the shares. The company itself was very successful – a market leader and remaining very entrepreneurial. A management buy-out was the preferred route for the founders as the company had a strong corporate culture which they wished to preserve. They were also anxious to find a buyer who would leave the company intact.

Another obvious source of suitable candidates for a management buy-out is the receiver – and in 1991 this was the source for buy-outs in nearly one in five occasions (see Table 8 on page 98). Sometimes the company itself has gone into receivership; sometimes it is forced into receivership because of the financial difficulties of the parent. In either case, great care has to be exercised to avoid mounting a management buy-out to protect your job, or those of your employees. Crystal-clear thinking is required, to examine the reasons why the company would be more successful under your ownership (or part-ownership), especially as the company will be saddled with more debt after the buy-out than before.

Roy Mitchell bought out the stainless-steel division of Carron, manu-facturer of kitchen sinks. In his view, the company had gone into receivership for reasons other than difficulties faced in that particular division. He says: 'I was aware of the way in which the accounts were made up in the consolidated group. They gave a different view of the stainless divisions, which was not descriptive of the inherent possibilities of this operation. In other words, they were taking money out to adjust this and adjust that and so forth – I was aware of what was really being generated at the sharp end.'

Since the start of the nineties, receiverships have spawned a significant number of MBOs. When some larger companies have failed, many of the subsidiaries have been trading profitably and have

Table 10: Numbers of Buy-outs from Public-sector Sources

Source	Number	Source	Number
British Aerospace	1	BTG/NEB	13
BL/Austin Rover	13	National Bus Company	39
British Rail	7	NFC	1
British Shipbuilders	12	Scottish Bus Group	5
British Steel	10	Local authorities	41
Port authority	3		

Source: Centre for Management Buy-out Research.

been the subject of buy-outs. For example in Chapter 13 you can read about the buy-out of Denby Pottery from Coloroll, which in 1990 was the source of eight MBOs.

Finally, during the eighties a new source of targets developed: public sector buy-outs. Some of the better-known names that have spawned buy-outs (and buy-ins) are listed in Table 10 above. The review of the operations of the civil service being carried out by the government implies that these opportunities will carry on emerging during the nineties.

One example of a public-sector buy-out is the company led by Stephen Hinton. He had been seconded to one of the working parties that were looking at British Rail's strategy for the building and repairing of trains. The option recommended for the Doncaster site, one of eight sites in British Rail Engineering, was to close it. Instead the team of four, led by Hinton, decided to buy part of the Doncaster operation, 'The Wagon Works', and turn it into RFS Industries. Stephen says: 'We got lots of personal encouragement from BR to go and buy.'

What are the Requirements for a Buy-out to be Achieved?

You may have a wonderful candidate for a management buy-out – and yet still not be able to achieve it. To succeed in buying out a company, all the people involved need to be positively in favour, or at least to be neutral to this outcome rather than any other. So who is involved? There is quite a long list: the management, the sellers, the employees, the customers, the financial institutions and the banks. What do they all want to achieve from this particular change in ownership? You, the management, need to demonstrate to each what the effect will be on them and what the likelihood of success is.

You will know better than anyone what the management team hopes to achieve from the buy-out, but it is likely to include job satisfaction and material gain. Job satisfaction should emerge naturally from the independence and freedom which owning your own business brings. Material gain may or may not happen. Certainly the financial structure which you agree with venture capitalists will be one determining factor. Another is the scope available within your target company to be more efficient, cut down on costs and generate more profits.

You will have to hope that the sellers are not hostile to the idea of the management buy-out – or you will have to convince them of the positive outcome if they support it. Some sellers are favourably dis-posed towards an MBO – as, for example, the sellers of Video Arts were. And the sellers of Eurocamp preferred an MBO to a trade sale, although a prerequisite was that the financial return remained the same. Most sellers will simply be neutral, requiring that the MBO gives them the best return. Of course, if the seller was not seeking to sell the business and an MBO is your suggestion, their reaction may not be favourable. You may have to carry out a fair amount of persuasion.

One essential group to influence in your favour is the employees. A negative reaction may well prove fatal to the chances of a buy-out occurring; it certainly would reduce the chances of the business succeeding, even if the buy-out was achieved. The *Financial Times* reported the hostile reaction from the employees of a division of BT Reprographics – the in-house printing division, when an MBO was mooted: 'Employees say they are concerned that their rights to redeployment within BT would be affected by the buy-out and that the cost of redundancy agreements has not been taken into account.' And the plans for the MBO fell through in 1990.

Bob Mottram, the former personnel director of Premier Brands, a buy-out from Cadbury Schweppes, described in *Personnel*

Management how he approached the task of involving the employees positively in the buy-out process: 'The management team had a clear run to arrange finance, negotiate the sale agreement and the various Cadbury brand franchises through to the end of January when Cadbury Schweppes would consider any counter-offers.

'The communication process started on Monday, 13 January, with a press release and face-to-face briefings covering all 4,500 employees. The key messages in that briefing process had to achieve the right balance between reassurance and a very clear, unambivalent call for change. The consequences of failure to change had to be spelt out.'

Of course, the buy-out of Premier was a substantial one – but the reaction of employees should not be ignored, even if the business you are targeting is significantly smaller.

One decision you need to make early on is whether you will involve the employees in the ownership of the business or whether you will concentrate ownership in a few key hands at director level. Mottram says: 'From the outset, the buy-out team was committed to an ownership dimension for all employees, and a key part of our message was that 15 per cent of the equity was set aside for employees in the form of share options.'

John Leighfield of Istel also was strongly in favour of involving employees. He refers to the buy-out as a management-led employee buy-out. A significant proportion of the employees invested in the buy-out (900 out of a total of 1,300), buying shares at the same price as the management, although in a package which included some preference shares to lower the risk. 'We put an enormous amount of effort into a dialogue with employees, not as early as we would have liked because we were bound by confidentiality. But as soon as this ceased, we produced a list of questions and answers which was sent to employees. We laid on sessions in groups of thirty, which I attended, and from these consolidated more questions and answers. We produced a "prospectus" for employees which explained our aspirations. This pseudo-prospectus looked an awful lot like a normal one. We also organized a video, with Brian Widlake interviewing me and putting me on the spot. This was shown at conferences to which partners were invited.'

Any change of ownership of a business is an uncertain time for customers. Part of your communication process before the buy-out, unless of course it is a secret negotiation, should involve key customers. You don't want to find that you have succeeded in buying the business, only to find that there is no business left to buy. In particular, you need to persuade your customers to carry on buying your goods and settling their bills in the normal way, otherwise the business will start its independent life with an instant cash crisis. As with all the others involved in the buy-out, your aim should be to convince your customers that it will be beneficial for them – better focus on your business, more efficiency, ultimately a better product or service.

A neutral opinion from the financial institutions would, of course, spell the end of your buy-out dream. They need to form the view that the MBO will provide them with the financial return which they require. They will satisfy themselves of this by intensive study of your business plan and an investigation of your business. Acceptance or rejection will be based on the internal rate of return which the institutions estimate will be available when they can exit from their investment – commonly for large MBOs, they are looking for a minimum return of 35 per cent a year. For many small MBOs, there is no exit.

The institutions' investigations will focus on the management team and the market, as with any other venture, but particular emphasis will be on the assets of the business, the cash-flow profile and the interest cover. Will it be capable of generating a strong and positive cash flow, sufficient to pay the interest on the debt you are taking on and repay the debt in instalments when it becomes due? Here are some specific points you should look out for which will indicate ability to generate a strong cash flow:

- able to earn high margins;

- low capital expenditure;

- low fixed overheads;

- high turnover of working capital;

- availability of tax losses;

- surplus assets which can be converted into cash;

- low research and development requirements;

- a mature product with little cyclical fluctuations often indicates ability to produce surplus cash.

How will Competition From Other Buyers Affect Your Buy-out?

One obvious result of competition is that you may end up losing your purchase to another buyer. Or you may succeed, but find you have had to pay more than you wanted. The buy-out team at Eurocamp had to raise their bid to match the Rank offer. And at Istel, the team found that once they had persuaded Rover to divest the business, they had to compete with other buyers, raising the purchase price in the process.

In almost all cases, buyers faced competition, the only exception being buy-outs from the receiver. Although there will be competition in these examples, too, very often speed becomes an even more important factor. The receiver will be looking to sell the business as a going concern and uncertainty about the future of the business will result if there is too much delay before the receiver finds a solution – customers and suppliers will defect with increasing speed until the business is effectively buried. Ed Hunter bought Penman Engineering from the receiver; it had been part of a larger group but Ed decided that once separate from the rest of the group Penman could shed a lot of the group charges and expenses and be profitable. The group went into receivership on 30 November and Penman was up and running as an independent company by mid-January.

This was a very tight timetable to achieve and the timetable was met because Ed adopted a pragmatic approach to raising the funds. There wasn't sufficient time to hawk it around lots of institutions to see which was the best deal that the management team could obtain. Instead, the team sat down and looked at how the deal could be structured. With this structure in mind the team approached the Bank of Scotland and a couple of institutions, the Scottish Development Agency and 3i to ascertain whether they wanted to invest on this basis. They just managed to satisfy the timetable required by the receiver. Hunter likens buying from the receiver to 'a juggling act, with plates on tall sticks. You are running through the sticks constantly adjusting – in the case of an MBO, suppliers, employees and customers.'

Another company bought from the receiver, Carron, also had to meet a very tight deadline. Roy Mitchell explains: 'For about two months I was working for the receiver – and he was bringing forward whatever interest he could to run the business as a going concern. But it became clear that the interest was very likely to evaporate very quickly – and that's when I put in a letter of intent to the receiver.' After writing the letter of intent, the deal was completed in twenty-one days.

Other buy-outs can take much longer, even where there is significant competition. For example, the buy-out of Video Arts, like Istel, took two and half years to come to fulfilment. 'The vendors' position kept changing and we had to stop and start again. It all became very emotional,' explains Tina Tietjen. And the buy-out of RFS Industries from British Rail also took two years. Of the other buy-outs described in this book, Exacta, Porth and Eurocamp were achieved in a few months, Denby Pottery and Straightset in a few weeks.

The experiences of the management who have finalized buy-outs must bring home forcibly to you the difficulties and hindrances that can emerge. But John Leighfield's tip is this: 'Stick to your guns. All sorts of opposition can emerge, even envy. There can be misunderstanding of what you are trying to do and ignorance, because others within the group have not done a buy-out.'

Constraints on Directors Involved in Buy-outs

The idea of buying-out the company you work for may be very exciting, but you should be cautious in how you set about fulfilling your objective. As an employee and director of the company you have certain duties towards it – and negotiating a buy-out could prove to put you in conflict with those duties. And, of course, there may be particular terms and conditions in your contract of employment which you should check. The fundamental message is: take legal advice before you talk to anyone.

Broadly, as a director you have a fiduciary duty to the company. This implies four specific elements:

– to act in good faith in the bona fide interests of the company;

– to exercise your power as a director for its proper purpose;

– to avoid a conflict of interest;

– not to make personal profits as a result of your directorship. The profit, or the opportunity to make the profit, belongs to the company.

Directors have a further duty to exercise their skills and to take reasonable care.

Areas which may cause you problems and about which you should take particular care include using the company's equipment to produce the information you need and producing that information in the company's time, not your own. A further hurdle appears where you need to use confidential company information to produce the necessary business plan or presentation. If you are simply reviewing it yourself, there may be no potential problem. But where you use it to make a profit for yourself or to reveal to others, there could be legal difficulties. While you may naturally wish to keep secret your plans to buy the company, there will come a point when this is no longer feasible – and certainly, once you need to reveal information to outsiders, you are probably at that point.

There is more about the duties and responsibilities of directors and employees in Chapter 3, 'Second Thoughts' and Chapter 6, 'The Board'. It is essential that you also take legal advice on this.

What Happens If the Management Buy-out Does Not Occur?

Success is not certain. You may suggest a buy-out but the owner may say no – or you may compete in a buy-out against other bidders and fail. What happens?

You may be forced out. And the management team at Denby Pottery faced this threat when they first proposed the buy-out. John Cavill of Logical Networks (see Chapter 15) had also tried to buy-out the business he worked for. The failure of this plan was followed by his abrupt departure. Carrying out clear planning and thinking before you reveal your intentions is advisable. This should encompass the likely chances of acceptance and rejection of the idea, as well as your fall-back plan if you fail.

Alternatively, you may be able to remain as part of the management team after another bidder takes over or after the owner retains control. The Eurocamp team suffered no ill-effect as a result of their first approach to the owners. And they were successful in their second approach.

The team who bought out Mohawk Computers was also able to have two bites at the cherry. Indeed, it was the very fact that they could see what mistakes they had made first time around that allowed them to succeed on the second occasion. Gerry Meredith Smith led the team and relates: 'There was an opportunity glaring us in the face; there had been problems since 1984. In 1985, we competed, along with seven others, to buy the company, but it was sold to an individual investor. The big problem for us was the pension scheme. The seller wanted the buyer to agree to an independent valuation, which meant there was an unknown figure. With hindsight we could have taken the uncertainty.

'We worked for the new owner for two years and we became unmanageable. For a year we were really fighting our parent company very hard. At the end, we were corresponding with lawyers.

'The sellers ran a couple of people against us, but we were the only ones who could act quickly.'

III

RAISING THE MONEY

Many businesses are established on the back of the investment of a few thousand pounds by the founder. These could grow into multi-million-pound enterprises, floated on the stock market in due course. So why raise money?

There are a number of reasons. One that is obvious is that some business ideas can't be developed with a small investment. They need hundreds of thousands, or even millions of pounds; in particular, businesses which involve production and manufacture may require substantial start-up costs to enable the goods to be produced in a low-cost way.

Other reasons for choosing to raise substantial venture capital include the desire to grow faster or to establish a leading market position or to seize a time-specific opportunity. One benefit, which may be less readily apparent, is of particular value to managers or executives immersed in the large-company environment. The small business is an alien culture; many excellent business people, well-versed in the management of the larger enterprise, will founder if they attempt to build a business with no infrastructure. Venture capital can provide you with the organization, no matter how stretched, which would enable you to operate closer to your maximum level of effectiveness.

There are concomitant disadvantages. Any outside investor will require some control over the manner in which their investment is used. Thus the introduction of venture capital brings shareholder agreements, restrictions on remuneration, responsibilities to account for the use of the money, an agreement to follow the plan outlined and remain within an agreed strategy and a duty to inform. These may prove vexatious.

More disturbing to you will be the realization that raising venture capital is usually a game. Some of you may assume that building a business will be in a partnership with the financiers. It would be naïve to rely on this assumption. Furthermore, the game has uncertain rules (at least, uncertain to you the protagonist). And you are at a further disadvantage when playing it. You are a tyro and the other player is assured and practised in this game; after all, the venture capitalist plays it every day.

The relationship with your investors can be a very difficult one. Some entrepreneurs will find words of praise. Some will be appreciative of the help and support. But some will doubt the motivation of the financiers. The basic point is to be clear in your mind what you want from the financing, to understand that you have responsibilities on your side and to understand that the viewpoint and interests of the venture-capital people will be different from your own.

There is many an anecdote of venture capitalists investing funds in a project which within a few weeks has gone to the wall. And there are tales of the dishonesty and failure of the duty of the entrepreneur. Equally, the venture capitalist has a responsibility to the people who put up the money, pension funds, life-insurance funds and individuals, to attain the best possible return. And this has to be achieved regardless of your own particular interest. On the odd occasion, in times of stress, both entrepreneur and venture capitalist are like the little girl in the nursery rhyme. When they are good, they are very, very good. But when they are bad, they are horrid.

With these words of caution in mind, it is readily apparent that the business plan, the choice of investor and the negotiations which surround the injection of venture capital become of paramount importance to the future of your proposed business. Spend as much time as possible visiting City people and advisers before committing yourself to working with one particular group. The advice you receive at this stage will be free – make the most of it.

10

The Business Plan

Richard Branson is a very, very successful businessman. And yet his views on business planning probably make the accountants, bankers and venture capitalists of the world shudder. 'I never actually set out to see how I can make the most cash. I've always merely tried to make the figures fit the ideas I've had rather than the other way round. I guess that's doing it backwards.' (Jeffrey Robinson, *The Risk Takers*)

So why should you draw up a business plan? And how should you do it?

Here are six good reasons why it is important to produce a plan. First, you won't be able to raise money without it. Second, if you produce a realistic business plan it should ensure adequate capitalization. Third, it's the easiest way to crystallize your thinking and enables you to set priorities. Fourth, you can use it to control your business. Fifth, you don't want to waste your time, energy and money on a business proposition which won't work and your business plan should allow you to evaluate the chances of success. Sixth, it will aid you in maintaining a long-range orientation.

The first reason in itself is sufficient to determine that you should approach the task of developing your plan as *the* major stage before you can launch or buy your business. But the next five reasons are very strong pointers that it is a vital task for the management team to carry out for their own guidance.

And the next question is – which way should you produce it? Top–down or bottom–up? The Richard Branson or the accountant's way? The advantage of approaching it from the top down is that you know what you want to achieve, say, sales of £15 million by year five, and you can proceed to estimate what management, marketing and funding are required to generate those sorts of sales. What this approach doesn't answer is the question of whether your chosen market will allow you to expand at the rate you want. And thus your plan may not be realistic.

It's very tempting to adopt this approach as you may be aware that the venture capitalists will require a minimum return on their investment and will normally be looking for an exit, say, in year five. The simplest way to establish this in your plan is the top–down approach.

However, to embrace this method wholeheartedly would be to throw all caution to the wind. First, you are not Richard Branson and may not possess his exceptional entrepreneurial quality. Second, the future outcome of your own personal investment of money and time after funding the business will be tied to your business plan. Fail to achieve what you forecast and your share of the equity will be under threat (and, of course, so may be the whole business). And never expect financiers to pass up an opportunity to take advantage of weakness.

The conclusion must be that your business plan must be very realistic, must concentrate on risk minimization, must not promise more than you can achieve and should be heavily based on the detailed market statistics. Yes, it must set aggressive targets and it must look for growth, but this must be firmly rooted in actuality.

It is axiomatic that the more conservative the business plan on which you raise the finance, the more successful you are likely to be. Post-funding, your performance is judged on how it compares with your forecast. And, for example, research that 3i has carried out into the factors which make buy-ins more or less successful confirms this. The most successful managers had conservative budgets – they forecast on average 40 per cent less profits at the end of year one. The more conservative the forecast the greater the chance that the money you raise will be the amount necessary for the successful completion of the task you have set yourself.

Lyn Davies, a non-executive director for a number of companies, points out that 'plans which are unrealistic are demoralizing. After the funding, management will be failing because they are being compared to a fairy tale – a plan that may be a dream, but it turns into a nightmare. You should concentrate on a realistic plan and the strength of the management team.'

It is because of the conflict which exists between the necessary appeal to investors pre-funding and the required ability to deliver the plan post-funding that it is impossible to treat the production of a business plan wholly as a science.

It is an art – a combination of scientific evidence backed by management judgement. You have to resolve the difficulties of using it as a marketing tool for the management and the business idea with its subsequent use as a total management-and-control tool.

What Should be in the Plan?

There are some excellent books and pamphlets available on what sections there should be and the detail of what topics must be covered. But over and above the detailed content of the plan, there are some tips which could greatly improve the chances of your plan catching the reader's attention – and holding it once attracted. The potential reader is a professional investor who receives hundreds of business plans, but will invest in only one or two of them.

Gail Croston, formerly of 3i, expounds the most crucial aspect of the plan and exposes some investor prejudices: 'A good executive summary is essential. If you can't explain your business so the reader can understand, it's hopeless. Remember that an investor can spend no more than two and a half hours on any business plan – and it may be only two minutes if the summary doesn't hit the right note. It's all about writing it for the audience.

'Investors have prejudices on plans. You should never put phrases such as "No competitors for this product", "Unique" in a plan, as they can't be true. You should beware of all apple-pie statements.

'Investors also doubt business plans which are based on computer programs such as Lotus 1–2–3; they don't always believe them.'

Many of the entrepreneurs also had tips to pass on about the tone and content of the business plan, so here is a miscellany of ideas:

– demonstrate a real feeling for cash – it must jump out at the prospective investor;

- 'make sure you've got enough working capital in because your business will go up and down; you need to make provision for that' (Derrick Bumpsteed);

- 'pay great attention to the detailed cash flows; they put great emphasis on this. Put in a pessimistic picture so you don't have to go back for more funds' (Ed Hunter);

- 'make sure you're damn conservative on the balance sheet, because it's the cash that will catch you out' (Derrick Bumpsteed);

- be market-led;

- be detailed about the sales – exactly which products and where are they coming from;

- 'sales figures in plans always sweep up at the end of the year: these are jam tomorrow plans' (Lyn Davies);

- focus on essentials, the non-essentials take care of themselves;

- focus on opportunities and explain how to deal with problems;

- don't over-rely on logic (competitors are not logical);

- 'management don't do sufficient research for the business plan; they are simply emotional about it' (Lyn Davies);

- 'put up a plan you believe in' (Gerry Meredith Smith).

Finally, should a suggested financial structure be included? Two contrasting views emerge. Tony Davies believes: 'Before you develop your plans in tremendous detail, try to work out the structure of a possible investment situation. If you don't, your proposal will have holes in it and will not be coherent, nor will it contain all the aspects of forward planning that it should.'

But Gail Croston expresses a contrary viewpoint: 'Don't worry about the financial structure of the investment, just the overall amount needed.' In any case, whatever route you plump for you will find that the terms of the financing will alter during your negotiations.

Producing the Plan

A business plan is the management's opportunity to sell themselves; it is the showcase for their talents. Venture capitalists back management teams which impress them, with the proviso that the plan must look sound and believable. So if the business plan is very obviously produced by a firm of accountants or advisers what can the venture capitalists interpret from that? The logical conclusion must be that the management does not have the ability to produce their own plan. And thus the management team is not very strong.

There is a clear prejudice, quite rightly, against plans which appear to be someone else's, not the management's, and you would put yourself at a disadvantage in the search for finance if you adopt that method.

Tim Waterstone gives further emphasis to this: 'I think it is essential that the initial business plan is written by the entrepreneur. It is of very little comfort to prospective investors to find that the business plan has been prepared by professional advisers. Accountants are there to check the detail and lawyers to check the law, but the entrepreneur really must have total clarity and grasp of the numbers on which he or she is asking other people to put up their money.'

While employing an accountant or adviser to produce the plan is not recommended, you could consider hiring an accountancy firm to help you in the task, although this is not essential. 'We didn't use professional advisers. Our prospectus was in retrospect a somewhat plain document, but it had common sense and was believable,' states Brian Gilda of Peoples.

However, most entrepreneurs have used accountants and have selected up-market firms in the belief that the name of the accountants matters and gives credibility to the plan. Allen Jones is one such believer: 'We used Deloittes. Their name and their sound advice were of great benefit.' And a similar opinion is held by Paul Bates of Straightset, who contracted Arthur Young to help prepare a three-year plan with which to interest the institutions in their buy-out (very small in size). To prepare this plan Arthur Young eventually charged nearly £10,000 in 1988, but Paul points out: 'You don't get taken seriously without good accountants.'

The *modus operandi* which seems to be favoured by most teams is that one person, usually the leader if there is a team, is responsible for putting the plan together and writing it. Each member of the team should provide the raw material for the section of the plan which refers to their particular area of expertise. The accountants' prime role is to challenge assumptions throughout the document.

So far this section has looked at producing and using the plan as a marketing tool to be presented to financiers. But, of course, it will be the basis on which you run and operate the business post-finance. You will be judged on it and the availability of further finance may depend on how your business performs compared with it. While producing the plan, it would be helpful in its use as a control tool to structure it so that the actual performance of every director can be monitored and measured – in this way each director is made totally accountable for the relevant part of the plan.

Elucidating the Risks and Hazards

No business plan will be taken seriously that does not highlight the potential risks and hazards which might throw your business off course – and, just as important, the steps which your team will take to protect the business. It is standard practice to incorporate a SWOT analysis (strengths, weaknesses, opportunities and threats). You may be very enthusiastic to explain the S and O, but less forthcoming about the W and T. The trick is to be clear about what they are, but use them as the platform to demonstrate your management quality. How will you counteract any weaknesses? How will you overcome the threats?

Here is a summary of some of the potential hazards which can overwhelm any business. Ensure that your business plan enlightens your reader on which of these (and any others special to your business) might affect your forecasts:

– absences or the loss of personnel with particular skills or experience;

– failure to obtain a reliable supply of some particular product or service;

- lower product demand due to marketing inadequacies;

- fluctuations in market demand or changes in tastes;

- inadequate finance;

- the timing of your market entry;

- competitive reaction;

- changes in your cost structure or your competitor's which adversely affect your market;

- too little or too rigid a production system;

- unsophisticated distribution structure;

- existence of restrictive practices or barrier to entry;

- technological changes;

- competitive changes;

- political interference;

- new legal requirements;

- changes in social attitudes;

- reliance on one or two major customers.

The plan needs to be able to present an overall picture so that the risk of the venture can be summarized in the reader's mind and compared to the possible outcome. An investor won't want to sink money in a high-risk, low-return business. And nor frankly should you. It is also for your own benefit that you can see a clear picture of the risk/reward ratio.

Most investors want exits – not all. All investors will want to estimate the return on their investment. The plan must provide the raw material for that calculation. It must recognize the requirement for an exit and indicate the time-scale that the management anticipates. And again this is also for your own benefit; you may not expect that you will ever want an exit, but many of you will subsequently be overcome by the desire to turn paper gains into real ones or simply to move on to the next challenge. To avoid later disagreements, when you find that your interests diverge from the venture capitalists, it would be fruitful to air these potential disagreements at the outset.

The time-scale that venture capitalists will consider varies. And there is a big difference between what they say they want and what is achievable. With large-scale MBOs the timetable may be as short as one to three years. Smaller MBOs may take between five and ten years for an exit, if any. MBIs are looking to take longer on average, say eight years or so. Start-ups could be ten years, plus. The plan will need to indicate your view of whether the expected outcome will be a trade sale or a float.

The Market Input

'Most plans spend insufficient time looking at possible market growth. Get someone with marketing experience to look at this side,' is Lyn Davies's view. Certainly many businesses find themselves off target, and hence underfunded, because the sales volume is lower than forecast or the gross margin too small. Lyn Davies refers to sales directors who achieve sales volume at the expense of margins as 'commercial undertakers; they will eventually bury the business'.

Unusually, Derwent Valley Foods raised funds to carry out the development work, including a market survey, over a nine-month period. Roger McKechnie spent £99 on a seat on one of the last Laker cheap flights to the USA, where he visited the main exhibition for the snack-food industry. He put the word around that he had $1 million to spend. 'I was entertained the whole time. I didn't have to spend a penny. I got lots of information and my suitcase was filled with products.' In addition, friends and family were also exploited in the task to find suitable products for the new venture. They were asked to bring home exotic titbits from faraway holiday destinations.

At one point more than 2,000 different snack packets were pinned to the wall of the shed. Eventually, twenty were short-listed. It was now time to look at the market itself. They carried out the market research themselves – to save money – and interviewed the public. Again, friends came to help; one was an experienced market researcher who showed them how to carry out the interviews. The message that came home was to go for quality, to break the rules on pricing that no one would buy a snack for more than 19p. 'Don't make extruded crap!' was the plea from the public.

Then the team talked to the buyers in the supermarkets. 'Tell us what is wrong with the snack-food industry.' Surprisingly, most buyers were extremely helpful and more than willing to explain the pitfalls. 'We got a lot of guidance on what not to do,' said McKechnie. 'No one was taking the position that Porsche does in motor cars. There were no up-market snacks. We decided to take the top spot.'

As a result of this very thorough research, the demand for their product was greater than their estimate, unusually for a start-up. While this market research was carried out post-funding, it may be possible for you to carry out a similar exercise pre-funding – if you can support yourself in the meantime.

Some ingredients for a successful market to launch a venture have been identified as:

– industries facing significant changes in technology or regulation;

– industries in which the smaller firms are relatively weak;

– industries in which it is possible to create subsequent barriers to entry;

– industries in which you can differentiate your products from others, especially in the areas of quality and service;

– industries in which you can aim to dominate your market segment.

Meeting any or all of these criteria does not guarantee success. Vamp Health entered the general-practitioner computer-systems market, which matched all these indications – but political interference meant that demand underwent wild fluctuation, famine followed by feast and vice versa, making life very complex and uncertain.

Nevertheless, if your business plan can demonstrate that the market which your business is in, or is proposed to be in, has some of these characteristics, it will be regarded as a plus factor. The other side of the coin is to illustrate clearly your marketing strategy to maximize your impact on the market.

The Team

'If you don't have the management team in place, the issue is where you are going to get them. Job descriptions are not particularly helpful,' points out Gail Croston. Chapter 5 looks at the composition of the team in detail, but some of the key points are that it must have a clear leader, it should be balanced and it needs someone strong on financial controls. It is not impossible to raise the funding you want if you are an entrepreneur on your own or if you have part, but not all, of a team. But it is more troublesome. And filling the spare role or roles post-funding is difficult.

It has already been explained in Chapter 5 how a strong financial person was missing from the Vamp Health team, which was very marketing-orientated at the time of the original funding. Part of the funding was to be dedicated to the task of filling that role. 'We advertised in the *Financial Times* and went through the whole interview procedure. We selected someone we considered would grow with the business but we got it wrong the first time around.'

11

The Venture-capital Organization

Venture capitalists are a multifarious bunch. With members dissimilar in size, time horizon, risk preference, interests and funding, the venture-capital industry resembles an amorphous mass. But there is one common thread. Given its preferences and within its own risk/reward criteria, the venture-capital fund wants to achieve the highest possible return. The achievement depends on selecting the entrepreneurs and companies in which to invest – and to structure the deal to enhance its investment.

What sort of return are they looking for? On the whole of their portfolio, the desired return may be around 30 per cent p.a. compound. A return of 20 per cent may be acceptable for a 'low-risk' deal; for the higher risks, the fund may expect a return of 60 per cent plus. In any venture-capital fund, some of the investments will fail. This implies that some very high returns will need to be achieved by some of the investments if the portfolio is to generate the overall return required and allow for the failures.

The estimated return for your venture will be worked out on the basis of your business plan, taking account of the length of time before an exit route will be achieved and a forecast of the size of the capital gain and discounting for its perceived over-optimism. With some invest-ments, a running yield will also be sought from the payment of dividends or interest.

A survey by Bruno and Tyebjee published in *Sloan Management Review* looked at the reasons given for the rejection of venture proposals. These were stated as:

– doubts about the management: 37 per cent

– market and competitive characteristics: 27 per cent

– financial characteristics (e.g. rate of return): 23 per cent

- other characteristics of the venture (e.g. location, history): 14 per cent.

This neatly summarizes what all venture capitalists are looking for to attain their required rate of return: a strong management team, a good market to enter and the specific financial characteristics of the deal which can be arranged.

Differences in Investment Policy

Each fund may have defined its own individual preferences and may stipulate criteria based on:

- size of investment;

- industry and region;

- development stage of the company and time horizon;

- monitoring procedures;

- majority/minority stakes.

An investment in the £250,000 to £500,000 range (or less) is considered small and few venture-capital funds will look at it nowadays, even though publicly they may say they will. Some venture-capital funds impose still higher figures, say £1 million. The rationale for these minima is that venture capitalists have to undertake the same amount of work no matter the size of the investment; thus an investment below a certain size is not an efficient use of their resources.

At the other end of the scale, there are investments which may be too large to be considered by one fund on its own, although one or two funds state that they can make investments up to £50 million.

Funds differ on which industries they will select as investments. Some funds will invest in any industry. Other funds specialize: health care, leisure, media, and defence are typical examples. Such specialist funds may have managers who are regarded as having expertise or knowledge in that particular industry. As well as the more positive approach to specialization, a fund may have a negative view of a particular industry. A survey by Gordon Murray and Jonathan Lott of Warwick Business School in 1991 revealed that venture capitalists were more reluctant to back investments in the information-technology sector. The acceptance rate for proposals in this sector was found to be only 2.9 per cent (the overall average being 4.3 per cent).

There may also be other specific differences in investment policy. A handful of funds are set up with a regional bias: for example, a fund might consider only investments in businesses based in the North-west. And these funds may look at projects requiring lower amounts of investment.

Another differentiation in the investment policy of funds is their attitude to the risk of the investment, which is closely correlated to the development stage of the business and the time horizon required by the investor. Table 11 below provides a summary of the potential risks and example returns required from the investor's viewpoint.

Many funds won't touch early-stage financing. Thus the choice among venture-capital funds for start-ups is more restricted than for a management buy-out, for example. Nevertheless, the statistics produced by the British Venture Capital Association for 1991 (see

Table 11: Investment Risk from the Viewpoint of the Investor

Type of investment	Time-scale (years)	Risk	Example target returns (% p.a.)
EARLY STAGE			
Seed capital	7–10	Exceptional	100
Start-up	5–10	Very high	60
Second round for start-up	3–7	Higher	40-60
DEVELOPMENT CAPITAL	2–5	Medium	30-50
MANAGEMENT BUY-OUTS	3–6	Lower	20-35
MANAGEMENT BUY-INS	4–8	Medium/high	30-40
TURN-ROUND	3–5	Medium/high	30-50

Source: based on information from Touche Ross.

Table 12 below) show that the number of start-up early-stage deals is around the same as the number for buy-outs and buy-ins. The amount invested is very much smaller, but all of the money invested in start-ups goes into the business for growth and the businesses are starting from a much smaller base.

A further differentiation in investment policy occurs because of different attitudes to the length of time the fund wishes to leave its investment. The British Venture Capital Association says: 'The timeframe from investment to exit can be as little as two years or as much as ten years.' But five years down the track, the need for an exit may be inconvenient for your business as it will divert attention from its management to fulfil a commitment to investors. For example, Roger McKechnie chose 3i to be the main provider of venture capital for Derwent Valley Foods because 3i was prepared to take the long-term view. Other venture capitalists who expressed interest in the scheme expected to be able to exit from the company within three to five years. The team weren't looking for an exit, as Roger explained: 'I didn't want to become another spoilt rich kid; job satisfaction is more important than wealth.'

Table 12: Early-stage Financing: Number of Deals, Amount Invested and Average Equity Investment, 1991

	Number of financings	Amount invested (£ million)	Average size of financing (£ thousand)
EARLY STAGE			
Start-up	158	35	223
Other early stage	115	23	195
Total	273	58	211
EXPANSION	570	333	584
BUY-OUT/BUY-IN	288	544	1,889

Source: British Venture Capital Association.

The control of the company is an emotional topic for many an entrepreneur. Generally speaking, few venture capitalists want a majority, although there may be the odd one or two who prefer that position, as Alistair Jacks described in Chapter 8. However, the financing may be such that losing control is certain. If that is the situation, you should be aiming to spread the shares around among two or more outside investors – and, in any case, most venture capitalists will want to organize syndication for the same reason. The survey by Bruno and Tyebjee in the *Sloan Management Review* in the United States found that on average the entrepreneurs had relinquished around 31 per cent of their equity to outside investors at the first round of financing, an additional loss of 20 per cent at the second round and a further 10 per cent at the third.

A final divergence in investment policy emerges post-investment: differing procedures for monitoring investments. All venture capitalists require management reports, but some require much closer involvement. This is described in more detail in Chapter 6, 'The Board'.

Other Variations in Venture-capital Funds

The most obvious difference between the funds is size: they range from the Big Daddy of them all, 3i, down to the very small. 3i, for example, makes about one third of the investment deals of the venture-capital industry each year (but not necessarily one third of the money invested).

The funds available to venture capitalists emerge from varying sources. For 1989, 1990 and 1991, the statistics for the British Venture Capital Association are as listed in Table 13 overleaf.

Another difference between venture capitalists which may not be readily apparent to the uninitiated is that they make their money in different ways. Some funds, especially the small independents, make their money from fees and on a transactional basis. Some make money by managing the funds. Some make money from the investments themselves. One entrepreneur gives the following example of fees charged by a small independent, investing £500,000 as a leader of a syndicate. On completion, there was a one-off fee of £43,750 plus

Table 13: Sources of Funds for Venture Capitalists, 1989, 1990, 1991 (£m)

Source	1989	1990	1991
Independent via unquoted vehicles*	887	580	625
Independent quoted investment trusts	143	137	111
Captive bank	242	249	127
Captive pension fund	63	32	67
Captive other	73	94	46
Government	12	14	13
Total	1,420	1,106	989

*Includes 3i and BES funds

Source: British Venture Capital Association.

VAT (in addition to paying all the costs of the venture capitalist). This was purported to cover the additional work of their appointed director in the first year (there was none). In subsequent years, as well as paying the £10,000 fee to the nominated director, there was a further fee of £7,000. This example may not be typical of the fees charged by all small independents but it illustrates a point which needs to be looked at closely.

The life of the fund can vary, too. Some venture-capital funds are for a specific amount: there is no continuing inflow. Once the amount is invested, there can be no subsequent investment from the fund (although the managers may retain a percentage of their funds to make a follow-up investment). The fund exists simply until its investments are sold, floated or liquidated. Once this occurs, the proceeds are paid out to the original provider of the funds. At first blush, this may not seem a disadvantage to a seeker of funds. However, you may find subsequent problems emerging.

At the outset, you may expect that you have estimated the correct amount of funds you need according to your business plan and that no further funds will be necessary to meet your targets. However, as most knowledgeable venture capitalists will admit, a majority of businesses will discover that they are not 'on-plan'. A few may outperform; a greater number may under-perform. In either case, you may require further funding. In general, it is assumed that most venture-backed companies need a further round of funding. The industry rule of thumb is between 1 + 1 and 1 + 3 – so for £250,000 raised first time, up to £750,000 will be invested as a follow-on.

It is much more helpful to turn to your existing backers to ask them to put up the money – after all, they should know the company better than a new investor. If your venture capitalists have exhausted their funds, the search will be on for new backers. And, as you will ascertain, searching for funding is very time-consuming. A couple of entre-preneurs who have started businesses from scratch estimated that, four or five years after the birth of the business, about 50 per cent of their available time was taken up with fund-raising.

It is not only the amount of time which may concern you. A venture-capital-backed business that needs a second round of funds (perceived to be for the wrong reason) is in a very weak position with its own backers, never mind new ones. You may be able to raise the funds from a new player, but the extent of the dilution of your own equity you may regard as usurious. This may be further exacerbated by the refusal of the first investor to accept dilution, resulting in you giving up even more shares. The conclusion is that backers with a predetermined amount of funds can have their disadvantages.

A final distinction which it may be useful to draw is between followers and leaders. Some venture capitalists will lead an investment; others will only invest once a leader is already in place. Leaders may be those funds which specialise in particular industries, so other venture capitalists may assume that they have expert knowledge.

The British Venture Capital Association produces an indispensable list of its members, giving names, addresses, telephone numbers, minima and maxima, preferences and so on. It is available free and you should certainly obtain a copy of it to help you in your search. (See the list of 'Recommended Books and Helpful Organizations' printed at the end of this book.)

How to Choose a Venture-capital Backer

If you are proposing a start-up in a market perceived as high-risk, you may have little choice; you may be delighted simply to raise any money at all. However, the lower the risk and the more developed the business, the greater prospect of a choice of backers. The financial terms you are offered will be a major influence on your decision. The investment policy and other characteristics will also be factors you take into account.

A survey by the London Business School carried out amongst entrepreneurs who had raised venture capital found that factors which influenced the entrepreneur's choice of investor included: (a) the terms of the offer, 64 per cent; (b) availability of funds for future expansion, 44 per cent; and (c) ongoing help, 22 per cent.

Interestingly, some of the entrepreneurs interviewed for this book cited the nature of the people working for the venture-capital organization as having some influence on their decision. For example, Tina Tietjen chose Barings because they were 'very supportive. The team had all worked in business.' And Derrick Bumpsteed and his team were introduced to 3i – and looked no further for their lead investor: 'We liked their style; they were good; they were very positive in the way that they went about things.'

Undoubtedly, the amount of respect which you hold for the representative of the venture-capital fund, either the account executive or an appointed non-executive director, will affect your investor relations after the funding. Unfortunately, just like anyone else, the employees of venture-capital funds move on. It would be wise to try to meet a number of the people, so that you can obtain a feel for the overall quality of the employees, not just the one representative handling your proposal.

What It Costs to Raise Venture Capital

It costs a surprisingly substantial amount to raise venture capital. Apart from the actual expenditure you will incur, you must not dismiss the work-hours spent by your team in raising the funds. In some cases, it can take many months and a substantial proportion of your time to finalize any deal. It can be extremely difficult to maintain any other job at the same time as arranging finance.

The other costs of raising venture capital in general include fees for advisers: your solicitors and the solicitors for the venture-capital fund; your accountants; and the cost of the due diligence and any other adviser who is helping to arrange the finance. One estimate puts the figure that will go in fees at least 5 per cent of the money you raise. As Stephen Hinton says: 'If you wanted to be, you could be extremely upset at the advisers who could make a lot of money by your efforts. But, if you like, it's the key to the club.'

One tip worth following if you are negotiating with more than one venture capitalist is to try to persuade them that they should agree to be represented by just one solicitor. This might help stabilize your costs. It's also worth trying to persuade your advisers to work on a contingency basis: no deal, no fee. However, this might mean that the ultimate fee you pay will be larger.

Straightset was a fairly small buy-out requiring funds of around £450,000, including overdraft and loan. Altogether the fees for the management buy-out totalled nearly £28,000, with solicitors taking £10,000, accountants £10,000, Midland Bank requiring a £3,000 fee for its overdraft facility and 3i an arrangement fee of £5,000 for the investment.

At the other extreme of the buy-out scale is the Eurocamp buy-out. The team had to raise £36 million to finance it. The costs and fees consumed £1.2 million of this.

Finally, there is sometimes a further cost which may not involve you in paying out money now but dilutes the capital gain which you can realize. Some venture-capital funds require that you give options or warrants to their individual executives as part of the price of the funding. Thus when you can turn your own paper gain into hard cash, you may also find yourself enriching individuals who work for venture-capital funds, whose only role was investing other people's money in your business. You carry out all the work as well as the risk of your own investment and the fund providers carry the risk of the money that is invested in you, but some fund manager, who takes no risk and carries out precious little work, takes part of the return from both – it doesn't seem equitable, does it?

12

The Money Timetable

The funding process is a version of a latter-day Pilgrim's Progress. Many trials and tribulations are faced and the Slough of Despond is a familiar phase. The process for a present-day seeker of venture capital is rarely smooth, frequently anguishing, commonly covers a very long period of time and is fundamentally dispiriting. 'This was a heart-breaking and frustrating period for action people like us. We kept on battering away. There were so many abortive meetings. You have to move through all the different levels in each of the institutions you contact. We never arrived at the right level. There are all sorts of red herrings which cross your path and endless meetings to see if that one was the way forward. But you need to go through all the available routes to ensure you have the deal you want at the end.' Thus Allen Jones of A J's Family Restaurants expresses most eloquently the frustration felt by most entrepreneurs who want to start a business.

The path may not be quite so tortuous if you are raising funds for a buy-out or buy-in. The opportunity may be immediate – and lost if the funds are delayed. So venture capitalists may pull out all the stops and focus their brains to meet any time requirements in buying a company. But, generally, with a start-up the entrepreneur recognizes the need for decisive activity, but not the financiers. There is no real end-point to focus on. But for the team this period may mean many lost openings. 'We lost all sorts of site opportunities the funding took so long,' says Jones.

Here are the stages for the funding process:

- initial appraisal;

- due diligence;

- negotiation of terms;

- syndication;

– formal-offer letter;

– the legals and the Shareholder Agreement;

– completion – hooray!

How to Approach the Venture-capital Funds

There's a dilemma here. Any experienced business person would have the instinct to create a competition, to be able to compare and contrast two or more offers – and yet many pundits advise very strongly against sending your proposal to numerous organizations. Their argument is that the venture-capital industry is a small one which has a lively network, passing on information and gossip. It is said that if the industry knows your proposal has been sent out extensively they will be less interested, less inclined to compete and more likely to consign your plan to the rubbish bin. This needs to be taken with a pinch of salt; nevertheless, it is more effective for you to target your plan carefully. The differences in investment policy have been explained in the previous chapter. Research your audience well; target your message productively. Raising funds is likely to be the biggest sale you have made so far. You are selling your abilities as leader, the team's skills and the strength of your business proposal. Make your strongest pitch to the audience most likely to want to listen. So, say, send your plan (or a summary of it, known as a pathfinder) to five or six venture-capital companies you have identified as being most open to your ideas. Follow these plans up with phone calls and meetings. You may at this juncture consider that you want to increase the number of recipients or you may judge that you will be able to generate a satisfactory number of responses with your initial 'hit list'.

Contacts can be important in this area of business just as in any other. The executive at Alta Berkeley, which funded Peter Gibson's Corin Medical, had been Peter's former boss and had already been to see Corin before the company needed to raise funds. And the people involved in Calidus sought and received funds from Baronsmead whom they already knew.

Lack of contacts however does not deliver a knock-out blow; it merely exacerbates the problem. The management team at Daton circulated its plans to a wide audience and hawked the business plan around the financial institutions. 'We did presentation after presentation,' recalls Tony Leach. Their hard work resulted in them having the choice of two institutions. They plumped for 3i, because, among other reasons, the latter wanted only 25 per cent of the equity (compared with 40 per cent required by the other institution) and their terms were less onerous.

With buy-outs and buy-ins, there may be more pressure on speed and thus less ability to develop a considered strategy to fund-raising. Roy Mitchell of Carron describes his approach, when he was buying the company from the receiver: 'I thought if I go down the road and knock on the door of the Royal Bank of Scotland, I'm very likely to be talking to the commissionaire for the rest of the month. If I go to the Scottish Development Agency, I suspect they'll treat me very courteously and be very interested and so forth, but things won't move terribly quickly. What I actually did was to pick up the phone and phone the manager at my own domestic branch of the Bank of Scotland. I said to him: "Bill, I've got an idea, I've got a proposal." Presumably he thought this gentleman is going to buy a car or move house. But I put my proposal to him and I remain full of admiration for his attitude. Whether he fell off his chair or not I'm not too sure, but his response was "Can you give me fifteen to twenty minutes?" He called me back and asked, "Can you be at head office tomorrow morning at 8 o'clock?", as the people who wished to be involved were at a senior level.'

Both he and Allen Jones have pinpointed a further problem. How do you speak to the real decision-makers, the right level? It's quite possible that you may spend a considerable amount of time and effort talking and selling to executives within the venture-capital organization, only to discover that they don't have the power to make the decision 'yes'. In some organizations, there may be a Friday meeting for the 'Investment Committee' or some other sobriquet: the executives put forward the proposals which they support and need approval to go ahead. The committee members are the real power; only they can approve investments. But your ability to influence their decision direct is very limited. Wherever possible, try to put yourself in the position of speaking direct to those with the power. Ed Hunter of Penman Engineering supports this view: 'Approach the institutions at the highest possible level, particularly the banks. Get to the senior level and get a quick decision.'

The Role of the Adviser

Some advisers are like teachers. It is said that those that can, do, and those that can't, advise. Perhaps this is a little hard – we all had one or more excellent teachers during our education and there are some excellent advisers around. But never assume that advisers know more than you. Your extra added ingredient is fear: the ultimate responsibility for success or failure.

This is a view that Malcolm Parkinson would surely endorse: 'It's never easy to raise money. It's easier for people in the City to say no. Do not accept that your professional advisers always know more about it than you do. They might know the front door, but not what goes on behind.'

Advisers have a number of potential roles to fill. In the first instance, you may decide to use an accountant to help you produce the business plan. It's not mandatory, but most entrepreneurs find it helpful and on the whole have been happy with the result of the collaboration, as Chapter 10, 'The Business Plan', explained in more detail. It is generally recommended that you select an accountancy firm with a well-known name and good reputation. A local firm may be even more helpful and experienced than one that is nationally known, but in the eyes of the venture capitalists, unfortunately will not have the same cachet.

Another obvious and clear-cut role is that of a solicitor to advise you in the legal negotiations and the legal agreements. A solicitor can also advise you on the formation or purchase of the company. Some of the entrepreneurs interviewed in this book have been fulsome in their praise for solicitors and have been vigorous in their recommendation to appoint a solicitor at a very early stage. For example, Tina Tietjen:

'The selection of a lawyer for a buy-out is crucial. He was like a terrier following up every point.' And Neill Bell: 'The financiers we were talking to started off by saying we'll give you 30 per cent and we'll have 70 per cent. Our solicitors walked in and said, "Tear up all your agreements. Management get 55 per cent or nothing."'

The entrepreneurs who have successfully completed management buy-outs have identified a further need for advice. With a buy-out there is a delicate tripartite negotiation – between the management team, the seller, and the financier. As Stephen Hinton says: 'We didn't understand soon enough that we were negotiating on two fronts, with our vendors and our backers. Which were the crocodiles?'

John Leighfield, as others have done, solved the problem by appointing a separate adviser (Arthur Young), who advised the management team on how to handle Kleinwort Benson, the institution organizing the buy-out. 'They appear to be simply on your side, but they're not; you need someone dispassionate to advise the management and employees, to make sure that you have the best possible deal.'

This advisory role is also present with start-ups and buy-ins; in general, this may be filled by the accountants who help you prepare your business plan. However, care needs to be taken that your accountant has true skill and expertise in this area of financial structures. Financial plans should be bread and butter to accountants, but the ability to analyse very complicated financial structures and advise on their effect on the business not just for the present but the future, too, requires a different kind of knowledge.

Particularly with buy-outs and buy-ins, but maybe also with start-ups, there is a well-defined role for an adviser to give you tax advice. Tax may play a part in the purchase price and negotiations for a business, for example, to maximize the tax efficiency of the sale for the vendor which will encourage them to choose your offer. You may also require some personal tax advice of your own. This role could be fulfilled by either your solicitor or your accountant.

Finally, there can be identified a much more contentious role for advisers – that of the introducer, the intermediary, with the key to the door. Here the opinions of entrepreneurs varied. Solway Foods was successful in raising £1.8 million finance for its venture. The team had used one of the top national firms of accountants in the UK to help produce their business plan, a role the accountants fulfilled admirably, but they were not so happy about their ability as introducers. The accountants were going to charge about £4,000 for a successful introduction, only payable if a firm deal was struck. But the only introduction the team thought the accountants made was to a US venture capitalist which it claimed was a specialist in start-ups in the food industry. When the refusal came from this venture capitalist it was on the grounds that it had never financed a food company before!

On the other hand, Tim Hely Hutchinson spoke warmly of the value of intermediaries. His family stockbroker had given him an introduction to Touche Ross, who had in turn introduced him to Rothschild Ventures and other big venture-capital backers. 'The venture capitalist will take you much less seriously if you are not introduced by an intermediary.' Certainly, Tim's experiences at raising finance have appeared relatively smooth and trouble-free compared with other stories. It was only three months, for example, from the introduction and the initial appraisal to the signing of the legal documents.

As well as accountants there is another mixed bag of organizations eager to help you raise venture capital: some of them are known as venture-capital sponsors, or they may call themselves corporate-finance experts. Whatever their appellation, you must examine carefully whether they can add value to your proposal and increase the chances of raising the funds you need. You have to pay for their services, the bulk of the fee usually being contingent on success. It may be a proportion of the amount raised and these people may also require options in your company. It's difficult to see how they can justify this latter demand and you should seriously consider whether nothing more than an extra pair of hands to help you with all the leg-work would not be sufficient. After all, detailed information about the venture capitalists is readily available from the British Venture Capital Association and in publications from other organizations, some of which are listed at the end of this book. Of course, some of these advisers have genuine skills to offer which will enhance your fund-raising – but thoroughly review them before taking them on board.

The Variety of Financial Structures

A luxuriance of creativity is apparent when financial structures are considered. Venture capitalists love new arrangements of capital. The uninitiated may believe that there are ordinary shares and there are loans and not much else. But there can be *preference shares, redeemable shares, cumulative preference shares, convertible preference shares, deferred shares, warrants, options, ratchets, reverse ratchets, kickers, 'A', 'B'* and *'C' shares, senior debt* and *mezzanine debt, voting, non-voting* and *two-votes-for-one shares* (see Glossary). Whatever difficulty emerges in negotiating the balance of control of the business, the share of the equity – the return required by the venture capitalists and the management team – can be solved by the ingenuity of the financial structure.

Sometimes, too much creativity can impose greater costs on the deal. For example, in the case of ratchets, legal fees can be sky-high. They are also extremely confusing; it can be difficult at the outset to foresee the full impact of a ratchet and reverse ratchet. If the financial structure is too complicated at an early stage, it also follows that there is an extra impediment to raising further funds, which will in turn be more expensive in legal costs.

The next three chapters include some examples of the sort of structures that can be available for start-ups, buy-ins and buy-outs.

Syndication

Sometimes a venture capitalist decides that it doesn't want to provide all the funding needed. This may be for a variety of reasons. First, the sum may be large and might be out of proportion to the size of the whole fund's portfolio. Second, the fund may consider the risk rather high and so want to spread it. Third, it may be that the level of funding requires the venture capitalist to take a majority. Most don't want this, and so will choose to syndicate to ensure that they remain a minority.

Finally, a fund may like your proposal but not consider that it has the expertise to evaluate it properly. In this case, the fund may be happy to provide part of the funds if another venture capitalist with the appropriate expertise has assessed it and considered the risk/reward ratio to be in balance. Thus the industry has leaders, who have the prime responsibility for assessing the proposal, and followers who will rely on the leader's judgement.

Syndication is not a curse. Most entrepreneurs will prefer to have more than one venture capitalist providing the funds as it gives more flexibility in any future funding and in any subsequent monitoring. However, syndication increases the length of time the proposal will take to bear fruit in the form of hard cash from the financiers and also increases the risk of the funding exercise breaking down. If you put any miscellaneous group together, all independent decision-makers, they will have a tendency to behave like a flock of sheep. You are herding towards the pen, when one suddenly veers away from the gate, with the result that the rest of the flock scatters in all directions. If the syndicate doesn't have a clear leader, ask it to appoint one. This also has the secondary beneficial effect of reducing the number of meetings you have to make.

The Due Diligence Process

When you reach this stage you have already accomplished a couple of manoeuvres: your proposal has been read and the venture capitalist is interested in your strategy and in you and your team. The venture capitalist may also have indicated an opening offer of finance and the sort of terms which might be available. All the processes from now on adjust this opening offer to your detriment and to the venture capitalist's advantage. Negotiate hard at the opening-offer stage and each subsequent adjustment.

Due diligence is the process by which any self-respecting financier will check out the facts you have so far presented and will evaluate the forecasts and estimates you have made in the preparation of your plan. The following are all areas to be ruminated over:

- past history of the business;

- management achievements;

- technical and product information;

- market-place.

The due diligence may be carried out internally by employees of the venture capitalists or externally by a firm of accountants. An independent market review may be undertaken by an 'expert' in that market and references may be sought from your customers. Checking up on the team's abilities may also be carried out by way of references. So-called experts produced to pontificate and judge your proposals, your product and your abilities are the running sore of the venture-capital industry. Nevertheless, tolerating them, appeasing them and convincing them are the premiums you pay to be able to raise the money. So bear this in mind in your dealings with them: you may consider you know far more than they do, and so you may, but it's quite irrelevant. This is all part of the sale you must make.

The venture capitalist will now proceed to use the results of the due diligence to adjust your terms downwards. You have a choice: negotiate hard, limit the damage and accept the revised terms or follow up some other source of funding. At this point you will realize the value of having at least one, preferably two, other organizations keen to work with you to develop your plan. However, too many organizations competing against each other will simply frighten them all off and consume too much of your time. So, play the game softly.

You may also want to follow up the opportunity to carry out a bit of 'reverse due diligence'. Approaching and talking to other businesses which the venture capitalist has invested in may give you guidance on their monitoring approach post-investment.

If you are negotiating to buy a company and inject yourself as the management of it, you will need to ensure that you have carried out the due diligence that you need to satisfy yourself that you have an accurate picture of its current trading position, assets and liabilities. In this area, your interest and the venture capitalist's coincide. The main message is not to rely too heavily on advisers; it is not their money which is lost if your purchase subsequently proves to be ill-starred.

Finally, negotiations and due diligence may be completed. The terms of the offer will be put in a formal-offer letter which marks the start of the legal process, the 'legals'. Every time you or the venture capitalist speak from now on clocks up pounds by the second. However, skimping on this part of the investment process is not advisable.

The Shareholder Agreement and Other 'Legals'

This is when you need your solicitor with the characteristics of a Rottweiler. The quantity of legal documents which a funding can produce is truly mountainous. The legal documents are the culmination of all the negotiation and need to be put under the microscope before signature on completion day. These legal documents will be based on the formal-offer letter which sets out the terms of the financing offered by the venture capitalist. Tina Tietjen's advice is: 'You must have time and space to review all the documents because you're stuck with the clauses. On signing our agreements, there were in total seventy lawyers attending plus all the legal documentation.' The purchase of Video Arts was a reasonable-size deal involving £43 million.

Further items likely to be included in the Shareholder Agreement and other legal documents to be signed at completion could be:

- undertakings on capital expenditure, the recruitment of senior staff, major changes in activities and so on. These are designed to guide you to keep to the business plan which is the basis of the investment being made;

- warranties by the directors that all the significant information has been divulged and is accurate;

- in an MBO, directors and auditors have to sign a warranty that the business won't go bust within a year;

- restrictions on your involvement in other businesses. This will stretch to 'connected persons', which is likely to include your spouse and an involvement with a similar business;

– restrictions on remuneration, directors, shareholdings and disposals of shareholdings.

Some of the latter restrictions are really quite absurd but are negotiable, so look out for them. For example, Paul Bates of Straightset complains that one clause in his agreement limits the earnings *and* expenses of the director shareholders to a total of £75,000. This is not a lot when split between them all. If any more is paid out, an additional sum has to be paid to 3i, the providers of the venture capital. This type of petty restriction can be negotiated away by an instruction to your solicitor to draw up service contracts and make them part of the legal documents.

Another undertaking which sometimes occurs in these agreements is to refuse to allow the management to sell any of its shares unless the venture capitalist can sell an equal proportion. At the outset, this may not appear too confining. But as you will discover, selling shares in an unquoted company is tricky. It can be impossible to convert any of your paper gain into hard cash until you sell the whole business to a trade buyer. But if perchance you find someone willing to purchase a small number of your shares, the deal can be scuppered by the insistence of the venture capitalist on selling shares at the same time.

It's difficult to understand what the venture capitalists believe they achieve by this sort of restriction. Their rationale may be that they must ensure that the funds are properly deployed and not used to enrich the entrepreneurs, by heavy expenses, higher salaries or capital gains, until the providers of the funds have received their proper return. And the venture capitalist won't want the management team it has backed to sell out leaving it with a stake in a company with a new, unwanted or unknown team.

However, many entrepreneurs accept lower salaries when launching a business or buying into a much smaller business than the one they previously worked for. And yet they still have mortgages and maybe school fees to pay. Selling a small quantity of shares to realize part of their gain is very unlikely to alter their determination to make their business the most successful that it can be. That is usually an emotional drive, not a financial one. Keeping entrepreneurs poorly remunerated is not an incentive which works and venture capitalists should recognize this. So a solicitor who can persuade the venture capitalist to remove some of the more asinine limitations is very valuable.

Completion

The day may finally dawn when negotiations are finalized and all there is left to do is sign all the documents. In practice, this often appears to take an inordinate length of time and small problems may emerge even at this late stage. A completion meeting for an average investment can take eight to twelve hours – they always seem to end at 11 p.m. or midnight – and often seem to take place just before public holidays.

13

Finance for a Buy-out

Financing problems for a management buy-out are likely to centre on:

- the nature of the three-way negotiation between vendor, management team and venture-capital organization;

- the required speed of the deal, which may limit competition and necessitate underwriting;

- keeping the gearing to a manageable level while enabling all to achieve the return they require;

- negotiating a structure for the management team which adequately reflects the contribution its members will make.

This chapter looks at these four problem areas and gives an example of a financial structure for a buy-out – bearing in mind that there is no such thing as a typical structure. At the end of the chapter are a couple of detailed stories describing how the management purchased and financed Straightset (a business which sells to the garage market) and how another management team bought Denby Pottery. It is also timely to remind you how technically complicated management buy-outs can turn out to be. It is crucial to take legal and tax advice at a very early stage: these elements can play an important role in the negotiation and valuation of the company.

Three-way Negotiation

How difficult it can be to negotiate the purchase of a business can no doubt be imagined. And the complications which will set in when trying to raise finance on a major scale for any venture can also be understood. But with a buy-out, you are trying to carry out both these negotiations side by side, culminating in an agreement from both parties which will take place at the same time. And, of course, with a buy-out you are still in the employment of the company carrying out your duties as a director. As Tina Tietjen puts it: 'Our biggest problem was time. We were trying to run two operating companies; we were trying to sell the businesses to a third party; and we were trying to buy it ourselves. You need an awful lot of stamina. During the negotiations, we had meetings starting at 7 a.m. and lasting until 11 p.m. And you've never seen such a paper chase.'

Gerry Meredith-Smith was in the unusual position of attempting a second buy-out for the same company, so unlike most management he was practised at the art of tripartite negotiation. Nevertheless, the purchase and financing of Mohawk contained some shocks.

'We were going quite strongly with 3i because the apparent deal was so much better than any of the other venture capitalists'. But 3i dropped out at the last minute and left us up the Suwannee. It got all very hot and suddenly they melted away and were not around.

'But Alan Patricof was a natural choice. The manager there was a salesman with me at ICL. My gut feeling is if you know the people and it's a small team, you can talk to the decision-maker. Communication is very important. They also had to take a gamble right at the end as the vendor couldn't obtain shareholder approval for the sale. Mohawk had a very dispersed shareholding and the company couldn't obtain the 70 per cent approval required.

'Negotiation is bloody hard work as you are carrying on two negotiations at once. At the last minute we tried to cut the price and the vendor threw us out and accused me of gross misconduct in a very emotional diatribe.

'The art of successful negotiation is to look at it from their point of view. What will they want?'

There is no general rule about the help which the venture capitalist might give you in negotiating with the vendor. At one extreme is the example of Roy Mitchell, who bought Carron from the receiver. His team, including financial and legal advisers, conducted all the negotiations with the receiver and the venture capitalists were never present at the table. The negotiations concentrated on what the value of the company was which they were buying, and although they had a strong hand because the company was in receivership and needed to be sold quickly, nevertheless, because of the product, they don't consider they got it at a discount price. As Mitchell says: 'Who can imagine their kitchen without a domestic sink?'

Compare this with Derrick Bumpsteed's experience, which was that the venture capitalists 3i took the lead role in the negotiations with STC, who were determined to sell the company at the right price. STC had commissioned a report from some accountants which helped to uncover two other possible purchasers for Exacta. The management team were bidding against these two competitors. Says Bumpsteed: 'I think we bid the right amount of money; I don't consider that STC let us have it cheap. The way the deal was set up as regards tax benefits came into it. There was a figure of cash and there were tax breaks that were beneficial to STC, so the two together gave them what they wanted. The 3i tax man worked out how the tax should be done when the company was sold.'

Competition and Speed

There are two aspects to consider. The first is that management buy-outs remain relatively popular as a vehicle for venture capitalists, so you may very well be able to encourage a competition to improve your terms. The second is that the speed of the decision-making in some cases may hinder the development of competition.

The purchase of Video Arts proceeded to completion at a snail's pace, so there should have been ample opportunity for enhancing the deal, and yet Tina and Maggie consider that they failed to capitalize on their strong position. Tina says: 'We had more clout than we thought we had. If we had had more knowledge about the route we were taking, we could have argued harder on some points.'

Neill Bell emphasizes the same point: 'No management buy-out team ever realizes that they are buyers themselves. They're buying from a company, the company is selling to them. All MBO teams that I've ever spoken to have the feeling, "Oh, my God, we're going to have to go and find finance!" What they don't realize is that there are people falling over themselves to give you finance and you really should shop around more.' Neill was speaking about the atmosphere in the late eighties and management teams will have found less competition from lenders in 1990 and 1991, for example.

The recognition that there is competition amongst venture capitalists led to the development of the beauty parade. In this, MBO teams asked various venture capitalists to come to pitch for the business, in much the same way as advertising agencies have to make a pitch.

However, there will always be buy-outs which need to be carried out at great speed. For example, Roy Mitchell completed the buy-out of Carron in just twenty-one days. In cases like this, it's more important to get the deal done than to try and negotiate so hard on every little point that you risk failure.

Where great haste is needed, with larger management buy-outs, you may find that a lead investor will agree terms and underwrite the deal. Post-deal, the investment will be syndicated.

Gearing and Financial Structures

Gearing has a Jekyll-and-Hyde character. On the one hand, it is beneficial because it increases the return to equity investors. On the other hand, it can be so high that it cripples a company with debt and interest repayments so large that they cannot be met. It's all a question of moderation.

The typical structure for a buy-out will include what's called senior debt and equity. In larger buy-outs, over £10 million say, there may also be mezzanine debt.

Senior debt is usually provided by banks, who demand in return a rate of interest somewhat higher than LIBOR; in 1992 some 2 per cent above. Some banks require full security for these loans; some will lend against projected cash flows.

Mezzanine finance ranks behind the so-called senior debt and carries a higher rate of interest. It will generally have some sort of option or warrant attached to it. Andrew Jackson of Intermediate Capital Group, specialist providers of mezzanine finance for buy-outs of developing companies, says: 'We would expect a return of around 20 to 30 per cent. The make-up of this return includes an interest rate of 3.5 to 4 per cent above LIBOR. The remainder of the return would be made up of warrants or the ordinary shares themselves. Warrants invariably add complications and so we are often as happy to invest in ordinary shares. The size of the warrant would vary according to the state of the company and the range of its expected growth. We look typically for 5 to 15 per cent of the equity, but it does depend on how much the mezzanine is in the total package.'

Mezzanine debt can be very flexible. There have been examples of notes which required no interest payments for the first three years. Senior-debt providers require interest payments, so they are less likely to agree to interest holidays. Mezzanine can also be provided in the form of preference shares, thereby increasing the share capital and lowering the gearing.

Mezzanine debt may be required if there are not enough assets to secure long-term debt, which together with the equity, would otherwise make up the purchase price of the business. Firms which provide mezzanine debt will look very closely at the cash flow of the business. Andrew Jackson again: 'There are some companies where you can't get senior debt, for example, "people businesses" which have no assets in the balance sheet. Mezzanine can substitute here.'

The amount of funds provided by debt compared with equity has fluctuated dramatically over the last decade. For example, KPMG Peat Marwick estimated that in 1981 £50 was lent against every £100 of equity; by 1989 the ratio was £469 of debt to £100 of equity; and by 1991 the ratio had reversed so that only £151 of debt was available for each £100 of equity.

Table 14 overleaf shows the percentage supplied by each form of funds for buy-outs costing over £10 million. These figures show that for 1991 the gearing for MBOs had altered significantly. Far less of the purchase price was provided by debt and mezzanine debt and a far greater proportion by equity and vendor loan notes. The figures for the second quarter of 1992 (not in the table) show that the proportion of funding provided by equity had leapt to 40 per cent. Thus structures are much more conservative with much lower levels of gearing. For smaller buy-outs, involving less than £10 million, the financial structure has always been more conservative. One third or more of the finance has been provided by equity since 1989.

Table 14: Relative Volumes (%) of Buy-out Fund Types, 1989–91
(involving at least £10 Million)

	1989	1990	1991
Senior debt	58.7	55.6	44.9
Mezzanine	17.9	10.4	6.4
Equity	17.4	24.8	24.0
Loan note	3.4	6.4	11.2
Other	2.6	2.8	13.5

Source: Centre for Management Buy-out Research (CMBOR).

How much of the funds do the management team put up and what share of the equity does their input secure? Statistics from CMBOR are shown in Table 15 on the right. The message which rings out loud and clear is that the management for a relatively small proportion of the funds can secure a much greater proportion of the equity.

Andrew Jackson gives the following guidelines for a £25 million deal (not forgetting that there is no typical deal and that it can be arranged to fit different problems). The funds might be distributed thus: £22 million as a purchase price, £1.5 million in cost and £1.5 million in working capital. The funding might be made up as follows, if the buy-out were occurring in the more cautious climate of the nineties: overdraft, £1 million; senior debt, £12 million; mezzanine, £4 million; institutional equity, £7.8 million; management equity, £0.2 million. He would expect that the management team would have 10–15 per cent of the equity in this size of deal at the outset. Usually there will be some arrangement to increase the management share to 25–30 per cent as a result of a ratchet. The basis on which the ratchet works varies. It is commonly based on the value generated at the time of the exit, but sometimes on profit or cash-flow measures and sometimes a combination of all three.

'Watch out for deal creep. It's important that the management team has some independent knowledgeable financial advice when the deal is put together. The terms can move against the management team while

Table 15: Management Equity Stakes in UK Buy-outs, 1989-1991

Size (£ million)	Year	Average management contribution (%)	Average vendor contribution (%)	Average management equity stake (%)
Less than 10	1989	7.5	6.6	60.4
	1990	7.8	7.4	57.0
	1991	7.2	8.1	53.2
10 plus	1989	1.3	5.3	32.7
	1990	2.5	8.2	31.7
	1991	1.7	15.3	30.1

Source: Centre for Management Buy-out Research.

the deal is negotiated. And no management backs out of a deal on the day of completion,' advises Jackson. Denby Pottery, for example, found that the terms altered – see the end of this chapter. 'Good advisers are the corporate-finance side of the big accountancy firms', continues Jackson. 'They know their stuff. They are also a source of deal flow and we want to be reasonably nice to them!' In other words, they all know each other very well, so the management team should use this to their advantage.

Some Specific Examples

Discussing 'typical' structures in the abstract can be rather unreal. To give a little more substance, here are some specific examples. Penman Engineering, bought out by Ed Hunter and his management team, is an example of a small-scale buy-out. Some £700,000 was required to purchase the assets and provide working capital. The management team put up £93,000 and this gave them 63 per cent of the equity. The balance of the equity was secured by two financial institutions, who also provided some long-term loan capital. The remainder of the funds was in the form of secured loan capital, £100,000 from Dumfries and

Galloway Regional Council. This illustrates the point that in some areas of the country you may be able to find funding from sources other than the traditional financial institutions.

RFS Industries required funding of £5 million. The four founders put up £25,000 each for ordinary shares. There was a ratchet in operation based on profit before interest and tax over a three-year period. Potentially, the four founders could have secured 36 per cent of the ordinary shares. A further 12 per cent was available for an ESOP scheme for the workforce and 8–10 per cent in management share options. Thus, if the ratchet operated as originally envisaged, the employees and management would have controlled 60 per cent of the business on the back of the £100,000 invested by the four founders.

The purchase price of Exacta for the team led by Derrick Bumpsteed was £8.1 million. The bank lent £3.5 million and the remaining £4.75 million came in a mixture of ordinary shares, redeemable ordinary shares and preference shares. Out of this amount the management team invested £120,000 and at the outset this secured 15 per cent of the equity. However, there was a ratchet for the redeemable ordinary shares which could have increased the management's stake up to 25 per cent. The ratchet was based either on profit figures or on a certain value obtained on an exit after three or four years.

Finally, Eurocamp was a substantial buy-out at £36 million. It has now floated, as Richard Atkinson, the managing director, had recognized from the start that the company should be floated at the earliest moment to avoid servicing a high level of debt on a long-term basis.

Part of the total payment at the time of the buy-out included the repayment of a £6.5 million internal loan to Next and the payment of a £3 million dividend, which because of the tax rules allowed a saving of about £1.2 million on the overall deal. This is a further example of the importance of tax considerations to buy-out (and buy-in) deals.

Some £15 million of the total finance was supplied as a straight mezzanine loan – unsecured, with an interest rate of 3 per cent over the bank base rate and an 'equity kicker' or warrant. The mezzanine finance was provided in equal proportions by 3i and Barclays de Zoete Wedd. A further £13,280,000 was provided by Barclays Development

Capital in the form of redeemable preference shares. Barclays subsequently syndicated about 50 per cent of these shares to other institutional investors. The shares were redeemable in 1992 (four years after the buy-out) or on an exit through a flotation or a private sale.

Next retained an interest in Eurocamp through a £5 million loan note, which received a beneficial rate of interest and had to be repaid in 1992, and some of the ordinary shares. Finally, £1.72 million of the funding was provided in the form of preference and ordinary shares, including £250,000 of the shares owned by the management. At the outset this represented 10 per cent of the equity, but this could have increased up to 50 per cent at the time of flotation.

Straightset: The Story of a Buy-out

Paul Bates was in many ways forced into a management buy-out when the holding company of the subsidiary he worked for decided to close down the business he ran. His horror at the decision was compounded by the fact that he had been asked to set up the business division selling to the garage market only six months before. Coupled with this, he had brought a loyal team with him to run the venture who would all be faced with redundancy.

This latest blow to Paul's career had come after several years of uncertainty and subjection to the vagaries of corporate decisions. Finally, the previous company, for which he had been sales director, had appointed a receiver. With all the difficulties he had experienced, Paul felt that all he wanted was to 'run an ice-cream van'.

Then came a job offer from a company called VL Churchill, part of the US Sealed Power Group. Churchill not only agreed to take Paul but also his team and allow him to build up a similar business. This seemed the ideal solution and with renewed enthusiasm and a lot of relief, Paul and his colleagues joined the new organization.

Just when Paul thought everything was set to run smoothly, the Churchill managing director called him into the office and explained that there had been a management decision to sell off the business Paul was in or to close it down. Paul couldn't believe his ears and said: 'I couldn't tell my people we were on the scrap heap.'

'I didn't know anything about management buy-outs,' explained Paul, but he contacted Arthur Young to help prepare a three-year business plan with which to interest the institutions. Armed with this document, Paul and his colleagues set out to raise £300,000 in overdraft facilities and a £150,000 loan. Arthur Young provided the initial contacts to Midland Bank for the overdraft and to 3i as the loan provider. Because of the speed with which the deal had to be made (Sealed Power wanted to get rid of the company very quickly) and Paul's admitted naïvety about buying a business, there was no shopping around for a better deal. Indeed, if there had been time it is very likely that Paul and his colleagues could have secured more favourable terms for the loan.

Midland Bank demanded personal guarantees and life insurance to cover its overdraft facility. However, Paul and his colleagues later managed to get an offer from Lloyds Bank for overdraft facilities without the need for this personal commitment and Midland offered to match these terms rather than lose the business.

They were so grateful at the time the offer was made that the team settled for the conditions laid down by 3i. This was £45,000 provided as shares, split into £15,000 of 'A' shares and £30,000 of preference shares, giving 3i a one third shareholding in the new company called Straightset. The remainder was a loan repayable over a ten-year period at a cost of 2.75 per cent over the base rate. There was also an eight-year capital holiday.

Paul and two of his close colleagues own the rest of the business apart from shares distributed to staff. It has been Paul's policy to give shares to several of his staff who he feels are important contributors to the business. Paying his staff well is important and he also has regular meetings to keep employees well versed on the progress of Straightset.

The company started trading officially in January 1988. It has already outperformed its original, admittedly conservative forecasts. Initially, it has selected a niche at the top end of the garage workshop market. It provides turnkey packages – everything a garage owner would need for his workshop from the bays and the lifting gear down to the screwdrivers. 'We tend to get the larger, more-involved sites,' explains Paul, 'costing typically between £20,000 and £120,000.'

A couple of years after the company was bought out it had reached a turnover of £2 million and a gross profit of 30 per cent, reduced to a net 10 per cent. In the sector within which he operates, he feels that the company could comfortably reach a turnover of around £4 million – any higher and the gross profit would have to drop to only 5 per cent, because he would have to compete in a more cut-throat sector of the market. The option is to diversify into other niche markets, for it is more important to retain a good level of profitability and keep in balance rather than simply grow turnover.

The Buy-out of Denby Pottery Co. Ltd.

There has been a number of spectacular failures of conglomerates built up during the eighties: foremost among those has been Coloroll, which called in the receiver in 1990. But Coloroll has subsequently spawned eight buy-outs, including Denby Pottery, purchased by a team led by Stephen Riley. It is a particularly hectic story – from receivership to buy-out in six weeks. And this included seeing off 180 other potential purchasers. At times, the team must have felt as if they were walking across an army training ground, with opponents armed with bazookas and grenades, popping up unexpectedly from all directions.

Stephen had been with Denby since 1988; previously he had spent fourteen years with Reckitt & Colman, with a typical management and marketing background. In 1987/8, he was becoming frustrated: 'I realized I didn't want to commit to a life of three-yearly moves around the world, even though this would be regarded as "success". So I thought I would do something rash and join a company where *something* would happen – either totally right or horribly wrong.

'Pretty soon after joining Denby, while it was prospering, Coloroll began to struggle. We could see that we were in line to be sold off, as we were not core strategy. It was a desirable division because we had high-quality products.

'Six months before Coloroll went down, and at the management's expense, we carried out preliminary investigations with Stoy Hayward to see whether we would be of potential interest to venture-capital providers. This proved encouraging. I knew how big companies operated, how very easy it is to offload divisions, if the company is not on strategy. We decided we must take the initiative – we didn't want to let our lives be determined by others. We couldn't see anything that Coloroll was bringing to the party; at that time, they were doing nothing to help us, but take up our time, giving information and making presentations. In retrospect, around 60 per cent of my time was spent pandering to Head Office.

'We made a tentative approach to the managing director of Coloroll, whose response was "Don't be ridiculous! We would want around £15 million for the business. You're on dangerous ground!"' This threat of instant dismissal ensured that the plan was dead in the water, so the team which also included Nick Steele, finance director, David French, sales director, and Richard Booth, production director, put their heads down and carried on with the job of managing Denby. Nevertheless, it was clear that power had shifted from the management of Coloroll to the banks and some of the other subsidiaries began to talk about and prepare for buy-outs: this included larger-scale plans, incorporating Denby.

'When Coloroll went down, it was a big shock – the first big receivership of the recession. We went out and celebrated – at last we had a willing seller.' The next step was the arrival of the receiver, who happily did not coincide with the usual characterization attributed to receivers, but was regarded by the team as helpful and constructive. 'We were honest with him and him with us. We helped him to sell the business to other parties. But we told him that we would leave if we didn't succeed with an MBO.'

The next step the team took was to jettison the parachute of the other larger-scale buy-outs. Stephen remembers: 'On the day of the receivership, I rang up the chap who was trying to complete a buy-out of four divisions and said "We're out". His response was, "You bloody fool! You'll never make it on your own!"'

The day after the receivership, the team took what they now regard as their most important step. They contacted the chairman of Aynsley China, who had staged a buy-out from Wedgwood, two years before. They had never met before, but the Denby team remain extremely grateful to him for the unstinting manner in which he passed on all he knew about the process. In particular, he had advised them: 'Watch out for ratchets and watch that the offer from the venture capitalist doesn't change.' He also gave the team various contacts, including the name of a solicitor, Tony Reeves of Kent, Jones and Done. He proved to be a valuable and experienced negotiator with venture capitalists. Says Stephen: 'Without Tony, we would have paid more for the business.'

Within two days of the receivership, the team had the business plan in the hands of merchant banks: the groundwork for this had all been laid six months before when they had suggested a buy-out to Coloroll. Stoy Hayward arranged all the contacts with the venture-capital people, but did not have much input in the plan. In all the team presented to six sets of potential financiers and banks. These involved the full management team and lasted approximately five hours. Stephen and the other directors were surprised during all these discussions by how much emphasis was placed by some of the financiers on the asset base of the company, rather than upon the growth and profit record and potential. As a rule they did not seem prepared to consider unsecured lending.

The buy-out process became very hectic, lasting only six weeks from beginning to end. Stephen and the finance director spent all their time on the buy-out, while the other two directors kept the business going. And every day, new prospective purchasers turned up to see the factory. The bids kept coming into the receiver and the team carried on gleaning snippets of information about the intentions and plans of the receiver.

While buy-outs from the receiver are not always successful, Stephen regards the receivership as a lucky break for them. He considers: 'Other teams buying from corporations may be tempted to pay too high a price because they're so keen to do it. In the case of Denby, I'm sure that some prospective purchasers didn't believe the figures, because they knew about Coloroll's accounting policies. We showed them the genuine figures – but maybe they discounted it all. Denby had the taint of receivership, but was profitable.'

The team were now close to fulfilling their plan but two further problems emerged. 3i was the front runner for the financing. Stephen comments: 'They recognized the need for speed and regarded it as a high-profile investment.' However, the terms of the financing offer were changed as the discussions with the receiver and prospective bankers progressed. This led to considerable concern and debate amongst the team especially after the comments of the chairman of Aynsley. However, finally, a formal offer was agreed and this did not alter.

The second problem arose from the last scheduled visit to the site by a competitive bidder, Hambro European Ventures. The Denby team regarded this as a formality, that would come to nothing once the management had made clear its intentions – unless the team bought the company, it would leave. However, Hambro adopted an aggressive stance and insisted that they would back a bid from a management buy-in team and that they would outbid the existing management. But the team called their bluff. However, that last play by the Hambro team had almost worked: the team had considered acceptance. Instead, the team wrote jointly rejecting the Hambro offer.

There were no further visits to the factory by potential purchasers, but the receiver still delayed. The Denby team thought that there were no more than a handful of serious bidders, but had no firm proof of this. Clearly, the receiver wanted the maximum possible for the business. Finally, towards the end of the sixth week of receivership, it seemed that a decision had been reached and the momentum of the deal speeded up.

The shell company was formed to buy the business and endless agreements, and minute alterations, were going backwards and forwards between the lawyers for the receiver, the board and 3i. However, despite all this activity and the clocking up of expensive legal time (to be paid for out of the finance raised), at any time a better offer could have emerged for the business which would have knocked the buy-out team out of court.

On the day of completion, all the advisers, lawyers, financiers and the management travelled to London to finalize the documents. One team of lawyers were at 3i's London offices and another with the receiver. Progress, painfully slow at times, was made during the day. With the arrival of the central administrative receiver at 6 p.m., the team thought the process was nearly complete. But it wasn't until 4.27 a.m. the next morning that the team became the owners of Denby.

Around £7 million was needed to complete the deal – £5 million to buy the business, nearly £1 million to provide working capital and the final £1 million to cover other items, including costs of £370,000. 3i initially provided all the finance required to complete the deal, apart from £160,000 from the management team.

The financing looked like this:

Management share	£160,000
3i equity and preference shares	£1,900,000
3i mezzanine loan	£1,000,000
3i underwriting facility	£3,800,000

The preference shares and loans are repayable over ten years. There were no ratchets, which had been a point of importance for the management team after the warning from the Aynsley chairman.

After the deal was done, the underwriting facility was replaced by £1.5 million secured loan from 3i, repayable over fifteen years and £2.15 million of loan and overdraft facilities from the Royal Bank of Scotland. There was a provision in the original deal for the directors to choose to replace some of the funding with a further £500,000 of equity and preference shares provided by 3i and this has occurred.

Four directors now control the business with 55 per cent of the equity split fairly equally between them. Comments Stephen: 'Control is lovely but the number of covenants in the agreements probably mean that if 3i wanted to take control they could!' The team all put up their houses as security, but 'I have never lost sleep, because the house is mortgaged. It's not so high that it would clean me out.'

Since the buy-out there have been two difficulties for the company. One occurred six months after the deal when the business had to go on a four-day week for a short period. The second difficulty emerged as a result of the original selection of the team to buy the business. There were four directors who took part, but Denby had six directors at the time of the receivership. Two were excluded by common agreement amongst the buy-out team. One was very disappointed, but left quickly. The other made no comment and has only recently left. Stephen advises: 'Make all those changes of personnel on day one. Even if it costs you and you don't think you can afford it, carry out the adjustments needed. The changes we have now made have released a more dynamic group of managers.'

Stephen's final piece of advice to anyone considering a buy-out: 'Ring up someone who has achieved a buy-out, go and see them, even if you don't know them.' The team at Denby has issued an open invitation.

14

Finance for a Buy-in

The problems you are likely to encounter in securing finance for a buy-in include:

- the difficulties of conducting a tripartite negotiation between the vendor, yourself (the purchaser) and the venture-capital organization;
- the conduct of the due diligence process and the warranties which need to be coaxed from the vendor;
- financing the purchase without overburdening the business with debt, i.e. keeping the level of gearing conservative;
- negotiating a structure for the management team which adequately reflects the contribution it will make.

This chapter looks at some of these problems and gives an example of a financial structure. At the end of the chapter, there is a case study of Fernox, a very successful buy-in.

Commonly, you will find that you are presented with a trammelled negotiation for the business you have targeted. A survey by CMBOR found that 57 per cent of those in the survey had faced competition from other serious bidders, including management buy-out teams. Where the buy-in teams were unsuccessful, almost half had been outbid by a trade buyer and a third had found that the vendor decided not to sell. A sensible working assumption is that you are always in competition – and you won't know who they are.

Competition and dithering sellers are not the only problems you are likely to encounter. Nearly two thirds of the CMBOR sample had reported major negotiating difficulties. The pricing, the final terms, the structure of the deal to meet the vendor's needs, the paperwork, the number of advisers and inadequate information about the target company were all highlighted as potential pitfalls in the survey.

The due diligence process and the wording of the warranties for the vendor are areas which will repay application of your brain power. It is not sufficient to employ accountants and solicitors to carry out the tasks allotted and rely on them to complete this function better than you can. You must direct them, using your knowledge of the industry, the sector, the vendor and the target company. This investigation process must be completely gripped and run by yourself.

Armed with this information you can negotiate a lower price, more stringent warranties, deferred payments or even conclude that this is a purchase you would be advised not to make. The buy-in team at CEC-Time found after the purchase: 'The figures weren't what we thought they should have been.' A writ was issued, but the subsequent negotiations, which lasted for eighteen months or so proved a distraction. Eventually, a settlement was reached. Terry Weston expands: 'The only way to protect yourself is to make sure your purchase agreement has warranties and that there is deferred consideration.'

Patrick Dunne of 3i emphasizes: 'Cases with huge skeletons turn up – the manager missed it, 3i missed it and a band of professional advisers, too. Part of the problem is that the manager does not grab hold of the process of assessing the company and relies too much on advisers. The manager has to focus hard on this – tell the accountants what to follow up. It is vital for the manager to drive the process and provide a clear direction to advisers. You can't rely too heavily on them. It's your life's work that is at stake!

'We've been trying to persuade managers to work for the company before the buy-in. Fifty-two per cent of the companies we finance as buy-ins are family-owned and they quite like seeing the manager in action and establishing trust.' No doubt this also enables the manager to see what horrors lie beneath the surface, thereby mitigating the risk of the venture.

Financial Structures

The structures for financing management buy-ins are similar to MBOs, although the CMBOR survey found they were more conservatively structured. Of the original funding, 29 per cent was provided by equity.

The rest of the funding will come from overdraft, debt and possibly mezzanine finance with bigger buy-ins.

Patrick Dunne gives an example of how a funding of £1.5 million could be arranged on a conservative basis. The funds might be spent as follows:

Purchase price	£1 million
Working capital	£200,000
Capital expenditure	£250,000
Fees	£50,000

The purchase price is only part of the picture. Particularly if growth is envisaged, you will need a substantial amount of working capital and capital expenditure. He would look at a debt/equity split of 50/50. Thus the funds would come from:

Overdraft/long-term debt	£750,000
Ordinary share/redeemable preference	£750,000

Interest cover of three times profit before interest and tax would be ideal, although some venture capitalists would accept cover of two or two and a half times, which are the typical levels for MBOs.

The CMBOR survey found that on average management put in £135,000 and this obtained for them 54 per cent of the equity. You can secure a greater percentage of the equity for your stake than does the venture capitalist because you will be entitled to subscribe for your shares at a better rate than the institution. This is known as the 'envy ratio' and is subject to negotiation, but typically will be somewhere between two and five. In the heyday of the eighties it might have risen to seven. If the ratio is five, every £1 you invest will secure five times as many of the ordinary shares as every £1 invested by the institution. The ratio will be less than five if the institution does not feel too confident about the management's forecasts, or considers that management has negotiated a price for the business which means it is being bought on too high a price/earnings ratio, or hasn't controlled the fees on the financing.

The absolute amount of the stake you invest is less significant as far as the venture capitalist is concerned than its relative proportion to the total of your assets: but the institution will want to know that it will hurt you if the business fails.

Here is one example of the financial structure of a buy-in. The total price was £2,125,000. The long-term debt provided £1,525,000 and the equity £600,000. The venture-capital organization put up £400,000 of the equity and this secured 20 per cent of the shares. The vendor retained 25 per cent of the shares and the management team invested £200,000 for 55 per cent – an envy ratio of five.

Fernox: The Story of a Management Buy-in

For William Stogdon and Edwin Davies, the opportunity to own their own business was basically a matter of chance. Edwin at fifty years of age would probably never have contemplated taking the risk, especially as he was happy in his job and had been with the same company for thirty years. William, on the other hand, was in his early thirties and had always felt that running his own business was the eventual aim. He had just been promoted at BP Chemicals when Fernox, a small, privately owned chemicals business, came on to the market.

Fernox, a twenty-five-year-old company, was set up by Peter Muetzel in the early sixties. Peter was a chemist and metallurgist by training who had spotted an emerging market for products in the central heating market. He had realized that central-heating systems were being redesigned to use thinner-gauge steel and that this would eventually lead to corrosion problems.

So, he developed a product to hinder the corrosion process. He sold his products to local merchants and basically, because Peter shunned professional advertising, the sales of the product grew on its reputation and quality alone. In fact, the name Fernox became synonymous with his anti-corrosion products and the company captured the lion's share of the market. Peter also gave many lectures to professional bodies on corrosion and related topics.

Peter realized in his early sixties that he had to think about the future of the company and decided that, because he had no children who could inherit his business, the best option was to sell out. He looked for people who could give some continuity to the business and had decided against offering his company to a larger group because he felt that being swallowed by a big fish in the chemicals pond would not give his staff any long-term security.

Edwin and William, as employees with BP Chemicals, were good candidates for the buy-in, because of their knowledge of the industry and their commitment to it. Edwin had been selling speciality chemicals while William was versed in the ways of management and corporate planning.

Edwin was known to Peter Muetzel simply because they lived in the same village. During one conversation, he asked Edwin if he knew of any suitable buyer for his business. Edwin, not really considering himself a candidate to take over the company, mentioned the idea to William.

William, on the other hand, felt that this was a good opportunity and soon persuaded Edwin to join in. They had complementary skills and respected each other, both important ingredients for a successful buy-in. 'Edwin was essentially happy, but I had always fancied running my own company. Opportunity was the critical issue,' explained William.

Edwin, being fifty, took early retirement with BP. The retirement scheme provided Edwin with a useful financial cushion.

The main problem was to raise the money and offer the right tax-effective package to Peter Muetzel. They prepared a package with their accountants, a local firm, and used this as a basis for raising the funds from the financial institutions. William said: 'We didn't get turned down by anyone.' This is not surprising – Fernox was highly successful with a leading position in the market and had no debts. In addition, both William and Edwin had enough pedigree in the business to convince most venture-capital companies that they could run a business of their own. The main problem was to present a deal to Peter Muetzel which would be the most tax-efficient in the long term and still allow Peter the opportunity to participate in the technical development of the business.

Faced with an enthusiastic response from the financial institutions, Edwin and William decided on a mix of funding for the purchase. This included equity funding from 3i and a long-term loan from Barclays Bank. The purchase was finalized in May 1984.

The 3i deal was £250,000 of £1 cumulative, convertible, redeemable preference shares. These were scheduled to be redeemed in five equal tranches between the years 1987 to 1991. How many of the shares were converted was related to the progress of repayment. If the two had paid back £125,000 by 1987, this limited the extent of the conversion to 15 per cent. If that target could not be met, 3i had the right to convert up to 25 per cent of the shares. However, the company easily met its repayment schedule, so that 3i's shareholding was pegged at 15 per cent. In addition to repayment, the shares were also interest-earning, at a rate of 11 per cent; and there was an element of profit-sharing – about 3 per cent on top of this using a simple formula.

Edwin and William and their wives also injected some £60,000 into the business in exchange for ordinary shares. Finally, the loan from Barclays came to £325,000 and an unused overdraft facility of £75,000. The loan from Barclays was for a ten-year period; it was secured against the assets. The interest on the loan was 3⅛ per cent over LIBOR.

Peter Muetzel, the vendor, received payment over a seven-year period and was offered a five-year contract with the new company. (Peter unfortunately did not finish his contract as he died at the age of sixty-three.)

In 1983, the year before the buy-in, the business was turning over £1.4 million. It has risen to £3 million and the purchasers planned to double the size of the business over the next five years. This was to be achieved by a series of new product launches into related and not-so-related markets.

Without Peter's technical know-how, the company had to increase the strength of its research team to maintain and improve the company's position in the market-place. In addition, Fernox employed professional salesmen out on the road, actively promoting the product for the first time in its history.

They also looked for opportunities outside the UK. 'We have representation in Germany, Belgium, Benelux and France and still want further coverage in Europe.' William considers that there are many European countries in which the original Fernox product could find a market niche.

In January 1989, the company launched a range of swimming-pool chemicals to act as a summer seller to balance the predominantly winter sales of its anti-corrosion products in the domestic market.

Later that year, in June, the Cookson Group made an offer for the original Fernox business, minus the swimming-pool chemicals which William and Edwin retained. The two felt it was an offer they couldn't refuse. 'It also served another purpose as Edwin was looking to retire and has done so subsequently,' explains William Stogdon. 'From the outside people said, "Wasn't your timing right?", but in fact the business has carried on being more successful.' Sales for the 1991 year were just under £5 million. Both William and Edwin signed a three-year contract to carry on running the business, although Edwin retired in June 1991.

'We got what we felt the business was worth up-front.' There was also an element of earn-out, but it was a difficult hurdle. 'It would have been the cream on the cake.'

So far William is happy to stay at Fernox, even though the business is owned by another group. 'Cookson's runs a devolved system of management and leave you to get on with it.'

For William Stogdon, buying into Fernox has been a satisfying step. He explains: 'The most satisfying aspect is that you are independent of anyone else. You live and die by your own mistakes. You can come and go as you please. You can work as hard as you want or as little as you want. But this is all based on the fact that it is successful.'

15

Finance for a Start-up

The difficulties a start-up is likely to face in securing finance are:

- lack of competition among venture capitalists, because start-ups are not as popular as MBOs and MBIs;

- long negotiations with financiers, because there is no apparent deadline to meet;

- inability to agree on the terms of the deal, especially if it involves loss of control on the part of the entrepreneur;

- differing valuations of the business, if it has already been established, and hence the terms on which the venture capitalist and the management team invest.

This chapter looks at these four problem areas and gives an example of a financial structure for a start-up – subject to the warning that there is no such thing as a typical structure. At the end of the chapter is a detailed story, recounting the founding and financing of Logical Networks.

Generating Competition

There have already been a number of examples showing how useful it can be to have competition among the financiers to fund your deal. The Solway Foods team have described in Chapter 12, 'The Money Timetable', how their accountant failed to fulfil the introductory role satisfactorily. Nevertheless, even though they were looking for a substantial amount of funding, some £1.8 million, they were able to ginger things up sufficiently by arousing the interest of more than one financier, to enable them to negotiate a better deal for their large-scale start-up. Corby Industrial Development Corporation proved to be fairly helpful in introducing them to the Leicester office of 3i. The team also had a few abortive chats with a high-tech venture-capital organization.

The members of the team each also looked at the possibility of raising money through their own personal banking contacts. As a result of this, three of the clearing houses' venture-capital arms became interested in the idea: Charterhouse, Midland Bank and County NatWest Ventures. Initially, it was Charterhouse and 3i which did all the running. The team recall clandestine meetings in hotel rooms – because all but one of them were still working – culminating in a Saturday-morning meeting with County NatWest in McDonalds, somewhere in the City of London, where the best offer they had received so far was put on the table along with the coffee and burgers.

The team gave 3i the opportunity to respond to this offer and 3i indicated that they could improve on the County NatWest terms; this tipped the balance in favour of 3i, especially as the team felt comfortable with the company. '3i wanted to know what was going on but didn't want to get quite so deeply involved in the company as the others.' In addition, 3i accepted the team's appointment of its own non-executive chairman and director without adding a director of their own. They also had a European loans manager who helped the Solway Foods team apply for the EC funding and another plus point was that 3i was the agent for some soft loans offered by the European Coal and Steel Community (ECSC) – available to Solway because it was locating in Corby, a former steel town.

Competition between venture capitalists also enabled the team at Corin Medical to obtain a better deal. Peter Gibson explains: 'One of the golden rules is to have more than one option. With a venture-capital fund you can get more improvement in the last half-an-hour of negotiation than in the previous six months if it is a two-horse race.' The Corin management opted for the Alta Berkeley offer, because Peter and the other founders were able to sell some of their shares and make a capital gain (they had started the company a year earlier by obtaining an unsecured overdraft of £70,000 without offering any personal guarantee and by asking for cash with orders from their early customers).

These two examples show how beneficial it is for your position if there are at least two venture capitalists interested in financing your start-up. Both Solway and Corin had obtained the same basic offer from the competing financiers, but some of the terms surrounding the financing were improved. In Allen Jones's case, competition played a slightly different role. 'Competition is a good thing. It didn't help us get a better deal, but it forced the venture capitalists to make their in–out decisions.'

'Sweat Equity'

The work already put in is the justification for the better terms offered to the management team for their investment than those taken by the financiers. You may be offered these terms to recognize the effort you have already expended in guiding the venture thus far or because the venture capitalist is keen to invest, recognizing the quality and calibre of your team.

There is no typical figure and the terms are quite individual to each venture. But, for example, at the initial round of financing for Vamp Health the management paid £1 for each share while the venture capitalists paid £4. (And in addition the venture capitalists put in larger sums in the form of loan stock and preference shares.) This was to compensate the team for the unpaid work they had already undertaken since establishing the business a year before the funding took place. Other teams have been able to negotiate superior terms or been forced to accept inferior ones.

The Shareholdings and Financial Structures

You won't find any debt in the financing for a start-up – just a chunk of equity, although some of it might be dressed up as preference shares or some sort of loan.

One possible structure might be as follows for a funding of £450,000, in addition to the investment of £75,000 by the management team for 60 per cent of the equity to retain control:

Management team ordinary shares	
(60 per cent of the equity)	£75,000
Preferred ordinary shares for the venture capitalist	
(40 per cent of the equity)	£50,000
Redeemable preference shares	£300,000
Loan stock	£100,000

As already pointed out in Chapter 12, there is a tremendous diversity of financial instruments, which allows the venture capitalist to satisfy many demands. For example, if loss of control seems likely, because of the amount of funds being raised, it is possible to offer shares with two votes for each share to the management and restrict the venture capitalist to shares with one vote for each share. Thus the founder can retain control, although the majority of the equity will be taken up by outsiders.

Derwent Valley Foods secured a mixed bag of financing first time around. The problem was as Roger McKechnie explained: 'We had no real equity ourselves. We needed half a million in capital but we could raise only £50,000 between us.' The rest of the funds were made up as follows: a £30,000 British Steel loan, £150,000 in public-sector grants like Regional Selective Assistance, £85,000 from Barclays Bank as a business start-up loan and £227,000 from 3i in equity and loans, giving them a 25 per cent share of the equity. The founders retained 75 per cent of the equity with their investment.

Solway Foods also raised their money in a variety of forms. The five directors put in £50,000 each and retained 60 per cent of the ordinary shares. 3i paid £167,000 for 40 per cent of the shares and put up a further £443,000 as preference shares at an interest rate of 10.25 per cent. As the business was set up in Corby, further money was raised from a Regional Development Grant of £212,000, a Regional Selective Assistance Grant of £50,000 and a European soft loan of £500,000. The terms of this latter loan were an interest rate of 6.42 per cent, with a capital holiday of five years and a repayment term of a further five years. There was also an overdraft facility of £250,000.

How Long It Will Take

'Everything takes a lot longer than you think it will. Once you've got a backer and an offer letter, it will take another three months to receive the cheque because the lawyers get involved,' explains Malcolm Parkinson. 'And you won't be able to do anything else while you're raising the money.'

While nearly all the entrepreneurs agreed with him, there was a great range of experience over the length of time taken. The shortest period to raise money was experienced by Tim Hely Hutchinson (three months). Derwent Valley Foods estimated that it took six months and Allen Jones had suffered nine months before receiving the capital injection the business required: 'Our biggest disappointments and heartaches have been from people agreeing to a deal and then at the last hour backing out. These sort of things take the wind out of your sails.'

Finally, Brian Gilda took eleven months to raise the initial £300,000 needed. But he says: 'I probably wouldn't be so commercially naïve again. I simply went to 3i, who directed me to Scottish Development Agency. I spent the time bumping between Scotland and London and eventually found more subscribers than I required, although by that time 3i had dropped out.'

John Cavill and Logical Networks

John is an engineer by training, but in his early twenties he moved into the sales side. His burning ambition had been to run a company by the age of thirty. But he found himself at the age of twenty-nine still working for a large company – and finding the atmosphere too political.

He put together a business plan and interested a US-based company, Data Translation Inc. in setting up a subsidiary in the UK. This sold the parent-company products and computer networking products. After a few years, sales of the network products were outstripping all other sales. The parent company went through a process of deciding what to do – and came to the decision to sell the networking business. John was asked if he would like to buy: and so began the process of a buy-out.

However, it all came to an abrupt end when the company changed its mind. John was given an ultimatum: he could stay on and focus on developing the parent company's traditional business only, or he could accept a payment but agree to be locked out of the industry for two years. Neither course was acceptable. And so he was fired.

John acknowledges with understatement: 'The timing was a bit difficult. My wife was just about to have a baby. But I gave myself six months to achieve what I wanted to do.' And this was to raise venture capital and establish a business selling a range of local area network (LAN) products and services to *The Times* Top 100 companies and value added resellers in the UK.

'I spent the whole six months raising money and taking legal action against my previous employer for wrongful dismissal. I had no income, but my wife was very supportive, as soon as she realized what I wanted to do. I did have some cash from the sale of some shares, but I knew I could only last six months.

'The first thing I did was to go out and buy an Amstrad PC. I was very busy and got up at the same time as when I was employed; I found myself on the phone the whole time. It would be very tough to raise finance and try to hold down a job at the same time. You could do it, but it would take longer.

'I was constantly pushing for the venture capital to happen. And I was also spending a lot of time with potential suppliers – showing them my business plan and getting their support. I needed to demonstrate to the venture capitalists that manufacturers would supply me with their products.'

John put together the business plan himself, but asked Arthur Young to advise. 'I got in touch with the person at the business development section, saying "I've got no money to pay you – but if you give me help and assistance you will get the audit at the end of the day."' One of the useful functions Arthur Young performed was to take part in a dry run, pretending that they were the venture capitalists.

However, generally speaking most of the contacting of venture capitalists was carried out by John. He explains: 'I went and bought a book which listed all the venture capitalists – and I talked to everyone I could find who had experience of raising finance.' He found that a lot of venture capitalists were interested only in mezzanine finance (John was raising money in 1988), and few were looking at providing seedcorn or start-up finance. He had many telephone calls, but sat down and had in-depth discussions with only four – Advent, BBHQ, Octagon and 3i. Once it became clear that John's plan was of interest to these venture capitalists, a management team of five was identified.

The final offer which came from 3i was for significantly lower funding than he had been seeking. His business plan had been trying to raise £1 million – but, in the event, he raised only £200,000 in addition to the money which he and the management team could put up, £150,000. The team scaled down the business plan and John explains: 'Once we'd gone through the numbers, we were happy we could still achieve the forecast revenue and profit stream by careful use of the funding, with equipment leasing and invoice discounting to ease cash flow.'

The funding looked like this:

Management team (75% of the equity)	£150,000
3i (25% of the equity)	£75,000
3i secured loan	£50,000
3i Loan Guarantee Secured loan	£75,000

There was an additional loan facility of £100,000 made available but this was never taken up – and this meant that a ratchet in favour of the management team could be sprung, which reduced 3i's equity to 17.5 per cent. (John, unlike the Denby Pottery team, was attracted to the idea of ratchets).

John himself invested £82,000, giving him over 40 per cent of the equity initially: he raised the money by selling some shares he held and by extending the mortgage on his house. He explains: 'We didn't want to put up our houses as security. It didn't bother my wife, but I felt it was important for the management team that we should be able to do this without risking our homes.'

Logical Networks is that rarity: the business plan approaches reality. Turnover was £1.5 million and profit before tax £5,000 in 1989; by

1991 turnover had rocketed to £6.6 million and profits were now £396,000. For 1992, the company is looking for revenues of around £9 million, increasing to £15 million or so in 1993.

The team have been able to raise further funding to enable them to develop an idea for a new product area 'messaging' – electronic fax, telex, E-mail – all resident in one computer. First of all, they were looking for a small amount of funding, say £150,000–£200,000. But none of the formulas were attractive. 'So we decided to raise more money to fund two or three projects. This helped to strengthen the balance sheet. If you're going to go for extra money, go for as much as you can – if you go for too small an amount, the venture capitalist is not interested.

'We wanted to minimize the equity position of 3i, so, for example, we got ratchets in the first and in the second rounds of financing. 3i didn't like the ratchets. But this time around we weren't desperate for money, so we could take our time to get the best deal. If you're desperate for money, there's no leeway. A couple of times we said, "That's not attractive", and left it. 3i were keen to invest as we were doing so well.'

Finally, the team were happy with the arrangement that 3i would increase their share of the equity from 17.5 per cent to 30 per cent, in exchange for a further investment of £500,000.

IV

SWIMMING – OR SINKING?

Here's a promise – the path of the first two years of your venture will match Tina Turner's description: 'River deep, mountain high.' The peaks and the troughs, the elation and the depression, the gloom and the buoyancy are exaggerated and heightened to a fine degree. Nerve ends twitch, adrenalin flows and hopefulness blooms. Life as an employee in a large corporation will now, by contrast, be recognized as dull, safe and staid.

And you will develop very rapidly as a business person. You will learn more in the first six months running your own show than you experienced in the previous ten years as an executive. Your learning curve will be nearly vertical.

'It's a most exhilarating process – starting a business. I did every job – opening envelopes, selling books, paying bills. And nobody could interfere!' is Tim Waterstone's description of the early stages of his business, Waterstone's Booksellers.

There is a somewhat unexpected hiatus between the drive to raise finance and finalize the purchase of the business and the drive to build or transform it. Completing the deal becomes the goal and the actual business an afterthought. Many entrepreneurs were surprised at the feeling of anticlimax once the money had been finalized. After all, there should have been euphoria and a sense of urgency to drive the business forward and put the plans in motion.

Stephen Hinton says: 'It was difficult to get going because we were all very tired. It was a difficult period.' And Tina Tietjen confirms: 'Post finance, the biggest mistake is to forget how much time is consumed during the MBO – the management is suddenly not there in the business. In the three months afterwards, we were still bombarded with meetings to sweep up the paper trail.'

The same experience has been met by teams carrying out management start-ups. Tim Hely Hutchinson explains: 'It's not all over on D-Day when you get the cheque. I had "postnatal depression" after I received the money as I was totally focused on raising it.' And Allen Jones advises: 'Have a plan to know what to do with the money when it arrives, otherwise you lose interest.'

Finally, what about the prospect of failure? It has to be faced: the statistics vary but somewhere between one in three and one in five businesses will fail in the first two years. And more established businesses fail, too – a few of the entrepreneurs who helped with this book have experienced the failure of their ventures during the severe recession and others have struggled to remain in business. The words of Stevie Smith seem apposite: 'Nobody heard him, the dead man, / but he still lay moaning: / I was much further out than you thought / And not waving but drowning.'

16

The Early Years

Managing a new business during its first two or three years is like taking part in a water-polo game. You're pedalling with your feet to keep yourself afloat while trying to throw the ball into the goal with one hand. With the other hand, you're warding off one opponent while another one jabs you in the eye with an elbow. Finally, under the water, another competitor makes a well-aimed kick. Survive it if you can.

Your abilities need to be multidimensional. If you can concentrate on only one task at a time, you aren't cut out for it. If you score the winning goal, it's the most exhilarating experience of your life.

Commonly with start-ups there is a critical period eighteen months to two years after you have started the business when there is the greatest likelihood of failure. Sometimes called the 'wobble', it seems a most inappropriate term. Essentially, it is simply a crystallization of the view that small businesses tend to be crisis-prone because they have no buffer or 'fat' which will see them through difficult periods. This buffer includes financial, as well as human, reserves.

The crisis reaches spectacular proportions a short way into the life of the business because the team can suffer a malaise – tiredness, exhaustion of ideas and an evaporation of confidence. On top of this, dwindling financial resources will be a pressing problem.

Many start-ups experience severe crises in the early years. At the end of this chapter is the story of Daton Systems, which illustrates vividly the survival instincts of an entrepreneur. Lesser mortals would have crumbled under the weight of all the setbacks. In Chapter 5 and later in this chapter you can read how the bank twice tried to close down Derwent Valley Foods. And Vamp Health were also threatened with closure by the bank and once narrowly avoided receivership (see Chapter 19). Peter Williams recalls the occasion when the bank threatened to foreclose: 'We were running out of money, but well on the way to raising new venture funds, indeed only a couple of days from agreeing terms. Despite this, the bank was threatening to close us down and to start bouncing cheques. We were summoned to a meeting with the manager. I persuaded the venture-capital company to fax through the details of the deal to our solicitor's office, around the corner from the bank. We were ushered into the manager's room – he sat at the other end, behind his desk, with a pile of cheques, which no doubt he was going to refuse to pay. Before he could say anything, I slid the fax over to him. It was all handshakes from then on.' Yet another tale which proves the maxim that 'a banker is a man who lends you an umbrella when the weather is fair and takes it away from you when it rains'.

Fast-growing businesses are vulnerable to that sort of threat to their existence because they tend to be chronically underfunded. All you can do at the time is to rethink your strategy and use every available resource.

Robert Wright of Connectair is a pilot and entrepreneur who worked really hard to make the business pay in its various stages. He made excellent use of all the resources to hand and kept his overheads as low as possible. He wrote a business plan but was unable to raise the money to finance the venture. However, he wasn't deterred and spent a couple of years trying to put his idea into action. At the beginning of 1984, with a £60,000 bank overdraft, Robert hired a Brazilian-made Bandierante fourteen-seater plane at a cost of something like £9,000 a month. He managed to get some work ferrying urgently needed spare parts to the various UK Ford factories. Only four people were involved in the business at that time: Robert, his wife, a commercial manager (employed on a commission-only basis) and another pilot.

The business was run under the name of Connectair, reflecting Robert's ultimate aim of carrying passengers to link with the major airline routes. Connectair's first real break in achieving that aim came when British Caledonian allowed the company to sublease the rights to a route between London and Antwerp. To a company the size of British Caledonian, the 10,000 passengers a year who used this route were insignificant and did not warrant the investment in aircraft and staff. However, they were enough for Connectair to make a profit and

British Caledonian benefited because these passengers could feed into the larger planes. Robert reckons that the larger company raised its income by around £1 million over a period of one year thanks to its agreement with Connectair.

To make this route pay, Connectair also had to use night flights carrying cargo. Eventually, it got a regular contract from the carriers, TNT, to ferry parcels to the Continent.

Robert realized that subleasing the route was commercially dangerous and a precarious way to make a living as British Caledonian could easily withdraw from the agreement at any time. So, Connectair tried to bid for the route in its own right. The Civil Aviation Authority, which issues the route licences, was persuaded to allow Connectair the rights to the London–Antwerp route provided that the company had enough financial security behind it.

Raising capital was now much easier for Robert as he had a proven business and potential for development. Connectair obtained £60,000 in government grants, a loan of £15,000 and an equity investment of £36,000 from a venture-capital group, in exchange for 24 per cent of the ordinary shares. However, the CAA did not think this was enough money and wanted a further £60,000 in security. To raise the money quickly, Robert sold his house, thus solving his financial crisis.

Fighting the War on Two Fronts

In an established business, you may face a major problem which can threaten its existence. In a new business, its special nature is that you are frequently dealing with not one, but two or more troubles at the same time. Very frequently, you will be dealing with the predicament of a slower sales take-up at the same time as fighting the battle to make your product a quality product. Many experienced executives have the capacity to cope with one life-threatening quandary – but two (or more)? Derwent Valley Foods faced such a dilemma. They paid particular attention to setting up the production facilities as the whole image of the company was to be built around quality. By January 1983, a year after their initial fund-raising the company had production facilities ready in a small 12,000 ft^2 factory at Consett – but no firm orders. They had missed the Christmas rush. The bank manager became impatient at this point, giving them six weeks to get orders or be closed down.

Fortunately, they managed at the last minute to get a small stand at the International Food exhibition as a late entry. They only had photos of the product, which they pinned to the stand wall. The response was tremendous. 'All the major multiples wanted to see us. Suddenly we were worried about not having enough production capacity.'

This initial difficulty for Derwent Valley Foods was resolved, although the company has had to solve a subsequent crisis (see Chapter 5). However, for some start-ups this fighting the war on two fronts in the early stage is too complex to solve: the business folds because the difficulties faced with production, or whatever, mean that all the funds have been used up before a viable sales operation is under way. Or, just possibly, you can raise some stretch finance to tide you over until break-even is reached.

Lyn Davies, a non-executive director of a number of start-ups, pinpoints another problem: 'The next area of concern is the rate of productivity, that is, what you can achieve in a day. How much can you produce per hour or per week and what are the losses? A company struggling to survive may be suffering from the law of diminishing returns – are the prices high enough, is the rate of productivity good enough?'

And there is another area of concern for him: 'Are the overheads too high? Are there too many Jaguars in the car park?'

Personnel Problems

The possibility of personnel problems in the early stages of a new business is recognized by Davies. He remarks: 'Within three to six months, you will know whether your plan is a dream, a reality or a nightmare. You and the team are now out on your own in a competitive world. A new team will be settling down and trying to sort out the chemistry.' Certainly, a few months after the start of a new venture weaknesses and conflicts within the team will emerge, if they have been latent before. The stresses and strains of trying to run the business will highlight any team member who cannot cope with the allotted tasks. The need for a stronger financial, marketing or production director will be clear.

Further personnel difficulties emerge while trying to recruit good staff and employees for the new business. As Peter Williams says: 'You come across a lot of very strange people while trying to recruit for a new business.' A start-up has very little it can offer to attract good-quality employees: no fringe benefits, no high salaries, no reputation or secure financial history.

David Langston of Blue Ridge Disposable Nappies was in the unusual position of creating a start-up himself without the backing of a management team. These were recruited once the venture capital was raised. He says: 'I looked for people with experience – both functional and personal scope – so we could apply big company expertise to a small company in the beginning. We were aware of the problems of growth. It needs guts and ability to build an organization around and under one person.'

One solution to strive for is to resolve to recruit the best possible people even if you have to provide better remuneration packages to attract them. Brendan Farrell, formerly MD of Noctech, explains what their policy was. 'You have to get share options in for senior management. Nothing drives people on like the prospect of a capital gain. You also have to offer incentives. And you have to persuade people to share your dream – in our case, a successful Irish diagnostics company.

'We have young people in positions which they couldn't aspire to in a large company. It's a meritocracy.'

Not on Plan

'Plans rarely materialize in practice,' says Davies. 'Management shouldn't be afraid to say, "We've got it wrong." But, too often, they are afraid of investors. Plans sometimes have major holes which you only discover afterwards.'

Despite the widespread acceptance that few businesses are on target, and that your ability to get to the right answer on day one is likely to be close to zero, venture capitalists kick up a fuss if you are underachieving your business plan. They may try to imply that you are only one of a few 'problem' companies and that because of this you are failing.

One of the best ways of dealing with the problem of a wayward plan is to adopt a very adaptable approach to the business. An entrepreneurial management team will not believe that the plan is the holy grail to be met at all costs. Instead, you need to keep checking the plot or navigation of the company. The speed and direction of growth need checking; you should be looking at how you can adapt the business in the light of the new business information you are receiving. Fine-tune and keep fine-tuning.

An article in a US magazine used the term 'convergent iteration' to describe the process of starting a business. This is defined as the ability to go down a track believing absolutely you are right, but still observing and making the necessary turns along the way which will develop into something really good. It seems an apt description of what the management teams of start-ups will find themselves going through. Constantly seeking new information, especially by listening to the market-place, they will adjust and adapt their product and the message they send to the market.

It would be a mistake to believe that every start-up underperforms its business plan. As for example with Headline, outperforming also occurs – although it is obviously a far more pleasant quandary to resolve.

Cash Flow, Break-even and Funding

Mr Micawber's understanding of break-even is clear and absolute: 'Annual income twenty pounds, annual expenditure nineteen nineteen six, result happiness. Annual income twenty pounds, annual expenditure twenty pounds ought and six, result misery.'

No doubt understanding of break-even and cash flow is an important part of any executive or manager's job in a large company. But it takes on a greater significance for a new business with venture-capital funding. It must be a preoccupation of the chief executive of any start-up; it is crucial that the business is 'cash flow crazy'. The premise on which you are operating is that the venture capital will fund you until you've reached your break-even point. But once up and running, you will find that break-even doesn't work as it is described in those neat little diagrams on theoretical business and finance courses. There seems to be a reverse gravitational pull: it's always moving up. The business has to be incredibly disciplined to prevent this happening.

In practice, this means being completely ruthless on every expenditure. Is this £10,000 purchase really essential? It may be the lack of £10,000 in a year's time which pushes you over the brink. And you have to be controlled over much smaller items of expenditure, as the little ones add up, too. This is an aspect of the management of a new business venture which will be quite alien to managers breaking out from the large company culture.

The final point about survival for the early period is that you will inevitably find that you are underfunded. You will be underfunded either because your business performs less well than you have expected or because the contrary is true – you have grown too fast. If you have underperformed, you will need to try and raise 'stretch' or 'bridge' finance. This is when you will be glad that you chose to be funded by a venture capitalist who has more funds available. It is almost impossible to persuade a new venture-capital fund to invest in your business when the reason for the funding is underperformance to the business plan. This obtains even though venture capitalists will acknowledge that it occurs in the majority of start-ups.

Of course, the fact that your investor has more funds available does not mean that they are available to you. The desire not to throw good money after bad is very strong, so you will have to be able to convince the investor that the business is now a sound one which is worth backing. And your own shareholdings will pay the price and be heavily diluted. Indeed, it is at moments like these when entrepreneurs under stress may consider that venture capitalists deserve the epithet 'vulture capitalists'.

Whether you need new funding because you have underperformed or outperformed, some start-up businesses, generally those which are fast-growing, have an almost insatiable appetite for funds. Brendan Farrell, formerly of Noctech: 'Most of the time in the last three and a half years has been spent in raising money. The greatest mistake is underfunding a start-up. If you think you want £3 million, ask for £6 million.'

And Tim Waterstone was similarly occupied: 'We were spending six months of the year raising money.' In total, he raised finance for the business eight times in eight years as part of a plan to raise money in stepped tranches to reflect the capital-expenditure programme. Because of this, the shares were sold at ever-higher prices, thus benefiting those investors who were in at the beginning. He rather doubts whether this approach is possible in the nineties and recommends trying to finance a start-up at a very generous initial level. This might be difficult as the pressure from the financiers is always to invest less money than you think you need, as John Cavill of Logical Networks found in Chapter 15, 'Finance for a Start-up'.

Why Businesses Succeed – and Fail

There have been a number of surveys looking at how owner-managed businesses succeed or fail. None of them looked at the specific issue of businesses started by experienced managers with the use of venture capital, although the guidelines from the research which has been done have been incorporated throughout this book.

One survey by Coopers & Lybrand in 1989 found that Britain's most profitable growing companies were wary of very fast rates of growth as rapid growth is very difficult to manage. The survey also identified the six most common factors of success. They were:

– an experienced managing director with a good knowledge of the market and industry;

– close contact with customers and a commitment to quality in both product and service;

– attention to good employee relations frequently backed up with bonus or incentive schemes;

– innovativeness and flexibility in the fields of marketing, technology and product;

– a focus on profits rather than sales. Good management systems were essential to keep down costs;

– operating in markets that were growing.

Another survey carried out by the London Business School for Stoy Hayward looked at the causes of failure. Rather oddly, the survey asked bank managers for their opinion of the reasons why particular companies had failed. Not surprisingly the main reasons cited for failure were financial ones: undercapitalization, short-term liquidity and high gearing.

The Story of Daton Systems

Daton was formed by Tony Leach and Eddie Moore, a former colleague, to become a computer dealer. In 1982 International Computers Ltd (ICL), was setting up a new scheme for distributors. It was offering to carry out all the marketing, a major cost for distributors, with attractive discounts and incentives to go with it. Overall, the two felt that ICL was a good company with which to have a working relationship.

In February, the small team developed their business plan. Tony and Eddie both had marketing backgrounds and it was evident that to set up the dealership effectively they needed three other skills: financial, programming and engineering. They found a good engineer, who had been running his own one-man computer maintenance business for a short period. And Tony approached someone at his former employer's to provide the necessary programming and software skills.

The man with the finance skills was found in the shape of Laurence Jones (not his real name). He had run a yacht-chandlery business which had gone out of business because of slack times in the boat-building industry. Nevertheless, Laurence had a proven track record of raising money and running his own business for several years, which none of the others had done.

These people formed the original business team. Tony was the largest shareholder with 40 per cent of the equity; each of the other directors had 8.75 per cent. That these people came together was more a matter of circumstances than of their ability to make a good working team. Tony Leach believes that the business would have worked better if the original shareholders had been reduced to two, with the rest employed by the company and offered a performance-related shareholding incentive.

The initial funding was from 3i, who put up 25 per cent of the equity. They also arranged a loan from Lloyds Bank, 80 per cent guaranteed under the Loan Guarantee Scheme. Tony and Laurence selected 3i, partly because of the better financial terms offered and partly because of 3i's positive attitudes towards working with and complementing the Daton team.

By April 1982, Daton had signed up with ICL as a distributor and with a company called Peach Tree which specialized in business software. Together, this provided a complete business computer package which they could sell and have operating quickly. The company paid for a source-code licence which allowed them to tailor the system for users.

The company's target was to be profitable within the second year with a modest £6,000 – and it seemed that this would be possible. By the second year, the company had taken on extra staff and sales were growing healthily.

Disaster struck when Peach Tree withdrew the software Daton was selling (although Daton could continue to support existing customers because it had the source code). Daton had also become a dealer for Omicron, but there was another bolt from the blue when that software no longer ran on ICL's new range of micros. As nearly all Daton's business relied on Omicron or Peach Tree, sales plummeted and Daton, instead of registering its meagre profit, announced a whopping £70,000 loss for the second year. The whole of the business plan would have to be rewritten if the company was to be saved.

Just as the directors were facing up to this crisis, Tony Leach got a telephone call from a solicitor – Laurence Jones had been arrested for alleged fraud carried out while he was running his chandlery business. The story was beginning to follow the most outrageous script from a TV soap opera. Shocked, Tony went to visit the solicitor to learn that

Laurence had been convicted the previous day and had now started an eighteen-month sentence. At Laurence's appeal, Tony acted as a character reference, having nothing but praise for the work he carried out at Daton Systems. Laurence resigned and sold his shares to Tony, however.

During this time, the remaining directors were assessing the future of Daton. They decided that they were really selling human skills rather than machines and felt that their best course of action was to become more of a software and systems house than a distributor. This would add more value to their work, enable them to control their own business and, they hoped, bring in more money.

The directors decided to adopt a more formal management of the business. Instead of a 'seat-of-the-pants' approach to accounting, financial objectives and ratios were set and monthly management accounts were to be produced – and performance was to be monitored. They also identified three market sectors: government, local authorities and *The Times* Top 100. They prepared literally dozens of presentations and took every opportunity to spread the company name within the target groups.

When the break came for the company, it was a matter of luck. ICL rang Daton asking for help with a bid for a Ministry of Defence contract. It was for a relatively small system consisting of only ten computer terminals and special software. But, if Daton could demonstrate a working system quickly, there was a potential for up to thirty repeat orders.

In December 1984, the system was demonstrated and the order won. But, just as the directors were breathing a huge sigh of relief, ICL's accounting department demanded payment of outstanding debts of £200,000 within thirty days, and put all further deliveries on 'stop'. Eventually, ICL agreed to freeze the debt but refused to give Daton any more credit, asking for cash in advance and for the outstanding debt to be paid in fixed tranches with a final settlement in March 1986.

Whether or not as a consequence of the violent swings in the fortunes of Daton, the other directors left the company. One left for the apparent security of life with a large electronics company. Eddie Moore set up his own company, as a result of an amicable split, and took some of Daton's customer base. The final director dropped out for personal reasons.

This left Tony Leach completely alone. Barry Merchant had joined a year previously on the programming side. 'We hit it off. Barry and I grew sufficiently close that after the last director left, I made him a director with the chance of equity.' A year later, the shareholding became 65 per cent Tony, 13 per cent Barry and the remainder with 3i.

The last years of the eighties saw Daton stabilizing, maturing and developing; as Tony points out: 'We became a completely different company from the way we started out.' The management team was considerably strengthened, notably by the appointment of a finance manager in 1988. Until that time, finance and accounting was managed solely by Tony and Barry with the help of the auditors. They maintained very tight controls and knew to the nearest £100 their cash position at any time. 'From our experience in 1984, we realized that financial and business management was what the company is all about,' says Tony. 'Selling computers was the easy part.' The directors also recognize that their role is to plan and manage the business and they give increased responsibility to key staff. By 1990, the business had fifty employees.

Above all, the aim is to remain in a healthy financial position. In 1987, the company's turnover was a little over £1 million with profits of £215,000. The following year, sales were doubled but profits dipped slightly to £165,000. 'Balance sheet and profit – that's what it's all about, not turnover,' says Tony. 'Part of the company's prudent accounting policy is to have at least three months' worth of overheads in the bank. I never want to go bust again. From small beginnings, we have built a company of significant market value. The market opportunity is enormous and we plan to grow at 35 per cent compound.'

In 1989, while preparing their business plan, the Daton team saw that the scope for their products and services in the government market-place was enormous. But the information-technology market-place is becoming less fragmented and small companies may be unable to take full advantage of the opportunities available. Tony discussed this with 3i who agreed that the business should be sold. 3i Corporate

Finance were instructed to find a partner. From a short-list of three, the eventual purchaser was AT & T Istel in July 1990. 'We couldn't have hoped for a more appropriate or more synergistic partner,' says Tony. 'Our baby now has the opportunity to develop into a major and strategic player in the government market-place.' And this is just what Tony deserves, for to survive the difficult early years, the vagaries of the turbulent information-technology market and to develop a sound and growing business from this platform is an impressive achievement. Hats off to him!

17

Unlocking the Cupboard

No one knows with certainty what you will find when you buy a business from the outside – what you will see when you unlock and open the door. Will it be a nice, ripe, juicy plum or a wrinkled-up old prune? This is where the fear lies. You may have carried out the due-diligence process with vigour, but nevertheless unknown information may emerge once you have taken control.

Of course, the additional fear factor with an MBI is that the business will now have debt attached to it, which means the business must be able to absorb the interest and capital repayment agreed for it. Nothing concentrates and focuses the mind like a looming date in the repayment schedule. (Buy-ins are on the whole more conservatively structured than buy-outs, but this aspect is nevertheless looked at more closely in the next chapter.)

Simon Unger bought into an office-supplies business. He ruefully admits that both he and the venture capitalists seriously underestimated the nature of the problems before coming into it. 'We didn't appreciate the scope of the problems in any shape or form. Just simple things like the company doesn't know what stock it has in the warehouse. And it moves on from there – there was no substance to the sales. You sort of blow at people and they fall over. Usually you would expect one or two of these problems in a company, but we found half a dozen all at once.' He continues: 'What we really found here is a hollow infrastructure – as it's so nebulous, it's not covered by warranties.' The business went into receivership in January 1990.

He discovered a particular problem that he now realizes he might have been able to detect prior to the purchase of the business. There was a list of 17,000 customers. But this turned out to be only 3,000 'live' customers, as the 3,000 changed each year. Only 100 or 200 of them were core customers. The 3,000 were genuinely different each year. 'Basically the company hadn't held on to any customers – at all, ever – which is a fairly significant factor.'

Initial Steps

How tempting it is to arrive on day one at a company and to instigate a radical plan to introduce all the changes required to meet the targets set in your business plan. But 'softly, softly, catchee monkey'. Patrick Dunne says: 'Some buy-ins have failed because the manager has tried to do too much at once. It's difficult if it's a turnaround – you need to change a lot immediately. But, in other cases, considered changes from knowing the business are likely to be more successful.'

A business has a delicate balance – disturb one element and it may soon be restored to equilibrium, at a higher level, if the change is correct. But disturb two elements, and it takes correspondingly longer to restabilize the business. It is easy to imagine that if you try to amend and alter too many factors at once you will end up like the juggler who misses one ball – only to find that all of them are dropped.

This need to move at a measured pace also reinforces the attractiveness of the idea that you might consider working for the company before you buy it. This helps the investigation process; enables you to judge the chemistry; and allows you to develop a plan, and the requisite amount of the funding, to move the business on to the course that you want.

Stuart Swinden is the managing director of EFM, a manufacturer of 'effective educational environments for youngsters'. He was able to achieve a very smooth transition when he purchased the business for £600,000 in September 1989. Prior to the purchase, he was able to work part-time in the business as the managing director for three months. 'No one knew why I was there, but understood that it was to see how the company could move forward.' He says that he was 'slightly walking on eggshells during this period', but that working part-time gave him the 'opportunity to see where I could go forward, as well as what surgery was needed. While you're up to your rear end in alligators, don't forget that you don't want to end up in the swamp.'

The first rational step for a purchaser to make, once the business is yours, is to absorb information. You may not have been able to gain 100 per cent insight before the purchase, so make sure that your knowledge of the business and the way it has been run becomes complete once you own it – and before you draw up your action plan. Once you have full knowledge, your business plan, on which you raised the finance, needs to be reviewed, and adapted, in the light of your greater familiarity.

One buy-in team which did not have the luxury of a smooth transition was made up of Colin Guy and his colleagues at Agripac. In Chapter 3, 'Second Thoughts', you will have read about the difficulties which arose on leaving his employers, Bowater. The purchase was completed in December 1988, but as a result of the negotiations with Bowater, Colin and his other two colleagues were not able to start work at Agripac until April 1989, and this weakened the Agripac business from the start.

For three months, the company was run by a 3i consultant. While doing the best possible, the consultant had not been able to achieve more than a holding operation. He couldn't reduce the haemorrhage of losses and the losses ballooned to around £250,000 in that first quarter (Agripac was a loss-maker; the previous year the company had lost £400,000 on a turnover of £1.6 million). Not only was there management drift, but as Colin drily points out: 'It cost us money; consultants don't come free.' It was a dreadful start.

Finally, when the team were able to take over the reins, there was this pressing problem of trying to stem the losses. The first day Colin spent entirely with the Agripac workforce, explaining what they were going to do. Apart from this brief introduction however, all their effort was initially focused on turning round the losses and stopping the cash outflow.

Their initial plan was to concentrate on three aspects to turn round the business: reducing the level of waste, increasing productivity (which was horribly low) and improving the quality and service to customers. In the first instance, there wasn't much time for Colin to absorb information and work out a long-term plan – but as the losses were staunched, he was able to turn his attention to this.

Setting the Course

You could buy a company with the sole intention of making cuts, making it profitable and leaving it at that. However, in most cases your business plan will have needed to show a long-term strategy to persuade the venture capitalists to fund the purchase. Stuart Swinden is very committed to the notion of a long-term strategy. He explains: 'I feel very strongly about anyone doing an MBI or an MBO – you must end up with your own vision of where you want to go. I could have come in here, done the surgery and left it at that. You must have a philosophy or a mission of where you want to take it.'

Colin Guy, too, has a clear long-term notion of where he wants Agripac to be. He would like to build a little group of some sort, by acquisition, in related areas. But this is a year or two down the line. First, the business itself needed to be developed and remotivated. Colin has placed great emphasis on the development of a corporate culture to enable him to introduce the changes he has in mind.

Businesses can be surprisingly resistant to change, as the Metalline team found. 'It's been very difficult to get the pace that we want in the company. It was pretty sleepy when we bought it. It was doing very nicely and people had always made a good living out of it. But it has the potential to perform much better. The biggest disappointment has been the rate at which we have been able to introduce changes,' comments Les Hunt.

Fairly extensive changes have been introduced at EFM in the two years since it was the subject of a buy-in. Products have been revamped, management altered, production reorganized and overheads cut – and Stuart Swinden has yet more work planned. He doesn't consider that the pace of change has been too quick. 'If I'd come in and tried to do it all in six months, the company would have collapsed, but spreading it over two years the company can cope.'

The Team

You don't need to be conversant with psychology to understand what the expectation and reaction of the existing management team will be to your arrival. Your approach to the management – and the workforce

– will be a crucial factor in the likely success or failure of the business. Staff members may resent your arrival. They may view you with suspicion and circumspection. They may doubt your motives. They may start to look for other jobs – and, of course, that may be your choice, too. But how do you avoid throwing out the good with the poor?

One method of mitigating the risk to the business of any good management leaving when you buy the business is to combine a buy-in and a buy-out (a BIMBO) and involve some of the existing management in the purchase. The disadvantage here is that you may not know the quality and abilities of the team in situ; they may prove to be not the stuff of which entrepreneurs are made. Resolving this could be a problem.

Certainly, both Colin Guy and Stuart Swinden considered that the existing management was not the right level for the task they had in mind of transforming and developing the business. Colin was accompanied by two other colleagues from Bowater and bought Agripac without any of the existing management (above senior supervisor level); he knew the business and its previous management from his time at Bowater.

Stuart Swinden started the process of evaluating the existing management team while he was working part-time before the purchase and during the weeks after completion. He recognizes that 'the existing management viewed me with a degree of nervousness. I started talking to individuals to find their strengths and weaknesses and to mould them into my way of thinking. The team was OK at a turnover of £3 million, but there were no high-flyers. They were reasonably competent. So I started to bring people in underneath.'

After fifteen months, Stuart felt that he had made a reasonably good start at EFM, but worried that progress was going to be reversed. At the time that he bought into the business, the company manufactured design and technology workstations for schools. He has moved the emphasis into the manufacture of 'effective educational environments for youngsters', including science labs and home economics workspaces. He says: 'I had introduced a couple of new products, such as the science lab, and they needed a different style of management. It was an opportunity to move the company forward on a dramatically better profit margin. So I took £30,000 a month out of overheads, including removing ten people from the management level. I relied on the people I'd brought in.'

With some purchases, as well as the management team, it may be that the founder or the vendor is still very much on the scene. The handover between the old and the new leader can cause difficulties, but not in all cases. Les Hunt comments that the old managing director had hardly been into the business at all since the buy-in, although initially they had expected they would need to have him around a couple of days a week.

The handover at EFM has also been amicable. The vendor was Keith Rhodes, a lone entrepreneur who had built up the business. Initially, he retained 26 per cent of the equity, but Swinden has since bought him out. Keith appeared a very willing vendor – it seemed that he no longer wanted the hassle of running the business. At first, he stayed on as development director, but after nine months, he decided he wanted a sabbatical for a year. He has since returned as a consultant on the product development side for EFM.

However, in the case of CEC-Time, the management buy-in made by Terry Weston and Bert Ramsden, the settling-in process had been very difficult. The buy-in team thought that the staff hadn't known who to report to and the new team had eventually asked the old managing director to stay away from the business. This purchase is one that proved to be disappointing, resulting in receivership two years after the purchase.

While Agripac was bought without the existing management, nevertheless the team has been left with the legacy of a position on the board which they would have preferred not to have – Bowater is entitled to a place on the board. Colin Guy comments ironically: 'We have rubbed along. To date the Bowater holding has not created the sort of problems I thought it would.' He continues: 'Fiduciary duty applies to any director appointed by Bowater!' The wheel turns full circle! The main legacy from the difficult start is that it will take a number of years to build up a credible balance sheet, although the team has not had to refinance.

The Workforce

Colin Guy has had to work very hard to make headway with the Agripac workforce. He explains: 'I was surprised by the attitude of the workforce. If we hadn't bought Agripac, it would have gone under. I expected to be treated almost as a Messiah. I spent the first day entirely with people, explaining what we were going to do. They sat there in the canteen and went "wibble, wibble, wibble" – they had heard it all before. They were very cynical and demotivated.'

A similar difficulty was faced by Nayyer Hussain and James Wooster at Martin's. 'There was an enormous amount of cynicism about our intentions. They saw us as two potential asset strippers.' There were inherent problems left by the previous management as well: 'There was a legacy of entrenched combative attitudes left by previous lock-outs and strikes and an enormous "us-and-them" attitude.' A further problem with the workforce was that 'they were all very old, with no one under the age of forty-five on acquisition. The secretary said, "People at Martin's – they stay here and they die."'

The Martin pair have approached the management and employee problems by operating in a 'push-you-pull-you' fashion (apologies to Dr Doolittle). Says Nayyer: 'My mission has been to communicate as much as possible, so that everyone knows what the goals are. We've put in an incentive structure, which will transform their earnings, if these goals are achieved.'

The Metalline pair also saw communication as a problem: 'The old MD ran it very much as an autonomy, in a dictatorial fashion. There's very little in the way of line management. There was very little communication between the top and bottom. The problem has been to get people singing the same song.'

The Agripac workforce are now almost singing in harmony thanks to perseverance by the management team. 'The most difficult task over time has been to establish a culture in the company. With companies which are not successful, it's a matter of culture – and that comes right from the top. To change an ingrained culture took much longer than I anticipated,' comments Colin Guy. 'I thought it would take the first year, but now two and three quarter years on I can say that the culture is reasonably well established. That culture is to operate as one team. As a team player, we all have responsibilities to each other and the company. I'm trying to promote the opposite of the traditional conflict approach, management versus labour, company versus customers. I'm trying to promote a cooperational model, where everyone is interdependent on each other.'

To achieve this introduction of a new culture, the Agripac management have held regular general meetings to show progress and to put markers for objectives. They have instituted a company council, which has elected representatives from each part of the business. The council has a constitution which includes the proviso that anything can be discussed. The minutes of the meetings are published. Recently, they have introduced quarterly team briefings, a team consisting of up to eight people. Once a quarter, a team can sit down with Colin for an hour and discuss the business. He is a great believer in management by walking about, but finds it more difficult as the company grows. The quarterly team briefings are one additional means of communication, albeit a slightly more formal one.

Customers, Products and Markets

These are all areas which incoming management target for a shake-up: there tends to be a greater focus on marketing after the buy-in. At EFM, there was extensive adjustment, both expansion and shrinkage, all destined to improve profitability. An office-lighting system has been dropped from the product range, new products have been introduced and the sales effort has been more concentrated on selling to the education market, away from all other markets. Stuart Swinden has also rethought what the company is selling. He has altered the message to make it clear that they are selling whole rooms and has dropped the notion that they are selling furniture. 'We've done this for the last two years and it must be right because it has attracted imitators.'

Stuart readily admits that the company has been lucky in that there is an enormous rate of change in the education market and change equals opportunity. One of the new products is an octagonal system for science labs, which is totally different from any other. 'It is high-priced, but we have gone out and sold it. We held our breath. But it has sold well. It's an attractive product designed to entice kids into the science lab.'

The changes on the marketing side, combined with the other areas which have been tackled, have certainly helped EFM to grow. At the time of the buy-out the turnover was £3 million and the profit £70,000. Currently, the turnover is £5.5 million and the business is aiming at a 5 per cent profit-to-sales ratio, with a mission to get it to a 10 per cent ratio. 'We haven't made as much profit as we would like, but it is coming. So far we've been concentrating on growing and developing.' Even though the pace of change has been swift, Swinden states: 'I told a company meeting recently that the changes over the next two years are at least as dramatic as the changes over the last two years.' These include monitoring performance in detail, working towards BS5750 standard and a total quality approach, reviewing every buying decision and the underlying manufacturing technology.

Agripac, too, has been making good progress after its difficult start. In 1989, there was a loss of about £250,000 on a turnover of £1.7 million; this has been turned around to a profit of £80,000 on a turnover of around £3 million for 1991. The recession has hampered progress by putting pressure on profit margins; the market has been horrendously competitive in 1991. The major task on the customer side was to change the market's perception of the Agripac product. Before the buy-in the name was a joke in the market-place. But the incoming team had a great advantage in that at least two of them were well known because of their achievements at Bowater in building up their share of the FIBC market. Explains Colin: 'We were known in the market. The three of us were seen as bringing something different to Agripac.'

Much of the sales growth in the business has come from increased sales to existing customers. A further increase has occurred from the development of new markets and applications. The company has created growth by increasing the usage of bags – the size of the total cake – rather than by growing at the expense of competitors.

How Some Buy-ins Have Performed

The Centre for Management Buy-out Research at Nottingham carried out a survey in 1990. Fifty-nine teams responded and their information provided this rare glimpse into life after the buy-in.

Following the buy-in there had usually been a period of intense reorganization. Over 90 per cent of respondents had identified new markets, increased the customer base and reorganized administrative and financial systems. Over 75 per cent had added new products or services and changed advertising or promotion arrangements.

Furthermore, there had been extensive changes in management with almost 80 per cent of the sample recruiting new senior specialist staff and almost half of buy-ins losing existing senior management. The going has been tough: over half had required further finance since the buy-in, the most important single reason being because of failure to reach original targets. A smaller proportion required more funding for higher capital expenditure or to make an acquisition.

Underperforming the business plan was rife: over half of the survey companies reported that operating profit was below target as expressed in the original plan, a level of underperformance which is considerably worse than that found in earlier surveys of buy-outs.

The survey threw up the following interesting connections. There was some evidence to link disappointing performance with particular types of background characteristics. Almost three fifths of buy-ins from private sources had operating profits worse than plan, but this was true of only 36 per cent of the divestments from UK PLCs.

Smaller buy-ins had also performed less well than larger ones. Some 60 per cent of buy-ins with an initial value of less than £1 million were failing to reach planned levels of operating profit. One explanation for this could be that managers from large companies have bought into the businesses and have found the small-company atmosphere difficult. Small companies are very vulnerable, even to one thing going wrong. The answer must be to raise sufficient funds, not just for the purchase but to provide the infrastructure which large-company managers need to thrive.

Turn-rounds are also disappointing. Two thirds of buy-ins which had operating losses before buy-in failed to meet operating profit expectations and none had achieved operating profits greater than 10 per cent above target.

The greatest chance of success for an MBI lies in following those points which have been catalogued already in this book. Successful buy-ins:

– pay 25 per cent less for the business, compared to the less successful ones;

– forecast a 40 per cent lower increase in profits;

– are locally based;

– match the incoming manager's experience;

– are conservatively structured;

– raise additional finance at the outset to provide working capital and capital expenditure required.

18

Manager Turned Owner

One day the management team are employees; the next day the owners of the company. Why should this change in the legal position make a difference to the success of the business? There are a number of interconnecting factors. First, the team want to succeed. They have declared publicly that they can make the transition from manager to owner; they have claimed that they can increase the profitability of the business, make a good return for the investors and thus enhance their own wealth. They have made this declaration not just to investors, but usually to vendors, employees, customers and suppliers. No one wants to fail after such a public declaration of intent.

Furthermore, the layer of debt imposed on the business also helps to focus the brain wonderfully. It's a more highly geared vehicle and swings in operating profits are now magnified by the size of the interest payments. In a sense, the safety buffer is removed. A touch of fear improves concentration, the ability to take tough decisions and the grasp and drive to perform the tasks needed by the business. Mike Clark and his team bought out Perex, a manufacturer of digital tape recorders and touch screens, for £1.4 million in May 1989. He says: 'I don't think there was fear, but there was concern to get our houses back, which fortunately only took about a year.'

It has to be the right amount of fear. Too much and you are simply paralysed and trapped in a marshmallow of indecision. But a feeling of uncertainty can herald all those entrepreneurial attributes which you require to complete your task. You feel free to make and implement decisions; the job becomes more challenging; and you are more involved in the fortunes of the business, its achievements and disappointments.

Uncertain as it may feel once you are the owners with a need to meet interest payments on the business, many buy-out teams have been suffering from even greater uncertainties in the months or years leading to the buy-out and the change in ownership simply heralds a substantive difference in management motivation caused by the removal of various threats. For example, before Brian and Christine Box bought out Middle Aston House, a conference centre, for £1.4 million in the middle of the Gulf war, their futures had looked fairly bleak. They had been running this centre for Dalgety for a number of years, when it was announced that the director to whom they reported was being made redundant. They discovered that he was negotiating a buy-out of the conference centre. This came totally out of the blue for the Box pair who had always stressed to this director that they would like to buy the centre if Dalgety was going to sell. The new arrangement would mean that Brian would be redundant. The Box's approached Dalgety who gave them a month to better the offer – which they did. So the two were highly motivated to make a success. And, of course, they have sunk the proceeds from the sale of their house into the business, too.

The buy-out team at Perex had also been suffering from very low morale in the period before the buy-out was mooted. In their opinion, the previous owners had been milking the business and treating it as a cash cow to support other businesses. The company had apparently been up for sale for quite a while. If the buy-out had not occurred, all the management would have left as they were all actively seeking other jobs. So the boost to the management motivation was tremendous when they bought it for themselves.

Other buy-outs had suffered from different uncertainties: Penman, Carron and Denby were in receivership, Straightset and RFS threatened with closure, Eurocamp and Video Arts were likely to have a change in ownership. The resolution of uncertainty would have had some impact on the motivation of the team and been one of the factors in helping them to improve the performance of the business.

Post-acquisition Malaise

The actual period of the buy-out is an especially testing time for a management team. Some have said that the process was the most difficult task they have faced. The delicate tripartite negotiation, the stress of running the business to meet their obligations as directors while trying to complete the purchase, the technical and legal complexities of the process and the need to communicate and consult so widely among customers, suppliers and employees are all factors which would suggest that the process is particularly harrowing. Small wonder that there is often a sort of lull in motivation and a loss of adrenalin once the purchase is complete.

It is not only a question of malaise which prevents you burying yourself in the business. This is Tina Tietjen's experience: 'December the 6th, 1989, was signing night. But we didn't really get back into the business until March/April. Most people feel on signing night "Whoopee! It's over!" But there are still lots of meetings to do with the purchase to keep you away from the business.'

A third difficulty which buy-out team members face is that their preoccupation with the actual process of the purchase may have limited the attention which they were able to devote to the business prior to the buy-out. The company may not be in such good shape as the team would have wished. Derrick Bumpsteed suggests that this may be an exaggerated problem: 'You're still aware of what's going on; you're still talking to people. The place itself carries on. It didn't distract us that much because STC realized what was happening, so I suppose the pressure came off on normal reporting.'

Mike Clark of Perex estimates that he and the finance director probably took the best part of a year out of the business. But he was happy that the three other members of the team were able to carry on the burden of managing the business.

The Perex team were also affected by a quite different sort of reaction right after the buy-out and initially found it difficult to settle to the old routine. Mike Clark says: 'For the first two or three months we ran around like headless chickens with all this new-found freedom. We were looking at all sorts of weird and wonderful areas of business we could look into – robotics, for example. Each one of us was bringing up silly ideas. Probably by about three months, we sat down and had a chat and worked out what we were going to do to take the business forward – concentrate on the core business.'

The Art of the Squeeze

The major management problem for the first two years for a buy-out is to survive and to meet the interest and capital repayments required without breaking your covenants. Brian Box confirms that it can be a hard task. They completed the buy-out of Middle Aston House in the midst of the recession, in February 1991. The first year of their ownership is the first time for the last twelve years or so that the business has shown a downturn. He says: 'It only needs two very bad months of business and life would be difficult. It would be onerous because the interest payments are enormous. But so far we've been able to avoid going into an overdraft.' He notices a difference between management as part of a large group and management as an independent business. They were obviously used to a formal budgeting and reporting procedure, but he explains, 'Being part of a large group, you weren't concerned by cash flow in the same way, although we monitored our own debtors. With a small, independent place, we watch it much more closely. The same applies to capital expenditure – we were charged depreciation, but you didn't have to watch which month you spent it.'

The Perex team also completed the buy-out in the recession, but they have not been so affected by the downturn, as much of their business is exported. They have not felt that the debt they took on was a major burden. Mike Clark says: 'We were fairly conservative in the way we handled the finance for the buy-out. In hindsight, we could have done without the venture-capital companies.'

The need to generate cash and keep a strict control of finance suggests that if there is to be any chance of meeting its targets, it is essential for most management that the operations are pared down as far as possible. 'Once they become owners, managers predictably become more cost-conscious. Often, there will be a rash of cost saving – switching off the lights, cutting newspaper and magazine orders, that sort of thing. And a very serious appraisal of luxuries like company cars and other perks. Nine out of ten managers, I have noticed, become remarkably sensible about rewarding themselves in the early days, although there are the cases where delusions of grandeur show up.'

This is Derek Sach, formerly of 3i, writing in *QED* about the change in the management's attitude wrought by the transition from manager to owner.

In the case of Perex, there wasn't that much more which the management could wring from the business after the buy-out. It had been squeezed very hard by its existing owners to generate cash. A year before the buy-out, for example, there had been some horrendous redundancies, with some departments decimated in size. Mike Clark explains: 'There wasn't a pot of gold. We'd always been a fairly tightly run company. There were no massive cost savings that we anticipated making, other than things like licensing products. And we always have targeted, and we always will, the purchasing departments to reduce costs every year. But there's been no real difference since the buy-out.'

But there has been a significant reduction in overheads at Middle Aston since buying the business. 'We have had a really satisfying result in pruning staff numbers, particularly on the management side. Almost all of them have been natural wastage. We simply haven't replaced and have expanded the jobs of other managers.'

It is a delicate balance – how do you squeeze as much cash as you can from the business, to improve the cash flow, without damaging the structure of the business? It's all too easy to cut back on activities like marketing and new product development, which may not radically disrupt revenues in the near future, but will do so later on.

Both the Perex and Middle Aston teams have been able to run a tight business – and look to the long term. Brian Box regards a much greater emphasis on marketing as one of the major changes which they have been able to introduce since the buy-out. 'We took on a marketing consultant from day one; she has been absolutely critical to our finding new clients. It's much easier to introduce a new strategy when the final decision is ours, rather than reporting to a director.'

The introduction of new products was regarded as vital by Mike Clark and was the major objective of the buy-out. Products tend to have a limited life – say three to seven years. 'You have to have the products to maintain the life blood of the business. There had been no serious developments for about two years. Part of the strategic plan was to reinvest some of the profits back into new products – and to get us to the point where we were spending a minimum of 5 per cent of pre-tax profit on new product development,' expands Clark.

Steering the Course

In contrast with the problems of a buy-in and a start-up, meeting the schedule of debt repayments by keeping a tight rein on costs and cash is a one-dimensional task – and is one of the major reasons why a buy-out is a less risky form of enterprise. There are other reasons why the riskiness of the management task is mitigated. While the initial reaction of the staff to a team *buying into* a company may be one of dismay, the feeling towards a team *buying out* a company tends to be far more positive. Furthermore, where a buy-in team has to absorb information to increase its knowledge in the early weeks and months, a buy-out team should be in command of the facts before the purchase is finalized. The management task is less demanding and therefore less prone to error.

Nevertheless there are risks in the early days and positive reactions of staff and customers cannot be relied upon. Ed Hunter of Penman Engineering remarks: 'We had to take care quickly of some risks at the beginning. First, we had to keep our customer base intact – and coming out of receivership, they were nervous. Second, we had to keep our suppliers. And third, we had to keep our institutions happy.'

Customers generally react quite positively to buy-outs. A survey of MBOs by David Clutterbuck (based on fifty-seven respondents) found that customer and supplier support during the change in ownership was widespread: 96 per cent reported good support from suppliers and 100 per cent from customers.

Nevertheless, no team would want to leave to chance that this will be the outcome. Customers and suppliers need communication, to demonstrate commitment and enthusiasm to improve the quality of the product and the efficiency of the business. The Perex team acted swiftly to reassure customers, for whom Perex was the only supplier of some products. Clark says: 'I believe that the previous owners had had us up for sale for about eighteen months – and these things get out. As soon as we exchanged contracts, we did a world tour to all our major customers to explain what we were doing, the reason behind it and to try and convince them that we were well funded. In most cases, we gave them management accounts, forecasts, prediction, business plans and balance sheet to reassure them. In certain circumstances, we agreed to lodge design rights in escrow to give our customers some degree of comfort. These actions were in hindsight probably a lot more important than we realized.'

This focus on customers at Perex lies behind their strong profits and turnover growth. After the initial three months enjoying their freedom, the team realized what they needed to do was to concentrate on improving the service and expanding the range of products sold to existing customers – three of which accounted for 70 per cent of revenues. 'We sat down and said, "Let's have a look at every major account and see what we can do to improve its long-term prospects." That precipitated a whole series of actions. Particular directors were assigned to particular accounts. That probably occupied more or less our first year,' explains Clark.

Brian and Christine Box had also taken positive steps to ensure that customers were happy with the new arrangement and found that they were very supportive. Brian elucidates: 'We were very keen to indicate that it was business as usual. From a customer's point of view there was no change whatsoever except the bottom of the notepaper. We also wanted to continue the process of refurbishment and improvement – and this we did as if there had been no break.'

Suppliers, like customers, are generally very positive. Mike Clark reports that a few people might have been a bit tighter on payment terms. As with the customers, they had contacted the suppliers to tell them what was going on and assure them that they were financially secure.

The managers who are not involved in the buy-out and the workforce may have mixed feelings. They may be uncertain about the future course of their jobs – conscious that improved efficiency may mean job cuts, different working practices and salary structures. Equally, they may welcome the purchase by the existing managers because it removes one element of uncertainty. They may thus wish them to make a success of it. Both Middle Aston and Perex confirmed that this occurred with their staff. Christine Box found they gave them great encouragement. She says: 'They were very sweet. They wished us well and did nice things like buy us Christmas presents as part of their encouragement, which was lovely.' And Mike Clark, too, had derived great emotional support from the staff: 'They must have come to realize that under the previous owners, the company didn't have a long-term future.'

The effect of the buy-out may be to make the workforce more flexible, willing to end ways of working, which they had resolutely hung on to before the buy-out. Keith Hirst of Metsec (a buy-out from Tube Investments) reports in *QED*: 'We got a tremendous response from the 150 members of the workforce we retained. The work ethic in the Black Country is still very strong. Our initial strategy was very simple: go out and get work even if it is on a wafer-thin margin and get the factory busy.' He continues to describe their actions in the early days: 'In the past there had been a lazy attitude towards the customers. At times, it was almost as if we were saying, "Are you really good enough to have our products?" We worked hard to put that right.'

Motivating employees at RFS Industries also seemed to have been enhanced according to Stephen Hinton: 'Our relation with people was easier. You can get the message across. People like working for a smaller outfit. The results of their actions have a bigger effect on the business as a whole.'

Some buy-outs, such as AT & T Istel and Video Arts, are very broadly based among the employees, further enhancing the possibilities for motivating them well. Tina Tietjen says of Video Arts: 'All members of the staff can participate. Over 60 per cent of the staff have taken up shares. People are very committed and enthusiastic.'

Not everyone believes that spreading the ownership of the company increases the motivation of the workforce. The Perex team saw no point in the staff participating in the buy-out. They have a significant element of profit-related pay (between 13 and 45 per cent of salary) and this was considered to be a more effective motivator than shares in a private company for which the owners at present have no realization plans.

A buy-out generally has a very positive effect on a management team. They have shared objectives and are less prone to rivalry and conflict; they are on the whole better integrated. Of course, there is always the possibility that the team may crumble if the buy-out is struggling or facing some difficulties. And it is quite common for one of the team to find it difficult to make the transition from manager to owner. Thus a hard decision may have to be taken to remove the member of the team who is perceived to be inadequate by the others.

How Some Buy-outs Have Performed

Most buy-outs perform well in the short term. The survey by David Clutterbuck found that 82 per cent of respondents reported a profit increase and 18 per cent a maintained profit. Productivity also saw wide improvement, with 81 per cent seeing a productivity increase. Other surveys seem to confirm the finding that in the short run profits and productivity are improved.

A survey which was supervised by Brian Houlden of Warwick Business School looked at the performance of buy-outs beyond the short run. The overall conclusion is that 'on average buy-outs have led to improved performance in the period up to three years after the buy-out. However, over the next three years, performance declined and was worse than the industry average.'

The CMBOR reviewed the evidence and found that: 'In the UK, the first studies of buy-outs considered the deals undertaken during the industrial recession of the early 1980s. These MBOs appeared to exhibit considerable resilience to recession and to show evidence of systematic performance improvements, together with some shedding of labour.'

The report continues: 'There is a view that short-term improvements are sometimes purchased at the costs of the longer-term growth with strong short-term incentives discouraging research and development, advertising, maintenance and other long-term expenditure.' And it goes on: 'It may be that debt-intensified incentives in an MBO do give managers a short-term perspective which is appropriate merely during a transitionary phase.'

19

Building on Firm Foundations

A business moves through a number of stages between birth and death, unless it fails prematurely. There is the start-up phase, when you are choosing premises, developing your product, evolving your marketing strategy and putting together the tangible and intangible assets which constitute a business.

The start-up phase rolls into survival mode. The business finds itself staggering through a series of crises: some self-inflicted, some meted out by competitive response, some administered by external factors such as the economy and some imposed by sheer bad luck. As the business has such limited resources, both human and financial, you may eventually mimic the 'headless-chicken' routine in your attempts to attain equilibrium. The longer the business stays afloat, the greater the chance that balance will eventually emerge.

Slowly, inch by inch, your organization will stabilize, although you may be unaware that this has been attained. It may come as a shock to realize that life-threatening crises have metamorphosed into dilemmas undermining profits: the changes can be so subtle that they emerge subconsciously. It is a very gradual process.

Stability does not imply standstill, but it does suggest the business is constantly on a month-by-month basis running at or over break-even. Cash flows are beginning to be systematically positive, albeit in a fairly small way.

Once stabilized, the business is poised – for what? Fast growth, double or quits, expansion, or the living dead? Which category will you aspire to? Which is the preferred route? What changes will you need in your business organization to enable you to achieve your choice? How will you finance the next stage of your business – from internal sources or development capital?

Your Choice of Growth Track

Your choice may be predetermined by what you presented in your business plan at the outset, although by the time you are moving from the survival phase to the established, your original business plan will be history. In all honesty, the shape of the business you have two or three years from its formation will bear little resemblance to your original proposals – so the choice may be yours.

The state of the living dead has a certain appeal, although pursuance of that track would be disparaged by venture capitalists; it would fail to earn the sort of return on their investment which they would look for. So you could come under heavy pressure to provide an exit for them – difficult to achieve for a company which is stable but unexciting.

From your point of view, pursuing a slower growth track could enhance the safety aspect of your business, provide you with a good source of income and the ability to follow a mixed life. The disadvantages are that it is dull – and you would be unlikely to enrich yourself with a capital gain.

The other extreme – double or quits – may also hold appeal. Your market, and your product, may have sufficient potential so that with a following wind your business could double, treble or quadruple in a short space of time. The drawback with reliance on a following wind is that it is dangerous: winds are fickle and could soon change 180 degrees in direction and become head-on. Thus, the double or quits dilemma faces you. Are you prepared to bet the company? At the end of this chapter is the story of Vamp Health. As a result of a competitor's initiative, the business faced a dilemma two years after its founding: accept the living-dead route or possibly even failure with resignation or look for the golden opportunity. It chose the latter and tried to create a second start-up off the back of the first one. Trying to fund the second business out of the first almost brought about its demise – although at the same time it was rated in the *Independent on Sunday* Top 100 as the fastest-growing private company in the five years to 1990.

Between these two extremes is a long scale from living dead, expansion, growth and 'double or quits'. Between these four categories, there is a continual, gradual drift. The optimum point on this scale is to be in the 'controlled growth mode'. Sounds easy, but inevitably it is not. Only a marginal misjudgement and you are over-trading – and only a short step from failure. In Chapters 5 and 16, you read about Derwent Valley Foods and the problems which they faced because of their uncontrolled growth. The founders realized it was vital to plan growth in a controlled manner. So the year after its crisis with the computer breakdown and its near liquidation, the company increased its turnover modestly rather than spectacularly.

Robert Wright also found it a problem to grow the business in a controlled manner. Once Connectair had secured the London–Antwerp route in its own right, it was a turning-point in its fortunes – the move from survival to established business. Subsequently, the company acquired the licences to operate two more routes to the Continent and turnover rose to more than £1 million. To support these applications, more money was raised in a convertible loan – and commercial and financial directors were appointed.

However, the UK airline scene was not a very stable one and Connectair, relying as it did on the success of the larger companies, could not fail to be affected by the turbulence. British Caledonian was facing financial problems (which eventually led to a merger with British Airways) and this had repercussions for Connectair. Its results fluctuated rather violently although turnover growth was rapid. In 1986, it more than doubled to £3.5 million and nearly doubled again to £6 million in 1987.

At this point, Robert faced a dilemma – to make the company grow further would need a massive rethink of direction and more investment, and yet this would be against the backdrop of an uncertain market. You can find out in Chapter 20, 'Preparing to Exit', what decision Robert came to.

The Changing Nature of the Management's Task

'Waterstone's is now a monolithic, grade AB company – it's 100 per cent different from when I started it. I don't know the staff names or the names of their children. Five years ago, I knew them all. People don't speak openly to me now: there is fear.' This is Tim Waterstone's view of some characteristics of the changing nature of start-ups.

It is undoubtedly a different game: the management of an established, if young, business compared with a new business. The emphasis switches from maintaining survival to managing growth. More layers of management are introduced so that instead of supervision by you of most tasks, there is delegation – and you will no longer be aware of the existence of some tasks. You must relinquish the minutiae of the business. And this is a lesson absorbed by the founders of Derwent Valley Foods: they have stepped back from the day-to-day running of the company. As McKechnie puts it: 'We want to delegate as much routine work as possible, thus giving maximum time for strategic thinking and new product developments.' For the founding four, most of the satisfaction comes from the creativity needed in setting up new ventures and looking for new ways to expand the business. This they intend to do in an aggressive, but financially prudent manner.

Similarly, Peter Williams gave up the chief executive role at Vamp Health, to concentrate on being chairman, bringing in an outsider as chief executive, as you can read at the end of this chapter. And Tony Leach also had to recognize that he should play a different role. There is now a formal management hierarchy and he is committed to step back from the day-to-day running of the business. 'It is hard. I try to delegate, but find it very difficult not to become operational and "hands-on",' he admits. 'Until a couple of years ago, we did all the accounts ourselves up to trial balance and then got in an accountant. I knew where every penny was going.'

As with the changing role of the leader, so too other aspects of the management task change. The organization structure evolves. In the early stages, there may have been little structure. During the survival phase, the structure may be very simple. But at some stage, as the business is established there will be a need to adapt to a more functional organization – although it will remain flexible.

The organization needs more information because the leader and the original team will no longer know everything which is happening within the business, because jobs are delegated. Thus reporting systems and data-gathering mechanisms have to be set up. Finally, the business may be looking outward from its original product to broadening the range to its chosen market; it may possibly be moving to new products for new markets. With Derwent Valley Foods, the bulk of their business comes from sales under the Phileas Fogg brand name and the supply of private-label products for the main super-markets. They have also made a couple of acquisitions – one is a manufacturer of croutons and the other a producer of dry, chilled and frozen Indian snacks. They consider this gives them a cheap entry into quality ethnic foods and access to chilled- and frozen-food technology for expansion into related markets.

The changes required for a business as it goes through the established phase need a more professional management approach, less entrepre-neurial and individualistic. Management teams which have experience in large and medium-sized corporations should be able to revert to that different management style. However, some management teams and some boards of directors will need to be adjusted and strengthened to cope with the altering demands of the management task. The team needs reworking as the nature of the company changes.

The Use of Development Capital

While this book has generally assumed that you are interested in raising venture capital to start a business, many start-ups do not follow this pattern. Many entrepreneurs start their business and at a later stage, once established and in the controlled-growth phase, raise development capital to fund the expansion. For example, Connectair was up and running before any funds were raised.

Raising development capital should take less time and should be raised on more beneficial terms than the initial finance or any stretch finance. After all, the business will be proved and the management team settled in, so the investment should be inherently less risky than a completely new start-up.

Some businesses raise several tranches of venture capital. It is the easiest in this case to raise the funds from your existing investors, assuming they have any more funds available, which is not always the case. You can increase the likelihood of being able to raise money from your investors by skilfully building their confidence in the business and the management team. Tim Waterstone advises: 'The skilful way of building confidence amongst your investors is to be totally open with them all the time about what is going on, and be fearless in giving bad news as well as good. Management accounts should be very frequent and very reliable. Shareholders will develop comfort provided they feel that they are being taken into the management's confidence.'

However, your funding can be in jeopardy if one of your existing investors declines to take part in a funding. Tim Waterstone relates the problem which occurred when one investor refused to take up their rights on one occasion: 'One dumb controller from 3i missed a rights issue. It created a three-week panic.' And Brendan Farrell explains what happened during one rights issue: 'We had to drop the share price. It is very difficult to explain away why your biggest investor won't put up the money.'

It can be difficult to persuade a new investor to invest in those circumstances. Potential investors become very discouraged by the refusal of another, who presumably should know a great deal about the business, to take up their rights.

Entrepreneurial Fade

Interest and enthusiasm for the business venture is not guaranteed to last for ever. There can be a loss of entrepreneurial oomph in the early stages of a business, when it is seesawing its way through the survival stage. This can be recovered. More damaging is the entrepreneurial fade which can occur when the business should be coasting along nicely and in its expansion stage. For a few, it becomes boring. 'The great skill in business is to continue enthusiastically when the interest has gone out of it.'

Peter Williams Tells the Story of Vamp Health

When I first met Dr Alan Dean, our medical director, late in 1983 I was very impressed with the astonishingly advanced computer system that he had built for general practitioners. But I was also interested in his long-term idea that, if you could get a large number of doctors working in the same way with systems which had compatible medical and drug dictionaries, it might be feasible to aggregate the data anonymously. This would create a medical research databank for monitoring drug safety and carrying out health planning.

So here we had two ideas – the second was dependent on the success of the first. The first idea in itself had difficulties; under 2 per cent of the doctors had computers at the time and, with hindsight, the system was three to five years ahead of its time. The second idea was an unproven long-term concept. It was an inherently complicated, difficult and risky business, but the underlying strategy looked absolutely right on a long-term view. We just couldn't resist going for it.

At the beginning, we had to raise the money based simply on the computerization of doctors and leave out the research side. I suppose our most important early lesson was that we had underestimated the effort it takes to educate a market. It was grindingly hard work; it produced very low sales. The difficulty was exacerbated from time to time in the early years by government intervention of one sort or another. This was generally intended to help the industry, but in virtually every instance was a hindrance.

I remember the first example. It was about three months after we had raised our first round of venture capital from 3i in 1985. The Department of Health announced that they would evaluate all GP computer systems and report on the result in about nine months' time. The day after this announcement, the market dried up to zero. It would, wouldn't it? 3i were understanding and sent in some people to evaluate in detail what we were doing on a daily basis. They concluded we were doing all the right things in the circumstances – tying costs down and carrying on selling hard.

After just over two years, we had revenues of about £1 million per annum and were looking for an injection of stretch money. The costs of educating the market and surviving the Department of Health's 'helping hand' had used up all of our first round of venture capital. We also wanted to complete our pilot project on the research business, which was being run by Dr Gillian Hall at the Centre for Medicines Research and was going well. We raised around £280,000 from

Octagon Industries BES Fund; the terms were agreed literally moments before the bank was about to foreclose on us. 3i hadn't followed, as our original controller had been promoted and the new one viewed the research side as too risky.

In May 1987, just a couple of months after the Octagon money was in, I was at home recovering from mumps (which I had caught from my seven-year-old). My phone started ringing – both from work and various contacts around the market. The rumour was that a major player was going to make a move on the GP market on a scale that would simply wipe out current suppliers, including ourselves. We were now one of the top two. Rumours like this were pretty regular around that time – and nothing had ever come of any of them before. But on Wednesday night, just before midnight, I got a phone call from one of our customer doctors. He had been returning by train from a health meeting in the south-west that night and had overheard the owner of the main competitive system describe how he had licensed his system to a huge public company. The story was that they were going to announce the following Tuesday that they would give away 3,000 multi-user computer systems completely free to doctors, in exchange for medical data and research work. That gave me enough to go on to make further inquiries and verify the story in the next twenty-four hours.

It was true. A large public company was going to inject around £20 million of equipment and systems completely free straight into our market-place starting next Tuesday. Dr Alan Dean, James Loch (commercial and financial director) and Ian Collins (marketing director) met me in my back garden to discuss the position. Apart from succumbing to blind panic, we decided that what the business needed to do was:

– to hold market share. At this stage, the market penetration was still only about 10–12 per cent. If we gave up substantial market share to a major player, we were unlikely ever to get it back;

– to create cash, as even after the recent funding the balance sheet was not very strong, and certainly not strong enough to fight in the market on equal terms with a major public company;

– to create time to see the results of our research pilot project which was due to end in a couple of months' time. (We already knew that the results looked pretty good.) We didn't like the research idea being taken over by somebody else.

We had a twenty-four-hour moratorium. Each of us was to think how we could achieve these objectives – and then we would brainstorm.

The following day we came up with a plan. First, we felt that what the competitor was doing was really setting a very high price for the data. The questions were: Was it worth competing and matching the price? Or should we shut up shop, and move on? Our calculations showed that the price set would appear to be in the £15–20 million range or, if you financed it, an annualized £6 million. If the data arrived and were correctly validated, they could be very valuable indeed and dwarf these costs. But it would be a long-term haul – several years for the database to reach maturity. In principle, we agreed that we should compete.

We moved on to the slight problem that we didn't have any money and were somewhat short of time to deal with this pre-emptive strike. To compete effectively, we decided to 'borrow' the competitor's marketing and PR platform. We would launch our own alternative 'free scheme' at the same time on the same day. Today was Friday; launch date was next Tuesday.

James Loch came up with a stroke of genius. At the time, it was tax-efficient for doctors to lease their computer systems – and nearly all did so. James suggested we simply write an entirely separate research agreement setting out the research protocol required, the necessity of participating in validation, dealing with confidentiality issues and so on. We would make the consideration for the data a monthly payment that exceeded the doctor's leasing payment by a small amount. Furthermore, if for any reason after an allotted time the doctor didn't keep up to the protocol, the research payment could be stopped. But the doctor had to understand that he or she had leased the computer, and would have to honour the lease.

This injected the necessary discipline and control into the research project. It also meant that we received the full price for the delivered computer system from the leasing company, around £15,000, but only had to pay out for the data on a monthly basis at around £500. This meant that we were cash-positive for about fifteen months!

Once we had conceived our plan, which we labelled the 'no-cost option', I phoned each of the investors to give them background, told them that we did have a plan and it was going to get extremely noisy. It would sound as if we were going to be spending millions of pounds, but our offer was not in fact particularly risky. If the doctors did not reach the right standards for the data, we would not have to continue payments and they would have enjoyed effectively a 30 per cent discount on their system for the first year trying to reach the standard. But if they did reach the standard, we would have a lot of good data, in which case one ought to be able to raise the funding for the project. Anyway, I explained that we didn't have time for explanations or committees; we would be grateful if they would simply sit on their hands and let us get on with it. To their credit, they did.

The weekend was spent with the respective managers planning and preparing for the launch. I continued to orchestrate from my garden with my portable-phone extension. Ian Collins ran a special private advance press briefing on the Sunday afternoon and we launched on Tuesday.

The response and furore that followed was like a tidal wave. We took something approaching 3,000 inquiries in the following weeks (the total workforce was twelve at the time). We had set our target as 1,000 systems under this scheme. This would give a 5-million-patient databank. On 20 May, eight days after the launch, we began installing one practice per working day and kept that up for ten months. Up until then, sales of five systems in a month was pretty good.

In fact, it took our competitor until September or October to get their first systems installed. Luckily for us, they had made the classic error and launched before they were operationally ready – presumably, they had hoped to shut down all the competition by their announcement. This gave us a chance to get ahead. I thanked my stars that I had got some really strong people in the management team, who were fully capable of getting on with the job while I started looking for a major backer to provide the next round of funding.

Almost fifteen months to the day after the launch of the 'no-cost option', in August 1988, we completed a £3 million investment from Lazard Brothers and the Pearson Group (owners of the *Financial Times*, Penguin and a variety of other interests) which gave them a 24 per cent stake in the company.

Now we could fight our competitor on more equal terms. We started to increase our rate of installations and to put in the infrastructure we required. In 1989, we increased revenues from £4 million to just under £12 million, which meant an increase in installations from thirty to nearly one hundred a month. It was a fascinating management exercise; I remember we did complete zero-based budgets every twelve weeks. Effectively, we ran at a planned level for three months and increased it by 30–40 per cent the following three months, and so on. At the same time, we were trying to keep financial ratios and service levels synchronized with the growth.

In the event, we got our 1,000 systems in faster than planned, but that cost more money in research payments. It also took longer than we had planned to gather the data and validate them correctly, so that they were reliable for serious medical research projects. Dr Gillian Hall, who had run the research pilot project, had happily agreed to join us, once the pilot was complete. She headed our embryonic research side and began building the team to gather and validate the data and bring the project to fruition.

The result was that by the end of 1989 the data were really starting to come and looking very good, but we could see that by the end of 1990 we were going to need a further injection of cash, to take us to the point when sales of the research matched its costs. Here we were pioneering yet again! We were educating a different industry this time, the pharmaceutical industry – one of the giants of the world, but pretty conservative.

Apart from needing more money within twelve months, I also felt that it was time to find a managing director for the business. It was now quite substantial and I was really feeling the strain of spending so much time raising finance, as well as trying to run two technically complex, high-growth businesses on a day-to-day basis. Basically, I was pretty tired. Anyway, if we were going to grow rapidly from here and deliver our vision, we needed someone to run the business who had different experience and style.

In August 1990, we employed Richard Goat as managing director. He was an Englishman with true multinational experience. He was at the time a vice-president of a major Texas-based software company. It was rather difficult trying to work out how a founder should hand over his business to a managing director. In the end, I decided to take three weeks' holiday with my family, the first week spent with Richard in Texas giving him background that I thought would be useful and the next two weeks travelling in the States. Richard flew to London and took over the company, without me to get in his way.

I've only occasionally interfered in the day-to-day running of the business. But I keep my hand on the key decisions. It is a hard transition to make – you have to bite your lip. By definition, there are a number of things which I would do differently, although not necessarily better. Overall, I think that between us, we've managed the transition well.

The economic climate had been dramatically worsening during 1990, with interest rates rising rapidly. Our bank chose to inform us ten minutes before our August board meeting that a necessary extension of our facilities, which we had asked for some months before and been led to believe should go through with no major problem, had been kicked up to a committee for a decision and unexpectedly turned down flat. The bank knew that we were already about a quarter of a million into the planned new facility and so we were technically insolvent from that moment.

Our investors were unable to help on that time-scale. I asked Charter-house Bank, who were advising us on the major fund-raising which I was carrying out, to put me in a room the following day with somebody who had the authority to provide a few million pounds on an immediate basis. At 2 o'clock the next afternoon, I was in the offices of Intermediate Capital Group, a mezzanine-finance house whom I had never heard of – in fact I don't think I had even heard of mezzanine finance!

I carefully explained our strategy, the current position of the business and our potential. At 7.30 that evening, I was still there. They held a board meeting and agreed the heads of terms for £2 million of mezzanine finance. This was subject to the bank maintaining the current overdraft facility and their due diligence – seven key phone calls to be made the following morning to check out other people's view of our research data, their validity and value in the long term. The 'legals' were tied up within ten days.

The fees were very high and were probably best summed up by Jean-Loup de Gersigny from Intermediate Capital Group (ICG). He said, 'I am sorry, Peter, we don't agree with rape, but I am afraid, in these circumstances, we have to pillage a little!' Despite the price, I was impressed. They got to the guts of the issues fast and were decisive.

In parallel with this, I had been negotiating since about June with two or three potential trade investors. The intention was that one of them would either buy the company outright or invest £7–10 million to see the research project through to profitability in the mid-nineties. The indications from Pearson were that they were now unlikely to take their investment with us further, but they would not stand in the way of our seeking new backers. I believe this was because they were totally preoccupied at the time with the cash haemorrhage at British Satellite Broadcasting. This placed me at the bottom of the fund-raising ladder once again – I was beginning to feel that this finance business was rather like playing snakes and ladders. The only trouble was that on my board there weren't many ladders!

However by September we had reduced a short-list of three multinational organizations to one. This company went forward on an exclusive basis and carried out full due diligence. The terms were that they would lend us £10 million on a phased basis over the next three years, with an option to buy the business at its market value in years four or five.

By the end of 1990 we were running out of cash fast, as predicted, as the profits from the systems business, while good, were not big enough to cover all the fees to the doctors participating in the research project. Our potential investor was an American corporation (sorry, no takers in Europe), the economy was getting increasingly bad and we were now heading into problems in the Gulf. We were supposed to complete in November and failed. Then, it was to be in December – but it was missed. They felt they would definitely complete in January, so we extracted £500,000 non-returnable at about 11 p.m. on 28 December. This would keep the company solvent, whilst the deal was completed in the next few weeks.

The Gulf war broke in January and the world went to the toilet. During that month, I went back to Pearson, Lazard and my other investors and we agreed in principle a £7 million rights issue as a fallback position, if the Americans didn't go through. By early February, the deal had still not been completed and we were trading on fresh air. One Monday afternoon in the second week of February, I got two phone calls. One was from the president of the US corporation saying that they had finally decided that they could not go ahead. The second call, about half an hour later from one of our major investors, asked us to go to a meeting at their head office at 6 p.m. The meeting lasted ten minutes. The rights issue had also fallen through.

I wondered to myself how I could possibly have designed a business that managed to need large sums of money at the absolute bottom of the economic cycle a few days after war had been declared in the Gulf. Probably any other moment in the previous decade and possibly the following decade would have been absolutely fine.

Two or three of us got together and sat down to see if there were any options. We decided that if we were absolutely straight with the doctors they might agree to renegotiate the terms of the research deal with us. We discussed it informally over the squawk box with the chairman of the user group and two or three other users. They felt it might be worth a go.

We talked it through with ICG, who were very supportive and who agreed to let us have £500,000 to work with to enable us to stay solvent whilst we were negotiating with the doctors. They also agreed to consolidate it into a longer-term facility if we got acceptance from over 90 per cent of the research doctors, by Saturday of the following week. If we failed, the £500,000 and their other debts would be called and the company would close.

We designed and produced all the necessary legal documentation for a new scheme. Our solicitor from Rowe & Maw sat up all night, drafting it. He faxed it through to my home at 4.30 a.m. We asked the doctors to waive their old agreement and the future payments due under it. In return, we offered them a new twenty-five-year profit-sharing agreement, whereby rather than receiving a monthly fixed fee, they would now share half the profits among themselves. In this way, they would get nothing if the business was loss-making but would be true participators in the upside over the longer term. If the doctors agreed, it would transform costs of the research project from £7 million per annum to £1 million per annum – and we had achieved sales of £2 million for research in the previous year.

The next ten days were rather like running an Anneka Rice challenge without any help from the BBC. We were negotiating with 3,000 doctors in 1,000 practices, geographically distributed from Scotland to Land's End and Northern Ireland. Doctors, in general, are an interesting but idiosyncratic and individualistic bunch, not at all given to consensus. That's probably why they are self-employed. Anyway, we designed and printed a complete explanation of the situation with fully detailed questions and answers on every issue we could think of. Together with all the necessary legal documentation, we mailed it on Thursday and Friday to the 3,000, some forty-eight hours after our decision to go for it. That left the doctors seven or eight days to decide.

We set up special telephone hot lines, which were manned about fifteen hours a day, and a computer network, training each operator to use it. This gave the full details on each practice, including what money we owed to them, what money they owed to us, what their standard of data was, how long they had been in the scheme and how long they had left to run. There was also a series of parameters and free-text areas, which could be completed in real time by the hot-line operator when discussing anything on the phone with the practice. This enabled future calls being taken by different shift operators to have the complete picture. On its own, setting up this network in forty-eight hours was a substantial technical feat, achieved by our technical director, John Evans, and his team.

We also forged very strong and open links to the user group. We met their national panel on the first Saturday morning and set up user-group meetings in every region of the country over the following five or six days. Communications with the doctors over the period were through the hot line (which was manned as far as possible by directors and senior management), area and regional meetings throughout the country on almost every evening, and continuous mailings.

The sand was constantly shifting with new issues and questions arising all the time. The competitors were stunned for two or three days, before taking advantage of our plight by fanning the flames of rumours designed to finish us off. And there were other predators circling around us.

The result was that we ended up doing a full-blown mailing every night, giving an update of the situation and the facts from our point of view. We had six or seven Prontaprint outlets in our area, pretty well dedicated full-time to us over the period. There were teams of temporary 'stuffers' filling the envelopes during the afternoons and early evenings and, on one or two occasions, the Elm Street London sorting office opened specially late for us to accept deliveries from our vans. Operationally, it was a whole new business – probably rather similar to running a general election, but in rather a compressed period of time.

The atmosphere in the building over that period was unbelievable. The lights were on twenty-four hours a day and people just dived in to the areas they were most suited to and worked till they dropped. You could quite often see people flat out asleep at their desks. Whilst some really shone and came to the fore with resilience and imagination, of course a few simply found it all too much and quietly faded away. Our computer database enabled us to have running totals so that anybody could see the scores at any time, and we announced them about twice a day.

A board meeting had been arranged for next Saturday afternoon to report the result to ICG. We were able to report that 92 per cent of the participating doctors had waived the old deal, relieving the company of something like £15 million of contingent liability over the following three years.

This result was a tribute to the doctors and their far-sightedness and willingness to make a sacrifice to support and develop a computer system that had served them well and to keep alive that exciting research project which no one else was willing to finance. But the doctors understood it.

As part of the renegotiation, we agreed to create two limited subsidiary companies: Vamp Health, providing health-care systems, and Vamp Research, a purely medical research company. We also gave three non-executive-director positions on each of those companies to representatives of the general practitioners. This has worked exceptionally well.

Shortly after this, the competitors who had started the whole thing by giving away systems free, closed down their research business, taking a £13 million loss, so we are now the only medical databank of this scale in Europe. The next twelve months was like entering a new world; we could concentrate on managing the business, improving the service, developing the software and looking at new products. Of course, we have had some heavy debts to pay and we have had to be very strict on costs. And both businesses had initially suffered from adverse PR (hardly surprising), but the tide has turned.

The systems business gives high-quality earnings, made up of maintenance of 2,000-plus systems, with over 11,000 screens, sales of other services and products, helpful to the doctors, such as training, communication products and software, and sales to new markets, like dentists and hospitals. The research business is developing a range of standard products we have designed, now that the databank is sufficiently mature. The research databank already has over 9 million man-years of validated information (at September 1992) and is one of the largest and most sophisticated in the world.

I think that the strategic vision which Alan Dean and I discussed over a pint in 1983 has worked out; Vamp is positioned in its final phase to become a really major player in health-care systems and medical research. Like many 'interesting' experiences, it is one of those that, had I known at the start what was going to be involved, I certainly would never have begun. However, once surmounted, the difficulties are soon forgotten and life in the organization moves inexorably on to the next stage. It is very satisfying to see the vision turn into reality, even if it has taken the best part of ten years.

V

EXITS FOR ENTREPRENEURS

How galling to be a paper millionaire one year and a paper pauper the next. And yet how commonly it occurs. Your paper fortune is only as tangible as this year's report and accounts. One of the trials of being an entrepreneur is that you may build a successful business, but unless you exit at the right moment, success can be very short-lived. One mistake, one year's bad results and all your achievements are forgotten. 'The toughest thing about success is that you've got to keep on being a success' (Irving Berlin).

No wonder that it can become tempting to convert paper wealth into gold – or at least some part of it at the optimum point in time. Unfortunately, finding an exit for the business does not automatically mean that paper gains are turned into real ones. For example, if you choose a flotation as your likely route, it can be difficult to realize any of your gain, and impossible to convert all of it. Even with a trade sale, you may find that you are swapping one lot of paper for another.

Timing and achieving an exit is difficult, very difficult. You may be fortunate if you receive an approach out of the blue from a company who wishes to purchase yours, as happened to the founders of Connectair. More likely, you will need to initiate either a flotation or a sale yourself. And this requires great skill in preparing the business, making the right approach, generating the right image for your business and setting the right price. Alistair Jacks has been successful in selling his buy-out vehicle BOS. He says: 'I've always had a theory that there is a time to buy and a time to sell, which is all to do with the life cycle of the business. It's difficult to recognize that point.'

He continues: 'Exiting skill is as valuable as the buying skill. The smartest thing I ever did was to flog the business when I did.'

20

Preparing to Exit

Some entrepreneurs don't want exits. Here is Roger Stubbs of MORI explaining at a conference why they decided to stay independent. 'We went through a year and a half or so looking at the alternatives, partial exits, realization of capital, infusion of capital in the business, in participating in the glamour and in the excitement of being a publicly listed company. The closer we got the more concerned we got. I was reminded of an animal fable.

'A pig and a chicken lived in a farmyard. One morning the chicken spotted a sign saying "Bedrooms to let" and rushed off to tell his friend the pig. The pig was unmoved: "So?" The chicken explained, "It's a wonderful opportunity for a joint venture." The pig pricked up its ears. The chicken continued: "People will come and sleep in the bedrooms and when they get up in the morning they'll be hungry." The pig still didn't understand. "Don't you see?" said the chicken. "They'll be hungry and we can serve them bacon and eggs." The pig sidled away – "I want nothing to do with it!" "Why ever not?!" "Look," said the pig, "if these people come and sleep here and wake up in the morning hungry and we serve them bacon and eggs, it's all right for you because you will be participating, but I will be involved."

'That is the way we felt when we got involved with the City. We felt we were being sliced up for bacon.'

There are many entrepreneurs who will sympathize with the feelings that the MORI people had when dealing with the City. And, of course, it's not just dislike of the alternatives which persuades businesses to remain independent. Concern for job satisfaction, the security of employees, the quality of the firm's product, the commitment to the customers, a desire to retain a long-term approach to the development of the business and the lifestyle of the management team are all important factors which might persuade you to retain your independence as long as possible.

Why Exit?

One fundamental difficulty which many entrepreneurs face is that the venture capitalists need an exit – not all, but many funds are run on the basis that they will be wound up in five years or so and the proceeds paid out to the original investors. There will come a time, if you have a venture-capital backer with this objective, when you will come under increasing pressure to provide an exit. The alternatives for you are:

– to float the business, with the venture capitalist selling shares at the time of the float; or

– to find a trade buyer for the whole business, with the management team possibly retaining an interest, whether by choice or not; or

– to find an investor willing to purchase just the exiting investor's stake; or

– to try to fund a purchase of the original investor's stake by the management team, inevitably with the backing of another institutional investor.

It is not only the venture capitalists who want exits. You and the management team may look for an exit. The squirrel instinct can emerge some years into your business venture. Both you, and the rest of the management team, could be beset by the desire to turn paper wealth into the real thing. How tantalizing to know that you are wealthy, but to be unable to use it as you wish, because it is unobtainable. There is fear, too. You have been able to make your business venture a success, but can you keep it up? Certainly Robert Wright of Connectair cites this as one of the reasons why he seriously considered an exit. He had built up the business until it had the right to some 6,600 take-off and landing slots a year – a number of slots quite out of proportion to the company's size. He realized that times were getting increasingly tough for small companies in the airline business and that the opportunity to capitalize on the slot allocations would not last for ever. This was because there was increasing pressure on runway space and he might lose many of his slot allocations to companies operating larger planes. So when an offer came from the

International Leisure Group, which had unsuccessfully bid against Connectair for one of the three route licences, Robert accepted a very generous deal, after some wrangling.

Alistair Jacks came to the decision to sell BOS, a computer software group, because both the venture capitalists and the management team (although not himself) wanted to be out. He says: 'Keeping the management team together for for ever and a day is not possible. I would have needed to reshape the business; it could have been done, but this would have put the business into a number of years of renaissance with all the inherent risk. We were at a fork in the road.

'I would have needed to carry the investors for another three years if I wanted to do this – so this was the time to cash in our chips.'

He continues: 'I personally didn't feel that I had had enough. But two of the shareholders had. They had got to the point where they believed that what they had in the business was of value, but it was landlocked.'

The squirrel instinct is not the only motivator. Sometimes the management team, or some members of it, simply wish to move on to other challenges. You may have a new idea or wish to move to a new location. You may also simply be tired of the stress and strain of holding the edifice together, because inevitably in most cases you provide the glue which keeps the structure upright. Finally, as the management task changes over time, you might lose interest.

With a start-up particularly, the nature of the management task changes from what it was in the early years. As each individual develops as an entrepreneur during the founding period, greater emphasis is put upon an entrepreneurial approach with its individual, directed style. Such a style is very seductive. When the business develops, it requires a more professional management approach, involving consensus and personnel development. An entrepreneurial leader can find this very boring, because it appears to be very slow-moving in comparison to the early days. So you may decide that you no longer have the patience necessary to carry on performing a good management task.

Another reason why the management team might decide that they, or one member of it, no longer wishes to take the business forward is advancing age. One of the buy-in pair at Fernox was already in his fifties at the time of the buy-in. After a few years the business became more successful, but Edwin Davies was looking to retire; it could have become a problem. The only sensible decision was to sell out at some point.

Whatever the motivation, financial or personal, which lies behind the desire for you or the management team to exit the business, it remains, however, a difficult feat to achieve. If you float, the stock market would be very nervous at the idea that you or substantial parts of the team were leaving or selling their shares. It's probably impossible to carry this off successfully. Indeed, Richard Atkinson of Eurocamp states quite clearly: 'If you float you've got to be prepared to see your future with the business. If you really want to cash in, you can't float.'

Even with a trade sale, the purchaser very often wants the founding team to carry the business forward, believing that in part what is being bought is the management team and its skills.

Personal reasons are not the only factors which determine the timing of an exit: business reasons are equally prominent. John Leighfield of AT & T Istel explains why they decided to look for a buyer two years after the buy-out. 'Originally the idea was that we would float around 1991/92. But by 1988 we were a lot more successful than our business plans had forecast; this had the effect of making us rethink and see what future there was for Istel in the nineties. We came to the conclusion that our industry would consolidate and companies would get bigger. One key reason is that customers are getting more global. So what would Istel do? We needed to find a partner. If not, we would be highly vulnerable in the early/late nineties. This wasn't a unanimous conclusion: there was lots of blood, sweat and tears in coming to a conclusion on this.'

Some businesses need the backing of a large parent company with its long pocket to enable them to carry on growing at the rate which will allow them to exploit their product or skills to the full. Waterstone's formed a four-year joint venture with W. H. Smith to enable them to carry on creating 'the best bookshops in the world'. The joint venture includes a fixed exit on a fixed rating.

There can also be a wish to raise a substantial sum of money. For example, Headline Book Publishing PLC floated on the main market of the stock exchange in April 1991. The float was combined with a fund-raising. The business raised £5.25 million gross (£4.8 million net) to finance future development.

With management buy-outs, the imperative motivation can be financial: the need to replace debt with equity. At the time of the Eurocamp buy-out the team were aware that because they were servicing such a high level of debt, there was significant risk in not floating the company at the earliest possible moment, because it would be difficult to sustain on a long-term basis. Richard Atkinson explains: 'It was very highly geared. This was important and useful in the short-term, but it was potentially hazardous in the long term.' The team achieved their objective, floating in July 1991.

Porth was another buy-out vehicle which threw off the heavy mantle of debt by floating within two years of the purchase. Says Neill Bell: 'It wasn't going to be a problem surviving but it was going to be a tremendous millstone around our neck. We were on loan stock 3¾ per cent above base rate. Flotation has been the best thing we ever did because we got rid of all those onerous sort of loans.' Despite shedding this heavy burden, Porth had problems in 1991 because of the recession, like many of the other companies which have been mentioned in this book.

Where is the Value? A Frank Look at Your Business

Generally speaking, the value of a business lies in the stream of profits and earnings it will generate over time. But trade buyers and stock-market investors look at other aspects in setting a value on the business. For example, Tim Waterstone, at a conference organized by the Employment Department, listed these factors which might hold value for a trade buyer:

- brand image, especially if you're recognized in the market-place;

- product innovation: a creative owner is always likely to expand the company;

- growing market share, especially if it's irritatingly fast;

- a high public profile makes it easier for the buyer to justify a high price;

- genius of management: that spark which is not always otherwise available to a large company;

- property assets.

Robert Wright discovered that his business had a far greater value than he had estimated by looking at the stream of earnings he was generating for himself and his family. In 1987, the idea of selling out was germinated when it was suggested to him, while attending a venture-capital seminar, that his company was worth around £6 million.

'I was flabbergasted,' said Robert. He had assumed that the company was worth around ten times less. The difference in the valuation arose because he had not valued the main asset of the company: the routes Connectair owned and the number of take-off and landing slots it was allocated.

All the other variables listed above may be strategically important for a trade buyer, who may place a much greater value on these than on the strict formula of profits. Institutional investors may look at the same factors and also may place emphasis in their valuation on items such as:

- the quality of the earnings;

- the company's growth visibility;

- the quality of the management team (lone entrepreneurs are not popular in the post-Maxwell era);

- financial controls and prudent accounting policies.

The quality of the earnings is an important factor. It covers a number of intangible items, such as the proportion of sales that are made to blue-chip customers, the persistence of the revenue stream (making further sales to your existing customer base), the barriers to entry which you have created in your market-place, the existence of strong distribution channels and so on. Some of the negative factors which investors might look at include:

- excessive dependence on a few large customers;

- insecure supply arrangements;

- exchange risks;

- cyclical exposure of customers;

- downward price trends;

- market saturation;

- single product with no follow-on;

- risks beyond the control of the company.

These positive and negative factors will affect the valuation put by investors on the company's earnings, increasing and decreasing the price/earnings ratio which is applied on an exit.

Preparing for an Exit

Sometimes it might seem that you spend the first three years surviving and the next three years looking for an exit. Of course, the time-scale is wrong. With start-ups and possibly buy-ins, you may not be able to achieve an exit in anything like that period – ten years is more likely (although Headline floated within five years of its founding, but the team do not regard this as an exit).

With buy-outs, the time-scale can be shorter. Indeed, the Eurocamp team were preparing for a flotation virtually as soon as they had completed the buy-out. They talked straight away to merchant banks, brokers and financial public relations companies and got the requisite non-executive directors on board.

However, the principle of preparing for the exit is sound. Certainly, if you consider that you may wish to seek a buyer or float, you should take a long, hard look at your business, at least three years before your intended time for disposal. Do you want an exit? Do you want to find a trade buyer, or would you prefer to float? What can you do to increase the attractiveness of the business to a trade buyer or a stock-market investor?

Buyers and investors prefer steady and good growth in earnings in the years before an exit. There may be ways you can improve the level of earnings, certainly you may be able to make the earnings more secure by focusing on existing customers as well as new ones. Richard Atkinson explains their thoughts: 'We were conscious that an uneven performance in profit growth would push the float back. We could more easily get away with fluctuations in earnings as a private company, or even as a public company, but not in the few years before flotation. We felt under quite a lot of pressure not to go backwards.'

There is also the clarity of your story to consider. Investors, whether stock-market, institutional or trade, like simple, straightforward stories. Complexity clouds the underlying issues of current and future earnings. Concentrate on ridding the business of any oddities or complexities in the years before an exit.

Your business may need to be adapted to cope with the more rigorous reporting requirements for a public company if you are aiming for a float. Review your advisers, too. Is your auditor appropriate for your business at this stage? Unfortunately, well-known names are of consequence to investors, so a national firm of accountants with a good reputation should be taken on as your auditors. This also applies to your legal advisers. At the time of the flotation, you will be required to produce a prospectus and your figures will be rigorously examined. Whatever you do, don't be tempted to fiddle the numbers, now or at all – you'll be found out.

Other steps you can take are to identify the main assets of your business: your brand, your market share, your premises and whatever. What steps can you take which will enable you to improve their visibility to potential buyers? You need to stand back and dispassionately consider your public image.

It's also helpful to improve the public profile of the business. Derrick Bumpsteed of Exacta is taking steps to achieve that. 'We try and differentiate ourselves, we give lots of information to our investors, we produce a glossy annual report and accounts as though we are a public company and we push those out and about. We usually have a press conference to announce our results – being in Scotland, we can normally get in the *Financial Times* even though we are unquoted. I think that's the fastest way to get any recognition.'

A Partial Exit

Some entrepreneurs don't wish to sell out completely and would prefer not to float, but would like to be able to realize part of their holding to consolidate their personal finances. Unfortunately, this is the most difficult of all the options to achieve. Indeed, the venture capitalists are likely to have written into the original shareholders' agreement that you cannot do this without providing an exit or partial exit for the venture capitalists at the same time. In any case, few individuals wish to invest in unquoted companies on what might be for them a substantial basis. Few venture-capital funds want to buy any of the founding team's shares. And trade investors are unlikely to be interested in what might be considered a very small stake in a company. Desire for a partial exit drives to the full-scale sell-out or float.

Flotation would appear to be the best solution to a partial exit. You may be able to realize part of your shares and still gain all the benefit of the future growth which you forecast. For example, the Eurocamp team realized 15 per cent of their shares on flotation. 'And we have income coming from our dividends, so no one is complaining!' says Atkinson.

21

Choice of Exit

There are times when it is impossible to achieve an exit; occasions when it might be possible but would be at a low value; and there is perfection – the opportunity, the right value and full steam ahead. In difficult economic climates, no matter how talented you are, there may be little that can be done to encourage a sale or a float. Part of the exiting skill you require is to be able to choose the right moment for your business.

The poor economic start to the nineties has meant a dearth of exit opportunities for private businesses. Values have dropped dramatically. Stoy Hayward calculates a private-company price index, published in *Acquisitions Monthly*. This shows that the price/earnings ratio attached to private companies had halved between 1987 and 1991. In the last quarter of 1991 it was 8.3 times earnings, but has shown some recovery in 1992. In the first quarter the P/E ratio rose to 9.2 times earnings and showed a further improvement to 9.8 times in the second quarter. What this means is that the same company sold in 1987 would have achieved a price tag double that which would be set in 1991 and 1992. The gap between the rating for FTSE 500 and private companies has also widened considerably and shows a discount of around 38 per cent (June 1992).

Some management teams have an extra incentive to time their exit to perfection. If part of the financing package includes a ratchet or reverse ratchet, one of the factors which might trigger the ratchet is achieving flotation by a certain date – and missing the date can considerably reduce the return to the management. This applied to the Eurocamp team. Richard Atkinson explains: 'From a personal point of view the quicker we found an exit, the better our position was. We missed the first step in the ratchet and if it had gone on a couple of years, it would have got much less attractive.'

The application of ratchets exaggerates the return to the management team. The Eurocamp deal included a ratchet element which applied to the value obtained for the shares. 'The difference between achieving a P/E of 9 or a P/E of 11 had a huge effect on our personal wealth,' explains Atkinson. In fact, the company was floated on a P/E of 10.8. 'It was past the critical gearing point as far as we were concerned.'

It is not only the values which have fallen, there have also been fewer completed deals. The CMBOR reported only forty-five takeovers of buy-outs in 1990, compared with eighty-two a year earlier.

Floating has not fared very much better for companies with, say, £10 million turnover. The Unlisted Securities Market has stalled and the main market doesn't always provide a very positive environment for companies of that size. The small market which can be generated in the shares inevitably means that it will be valued on a low rating. And as with trade sales, there has been a great fall in the amount of activity – only three buy-outs floated in 1990, compared to eleven in 1989. Atkinson again: 'The original target was to float after two years and we were aiming for October 1990. We had had two very good years. But the stock market went down the tubes and then there was the Gulf war – and this affected our business. But everything recovered after the war. This gave us the opportunity to float. We were advised that the opportunities would be very fleeting. So we set July 1991 as flotation date.' This failure of the USM to provide a steady exit route for private companies continues. *Acquisitions Monthly* reports only two companies were admitted in the first quarter of 1992.

It is a cliché, but times change. The underperformance of small company shares on the stock market in the 1988 to 1992 period is a reversal of the long-term trend. It may be sheer optimism to expect that the attitude to small companies will turn full circle, but surely it will happen at some stage. Conditions will alter in the trade-sale market, too. Companies acquisitive in the recession are looking to pick up fundamentally sound companies on very low ratings. When the economy is in a healthier state, there will be a re-emergence of companies acquiring for strategic reasons. And this reassessment may have begun in 1992. *Acquisitions Monthly* reports that there were 101 completed private acquisitions (excluding buy-outs) in the first quarter of 1992, compared with 56 in the final quarter of 1991.

A trade sale and a float fulfil quite different objectives. And neither might meet your wish to release all, or some, of your capital. So at some stage in the evolutionary process, an assessment needs to be carried out covering personal and business objectives. An exit needs planning.

A Trade Sale – Why and Why Not

Other things being equal, a trade sale will achieve a higher valuation than a sale on the market. John Leighfield explains that with a trade sale, 'there is always a control premium, so you get a higher value. It's always easier to sell the idea to one purchaser than a market.'

Values can be enhanced even more if there are several companies interested in acquiring yours. If your business is considered to be very strategic for a much larger business such that the bidders are very keen to ensure that you don't fall into a competitor's hands, ratings can go sky high. Tim Waterstone relates that they had worked out a possible price for flotation in the spring of 1991, but the deal which W. H. Smith offered doubled this. And there are apocryphal tales of companies being sold on ratings of 60- and 70-plus at the end of the eighties – how this compares with the average of 8.3 reported in the Stoy Hayward index for the last quarter of 1991!

Higher values are not the only advantage. If the trade buyer is a large business you may be able to negotiate a cash payment, or even if it is the other company's paper, the restrictions on selling the shares may not be too onerous. Within a short space of time you may have converted them into cash. With a smaller company, this may not be a possibility.

There is a further advantage. You may not wish to stay full-time or at all with the business. Not only may you wish to take out your investment, you may also have decided that you want to be out of the business altogether. It's not guaranteed that you may be able to achieve this with a trade sale, but it is more achievable than by floating. Some purchasers may be quite happy to see the back of the founder; they may wish to bring in their own management. Other purchasers, however, may be insistent that you must stay, and even the suggestion that you have lost interest or your appetite for further growth may be sufficient to frighten off buyers. So proceed with care.

The final advantage of a trade buyer is that they may bring 'something to the party' – they may have international presence, a deep pocket, or strength in a market-place. You may be able to take advantage of these, grow your business further under their umbrella and at the same time earn yourself further payment, although earn-outs need very careful thought.

Of course, there are disadvantages in trade sales. These are funda-mentally focused on the potential loss of independence, which can lead to bitter disputes, ending with the founding management team being kicked out of the business. Great attention needs to be paid to these areas in negotiating any deal.

How to Approach a Trade Sale

Some businesses just attract purchasers. William Stogdon relates how a number of buyers sniffed around Fernox before they finally sold out to Cookson. And Connectair had not been actively seeking buyers when they received offers.

However, it is possible to generate interest if none has so far been displayed by potential purchasers. One approach is to work out a short list of businesses which you consider might be interested, once they know your story. Contact the chairman of the business and ask if you can meet them to ask their advice on floating or selling the business. If you carry this out in a subtle way, you may find that the business suddenly wonders why they don't purchase your enterprise. This was the approach which worked for Alistair Jacks. He explains: 'I didn't do a major exercise to find a buyer. I had to sell to a public company, because I reckoned that paper would be involved and I would be tied in. I targeted three companies which had floated on the USM in the previous two years. I went along and asked their advice on floating – that was the pretext – but two of them said, "Why don't we buy it?"'

John Leighfield adopted a more structured approach, after all it was a much bigger sale to make. 'I went round and talked to lots of people who had sold out to gain their advice. I chose a traditional merchant bank, Fleming, and a US company, Broadview, which specializes in acquisitions in the information-technology field. Together we came up with a list of sixty companies which might be possible purchasers. This we reduced to twenty. We sent around a selling memorandum, setting down conditions under which we were prepared to be acquired, which was a bit cheeky. We effectively said, "We might talk to you if you fit what we want!"'

A selling memorandum is a document which needs to be prepared with the same care as a business plan. Essentially, its aim is to attract a potential purchaser's interest and to encourage a closer look at your business.

Do you need advisers to help you find potential buyers? Perhaps you should hesitate for a moment. It's very likely that you will know the businesses in your industry that are going to be interested in your company. Whether the corporate-finance advisers will really earn their fee may in this situation be debatable – and their fees are large. Clearly excellent legal and tax advice is required, but as with raising venture capital, the value of an introducer is less certain.

Negotiating the Trade Sale

The simplest deal is the straight cash purchase with the founder leaving on the day of completion. More likely, there will be a purchase with shares with a time restriction placed on when you can sell them. This could be hazardous. Who knows what will happen to the share price of the purchaser in the next year or so? And don't forget that you are not the major influence on what happens to the value of these shares.

Another potential restriction might be a requirement for the founder to stay on in the business. Two years is the common period. Tony Davies was required to stay for two years on selling his company, as was Alistair Jacks on selling BOS. After leaving there may be some sort of non-competition restriction. For example, Robert Wright on the sale of Connectair agreed that he would not set up operations at any

London airport for two years, which he did not consider an onerous limitation.

However, life gets very complicated if the vendor and the purchaser want to complete the deal but can't agree on the price. Towards the end of the eighties there was a plethora of deals involving earn-outs – and this is dangerous territory. To a vendor and a purchaser, they can be a manacle or an Aladdin's lamp. One of you will be a winner and the other the loser. Your task during negotiation is to ensure that you end up with the benefit.

You will need to agree a period for the earn-out. Some propose five or seven years, which seems completely ludicrous. During the earn-out period, it is in the vendor's interest to maximize the profits of the business, even if this is harmful to the interests of the group as a whole. The buyer may decide that he wants to integrate the business into the group. Five to seven years is an awfully long time in the history of any business. Most people would suggest that one to three years is a more realistic period. Tim Waterstone views it rather differently. At a conference, he said: 'The period of the earn-out should bring your company to an optimum profit point (e.g. at the end of a maturity cycle of capital investment, and before the next one begins). In practice, this is likely to be three to four years.'

Another likely problem area to focus on closely is the definition of what constitutes profit. What happens if the purchaser operates different accounting rules? Or wants to take over responsibility for the accounting function at head office? Common areas of disagreement in the calculation of profits are the valuation of stock and work in progress. Pre-tax profits should be the basis for the earn-out calculation, not the after-tax figure. Again this mitigates the likelihood of future disagreement and disappointment.

The purchaser might want to set a limit on the maximum which could be paid out. This is on the basis that if there is no maximum, there is too much incentive for you to run the business to maximize your earn-out payments rather than to emphasize the health of the business.

How much independence will you have during the earn-out period? Any integration inevitably muddies the picture and means the earn-out is impossible to calculate correctly. Many earn-outs are negotiated away after completion because of the difficulties of independence and integration. It depends on the reason for selling your business, but if it partly stemmed from the desire to capitalize on some of the advantages obtained from the larger business, it can be difficult to utilize these while staying independent. These issues need clarifying before completion.

Major problems could emerge for you later on if it transpires that the purchaser cannot pay for the business at the end of the earn-out period – a notion which is not impossible to imagine. Some publicly quoted companies have disclosed that they have sizeable earn-out liabilities. The possibility of your buyer not being able to come up with the goods should be catered for in your agreement. For example, you might specify that if this is the case, you can regain control of the business and the terms on which this can be done.

Finally, the earn-out should not be the whole deal. There should be a guaranteed minimum value for the business regardless of what happens during the earn-out period. This price should reflect the present performance of the business. Any additional payments earned during the earn-out period should reflect further improvements in the profits. Try to negotiate that the guaranteed minimum is a cash payment.

A Flotation – Why and Why Not

You must know why you want to float. If you or the management team want cash, floating may not be the answer, as there is a loss of credibility if the management team sell a major proportion of their holdings at the time of the float. One major advantage of seeking a quote is that vendors of other businesses will accept your shares as payment, but would not accept the shares of an unquoted company in the same way.

This is one of the reasons for the flotation of Headline. Certainly, Tim Hely Hutchinson does not view the flotation of Headline as an exit, but as a stage in its development, considering that there is still considerable growth to come. Indeed, the directors did not sell shares. On the contrary, seven out of nine of the directors bought more at the time of the float. He says: 'We wanted to retain day-to-day control of the business. We saw the float as preparing for the next stage, strengthening the balance sheet and making ourselves look more attractive to make acquisitions.' Headline was floated on the main market, not the USM, although the company is still quite small. His reasoning is as follows: 'The requirements for the USM and the main market are so close that there is relatively little cost difference. And it is more prestigious to be quoted on the main market.'

Another reason for deciding to float the business is to exchange debt for equity or to raise fresh equity. So Porth and Eurocamp wanted to reduce the debt levels; Headline wanted to raise fresh funds for expansion.

Autonomy and independence are other factors influencing the choice of exit in favour of a float. For entrepreneurs who have left the large-company environment, and have relished the ability to determine their own destiny, retreating to the corporate fold is a difficult decision. Richard Atkinson again: 'We seriously considered a trade sale but flotation was the favourite. The reason was partly the desire for independence and partly the desire to avoid disappointment for the staff.'

Mike Stalbow, the financial director of Tibbett & Britten, identified at a conference six reasons why this management buy-out chose to float in 1986:

- new equity capital was needed to assist in financing a major expansion programme;

- paper could be used for acquisitions which would provide flexibility in financing the diversification programme;

- share-option schemes could be introduced for management and employees;

- flotation gave the company status and credibility with its customers and other blue-chip customers;

- the stock market was buoyant;

- gearing could be reduced.

He identified a further benefit which was that the MBO team could sell some shares and use the proceeds to 'buy back' their houses from the bank which had taken them as security against loans to finance MBO.

However, flotation is not all roses. There are concomitant disadvantages. Tim Waterstone pinpoints one which may not be readily apparent. Before his deal with W. H. Smith, he says 'We were getting three offers a week. This is OK while you're a private business, but once you're a public company it would be difficult to ward them off. We couldn't have defended ourselves against a takeover.'

While this is a very practical objection to flotation, other entrepreneurs are fundamentally opposed to the idea, because of the extra restrictions and the extra publicity. William Stogdon sold Fernox to the Cookson group. He says: 'I was never interested in a float. I didn't want my company to go public with all that it entails. It's hard enough running a business without the added pressure of outside shareholders, the City and the press on top.'

Richard Atkinson explains the differences as he sees them so far between being private and being public, but he stresses that he has not been in charge of a public company for long enough to give a definitive view. 'Both the financial director and I have to spend a fair bit of time making presentations and talking on the phone. We also have to be more formal in procedures (we had to do that anyway to get prepared for the flotation). And there are certain professional costs which are incurred: the report and accounts, financial PR, registrar's and so on.' Tim Hely Hutchinson makes a further point: 'We have to be more careful in what we say in public about the results, so that no one knows more than the market.' He also considers that if you have always consciously run a private company as if you are looking after other people's money rather than your own then you could seriously consider floating rather than a trade sale.

There is also the question of the value you can obtain if you float rather than sell to a trade buyer. The conventional wisdom is that you will obtain a higher value from the latter – and a number of the entrepreneurs who have helped with this book would concur with the view. But Richard Atkinson felt that this didn't apply for their business. 'I think, in our case, it was a myth that you would obtain a higher value from a trade sale. Our business is a people business. Its value is in the goodwill of the customers and the skill of the management. An immediate problem on a trade sale is the loss of motivation of the management.'

A further disadvantage which is often cited is the cost of flotation. Roger Stubbs of MORI explains their objections: 'We were, among other things, frankly frightened by the cost. The out-of-pocket costs alone frightened us, but you should add the opportunity cost. The Bank of England quarterly report at the end of 1986 said that the average cost of ten offers for sale on the main market raising between £3 and £5 million was 27 per cent of the amount raised, including an underpricing element of 15 per cent. Underpricing was the norm in USM placings: 8 per cent, which doubled the out-of-pocket costs.'

He also relates that the people in the City with whom they were dealing said: '"Don't worry about the flotation expense, it comes out of the money you get on the flotation." We reckon we work damned hard for our money.' He continues: 'The idea that this "funny money" concept existed – where it is not really £200,000 because it comes out of this or that or the other thing – didn't wash with us. Perhaps we're just old-fashioned, but it struck me, frankly, as being a bit of a carve-up.'

There is also the supposed short-termism of the City to antagonize you further. Even with venture capitalists it can be a problem persuading them to back a venture with a long period before the payback. But, once floated on the stock market, you have to contend with the fluctuations of the share price and the pressure if performance in the short term is depressed because of a long-term commitment to a new product or a new market. Both Andrew Lloyd Webber and Richard Branson disliked their companies being public and returned them to their private status.

Finally, there are some other negatives about flotation. For example, there is the pressure from the City to produce an increase in earnings year after year. Furthermore, share prices may be very volatile – and for reasons quite unconnected with what you are doing in the business.

How to Approach a Flotation

Planning needs to start three years or so ahead. 'Preparing to Exit' (Chapter 20) outlines some of the stages which you will need to process in bringing your company to market.

The first step probably is to appoint advisers – or to review your existing ones to assess their appropriateness for this new stage. Sometimes when people get in the City environment, they get overawed and fail to use their common sense. You have to focus on the fact that you are buying a set of services, like a window cleaner. You should make people present themselves very carefully and put them through the mangle. Make them tender. Consider using a beauty parade to sort out which advisers are likely to be the perfect fit for your business.

Neill Bell of Porth has a clear view on choosing brokers. He says: 'In picking your broker, look at the size of the company and look at the size of the broker. I think a lot of people make major mistakes by trying to go with a big name. Whereas if you're a small minnow, you must be a realist about these things. If you're a Mickey Mouse company, where are you going to get the best service? You should look at the broker, at the type of account that they handle and the size of the accounts and pick accordingly.'

The position of venture capital backers as you approach flotation needs careful negotiating. Will they want to sell their shares? Will they hold on? In Headline's case, only one of their backers made a minor adjustment at the time of the float – although subsequently one sold out completely as the share price rose by over 30 per cent. Richard Atkinson found their venture-capital investors troublesome. He says: 'We had always had a good relationship with the venture-capital investors but when you get nearer to the float there is potential for interests to diverge. They had a stronger preference for a trade sale than us. There was also a big reluctance on their part to give reasonable guarantees to hold on to their shareholding once the company was public.'

A Note in Conclusion

This book is about some normal people who took the plunge and bought or started a business. Many difficulties were faced – but most were surmounted by a level of resilience and imagination that the protagonists may not have realized they possessed.

For a few, the adventure didn't end as they wanted – administration or receivership rather than growth. But it is fascinating to note that they have gone on to plan new ventures (or, in a couple of cases, returned to corporation life).

The experiences of all those who have helped make this book will have highlighted what is involved in making the transition from manager to entrepreneur – including the cultural change as well as the practical steps which need to be taken. Perhaps the book will inspire you to take the plunge too. If so, you can learn from the experiences described and, I hope, increase your chances of success.

Glossary

Beauty parade

Management buy-out teams ask venture capitalists to attend a 'beauty parade'; they will be required to make a presentation, including outline terms for an offer of finance.

BES

Business Expansion Scheme. In earlier years, an important source of finance for new companies. The scheme is being wound up in 1993.

BIMBO

Buy-in Management Buy-out: a mixture of the two forms of purchase. At least one outside manager will buy part of the company; at least one existing manager will buy part of the company.

Bridge finance

Short-term funding for a company which is on the point of raising new long-term finance or floating.

BVCA

British Venture Capital Association: the trade association for venture capitalists.

Close company

Broadly speaking, if there are five (or fewer) people controlling a company, or it is controlled by its directors, it is likely to be a close company.

Completion

The meeting at which all the legal documents are signed by the directors and the representatives of the venture capitalists. Money is exchanged for various forms of share certificates.

Convertible preference shares

Preference shares with the right to convert into ordinary shares, under some specified terms.

Corporate venturing

This is when a large company buys a stake in a small company, possibly through a venture-capital fund. The intention is to look for new products or markets, or to build a stake which can be used as a springboard for a subsequent acquisition.

Cumulative preference shares

If the company is unable to pay the dividends on these shares, they will be accumulated until the company has the funds to do so.

Deferred shares

Shares, usually issued at a discount, which do not receive dividends. They can generally be converted into ordinary shares at a later date.

Development finance

Finance for growing companies which are profitable, or almost profitable. The funding will be to expand current operations or enter new ones, not to rescue a business.

Due diligence

Detailed analysis and appraisal of the management team and the business plan carried out before the venture-capital fund will invest in the company.

Earn-out

Deferred consideration for manager–shareholders when they sell their business to another. Payment is dependent on the achievement of certain targets.

Employee buy-out

The purchase of a company that extends very widely (beyond the senior management team) among the staff and workforce.

Envy ratio

The ratio at which you can subscribe for shares in a buy-out or buy-in compared to what the venture capitalist is allowed. For example, if the ratio is five, every £1 you invest will secure five times as many of the ordinary shares as every £1 invested by the financial institutions.

Equity kicker

An opportunity to take a greater share of the equity under certain terms. This can apply to either the management team or the venture capitalist.

ESOP

Employee share-ownership plans.

Exit

Selling shareholdings through either a company acquisition or a sale in the stock market after a float.

Fiduciary duty

As an employee and a director of a company, you have certain legal duties towards it, for example, the duty of acting, in good faith, in the best interests of the company.

Followers and leaders

The venture-capital industry is divided into those who will act as lead investors in a company and those who will only follow other investors. The leader may have particular expertise in an industry, for example. The follower may not have the resources to analyse a business proposition in a particular market and may rely on others to carry out the proper assessment.

Formal offer letter

This will set out the investment terms in some detail and form the basis for the legal agreements.

Hands-off venture capitalist

This type of investor uses financial skills to pick winners and treats its investment in the traditional portfolio way, that is, it does not try to interfere in its management.

Hands-on venture capitalist

This type of investor tries to add value to its investments by participating in the management.

Kickers

See Equity kickers.

Leaders and followers

See Followers and leaders.

Legals

The legal formalities which need to be completed before an investment is made by the venture capitalist.

Living dead

Companies which are just managing to trade profitably, but unlikely to become star performers.

Mezzanine finance

An intermediate type of funding, halfway between debt and equity.

NXD

Non-executive director.

Options

Ways of giving management, venture capitalists or intermediaries a chance to get a greater percentage of the ordinary shares of the company.

Pathfinder

A short document summarizing the business plan, which is sent out before the plan to generate interest among venture capitalists without overburdening them with paper and figures.

Preference shares

General term for any share treated preferentially to ordinary shares, for example, often they carry a fixed rate of interest which must be paid before dividends can be paid on ordinary shares. There are many different types: redeemable, convertible, participating.

Ratchet

An arrangement whereby the management can attain a greater share of the equity of the company, by meeting certain targets. These could be targets on profits, exit values and so on. Ratchets are very complex animals.

Redeemable shares

At specified times, the company will have to pay back these shares out of its P&L reserves.

Reverse ratchet

An arrangement whereby the management share of the equity will fall if management fail to meet certain targets. See Ratchet above.

Selling memorandum

A document which is prepared about the company if it puts itself up for sale. It is usually prepared by an independent firm of accountants.

Senior debt

The security for this debt ranks before all other forms of debt in the event of liquidation and receivership.

Shareholder Agreement

A detailed legal document which will govern the relationship between all shareholders, such as the institutional investors, and the management team. It will set limits on the management's authority to carry out certain actions.

Spin-out (or spin-off)

An arrangement whereby an established company will allow a unit to operate more independently, giving a share of equity to the management. This is most likely to occur in areas of new product development.

Stretch finance

Extra funds provided to a start-up which has underperformed its business plan and is not yet at break-even point, but which the venture capitalist assesses that it will soon reach.

Sweat equity

Extra equity, over and above what the managers pay for, which they get in a funding.

SWOT analysis

An analysis of the business's strengths, weaknesses, opportunities and threats which should be incorporated in a business plan.

Syndication

The process by which an investment that is too large to be handled by one investor is spread amongst several.

Tranche

A round of funds that are payable in successive stages, sometimes if the company meets certain targets.

USM

Unlisted Securities Market.

Vendor loan notes

The owner of a company being sold to its management may provide part of the funding or retain an interest in the business by the use of vendor loan notes.

Vulture capitalist

A term of abuse applied to venture capitalists if it is considered that they are being too greedy in their demands.

Warranties

Before funding is provided, various parties who have supplied information on which investment decisions have been based have to "warrant" the accuracy and completeness of the information. They can be sued for damages if they are found to be in breach of the warranties.

Warrants

A right to a share in the equity is given to the holder of warrants when certain events occur.

Recommended Books and Helpful Organizations

Books and Publications That May be Helpful

Colin and Paul Barrow, *The Business Plan Workbook*, Kogan Page, 1990

British Venture Capital Association, *A Guide to Venture Capital, Business Plans and Financing Proposals* and *Directory*

David Clutterbuck and Marion Devine, *Management Buy-outs: Success and Failure Away from the Corporate Apron Strings*, Hutchinson, 1987

David Franks and Lance Blackstone, *Management Buy-outs and Buy-ins*, Kogan Page, 1990

Garry Sharp, *The Insider's Guide to Raising Venture Capital*, Kogan Page, 1991

Sara Williams, *Lloyds Bank Small Business Guide*, Penguin Books, 1992

Organizations That May be Helpful

Alan Patricof Associates, 24 Upper Brook Street, London W1Y 1PD

Alta Berkeley Associates, 9/10 Savile Row, London W1X 1AF

Baronsmead PLC, Clerkenwell House, 67 Clerkenwell Road, London EC1R 5BH

British Venture Capital Association, 1 Surrey Street, London WC2R 2PS

CINVen, Hobart House, Grosvenor Place, London SW1X 7AD

Corporate Venturing Centre, Morgana House, P.O.Box 134, Winterhill, Milton Keynes MK6 1YX

Intermediate Capital Group, 62–3 Threadneedle Street, London EC2R 8HE

Prudential Venture Managers, Audrey House, Ely Place, London EC1N 6SN

Rothschild Ventures Ltd, New Court, St Swithin's Lane, London EC4P 4DU

3i plc, 91 Waterloo Road, London SE1 8XP

Latest News on Entrepreneurs

Richard Atkinson

Now: managing director of Eurocamp PLC, camping holiday specialist.

Deal: MBO from Next, aged 35, in November 1988, raising £30 million.

Previously: managing director of Eurocamp.

Latest news: the company was floated in July 1991. 'Approaching the end of our first full year and expecting to be able to report a very satisfactory result. Still working with the same senior management team and enjoying "quoted life"(by and large!).'

Paul Bates

Now: managing director of Straightset Engineering Services which provides workshops for garages.

Deal: MBO, aged 35, in January 1988, raising £450,000.

Previously: general manager of VL Churchill.

Latest news: 'The company turnover is now £3.5 million and we employ 40 people. Has cash reserves of £500,000 and net assets of £900,000. The company now resides in its own office and warehouse complex which is wholly owned by Straightset (paid for). Although trading conditions are now difficult, the company is enjoying success with its own range of waste-oil handling products.

'Still working in the business, a little wiser, older and balder and hoping the recession will end soon.'

Neill Bell

Now: managing director of Porth Group PLC, Christmas decorations.

Deal: MBO from Gooding Group, aged 39, on 30 June 1987.

Previously: managing director of Porth.

Latest news: trading difficult in the recession. Has split roles of chairman and managing director, with Michael Edwards as chairman.

John Bladon

Now: managing director of Solway Foods Limited, chilled foods.
Deal: start-up, aged 39, in January 1989, raising £1.8 million.
Previously: development director, Freshbake Foods PLC.
Latest news: 'Turnover quadrupled in three years. First factory reached capacity during 1991. Total factory capacity doubled in May 1992. Funds raised by subscription – all shareholders took up their full rights. Company trading profitably.

'Still in harness and looking for acquisitions.'

Brian and Christine Box

Now: Brian – managing director, Christine – director and company secretary of Middle Aston House, a training and conference centre.
Deal: MBO from Dalgety, Brian 58 and Christine 43, in February 1991, raising £1.4 million.
Previously: Brian, principal, and Christine, site manager, both of Middle Aston House.
Latest news: 'After a loss-making first six months, we are now in profit – just! Both working all hours.'

Derrick Bumpsteed

Now: managing director of Exacta, producing printed circuit boards for electronic equipment.
Deal: MBO, aged 44, from STC in April 1986, raising £4.75 million plus bank facilities.
Previously: general manager, STC Exacta.
Latest news: 'Company still trading successfully; made acquisition of BEPI circuits in 1989, now fully integrated with Exacta. Turnover now £30 million.' Derrick still at Exacta.

John Cavill

Now: managing director of Logical Networks plc, selling network products to end-users and value added resellers in the UK.
Deal: start-up, aged 39, in October 1988, raising £200,000.
Previously: managing director, Data Translation Ltd.

Latest news: nominated for the 1992 Venturer of the Year Award, small start-up category.

Mike Clarke

Now: managing director of Perex, a company manufacturing digital tape recorders and touch screens.
Deal: MBO, aged 39, from Sintrom PLC in December 1989, raising £1.4 million (£800,000 venture capital, £600,000 invoice discounting).
Latest news: revenue 1989 £6.1 million, 1990 £6.4 million, 1991 £8.4 million. Profit before tax 1989 £440,000, 1990 £680,000, 1991 £1.13 million. Still under management ownership. 'By this December (1992) all but £200,000 of venture capital paid off. Healthy cash balance.'

Peter Gibson

Now: chairman and managing director of Corin Medical, a manufacturer of orthopaedic devices.
Deal: start-up, aged 39, in May 1985, raising £400,000 in April 1986.
Previously: vice-president of Zimmer International.
Latest news: company continuing to grow. 'This year, we will have turnover more than £5 million, with earnings over £1 million. We have joint venture subsidiaries in France, Denmark and the USA.'

Brian Gilda

Now: chairman and managing director of Peoples Limited, Ford main dealers.
Deal: start-up, aged 33, in July 1983, raising £300,000.
Previously: director Gael Motors (Glasgow) Ltd.
Latest news: group turnover in excess of £65 million. Brian is 'even more determinedly leading group from front'.

Colin Guy

Now: managing director of Agripac (Dundee) Ltd, manufacturer of flexible intermediate bulk carriers.
Deal: MBI, aged 46, in March 1989, raising £600,000.
Previously: managing director of industrial packaging division of Bowater PLC.

Latest news: turnover doubled since buy-in. Has traded profitably in 1990 and 1991.

Stephen Hinton

Now: chief executive of RFS Industries, manufacture and overhauling of railway equipment.
Deal: MBO from British Rail, aged 34, in October 1987, raising £5 million.
Previously: deputy works director, British Rail Engineering.
Latest news: grown to £50-million-plus turnover. Last two years difficult, but full order book for 1993 and trading profitably.

Les Hunt

Now: sales and marketing director of Metalline International Ltd, manufacturers of airfield lighting and electronic equipment for aviation business.
Deal: MBI, aged 37, in November 1988, raising £1.2 million.
Previously: rental depot manager of Zahid Tractor Co.
Latest news: turnover now at around £3 million. Business still in hands of buy-in team and 3i. Les is 'still in harness and likely to be for some time to come'.

Ed Hunter

Now: managing director of Penman Engineering Ltd, manufacturers of safety cabs for construction equipment and specialist vehicle bodywork.
Deal: MBO, aged 40, in January 1984, raising £700,000.
Previously: managing director of Penman.
Latest news: 'Purchased two further small specialist engineering companies in 1991 and consolidated them into a "Penman Engineering Group". Further focus on niche markets for our range of specialist vehicles and export opportunities being vigorously pursued.'

Ed is 'still at the helm'. Awarded an MBE in 1992 New Year's Honours.

Nayyer Hussain

Now: managing director of Martin Electrical Ltd, manufacturers of resistance welding equipment.
Deal: MBI, aged 26, in April 1988, raising £300,000.
Previously: group financial controller for Cundell Industries PLC.
Latest news: 'Doubled Martin's turnover over three years. Commensurate rise in profitability. In November 1991, again with 3i's backing, acquired second engineering company, Don Engineering Ltd, manufacturer of combustion engineering products. Size of total financing £1 million.

Nayyer is 'older, greyer and having integrated our second acquisition actively searching for further opportunities'.

Tim Hely Hutchinson

Now: managing director of Headline Book Publishing PLC.
Deal: start-up, aged 32, in May 1986, raising £1.3 million.
Previously: managing director of Macdonald & Co. (Publishers) Ltd.
Latest news: floated April 1991 and continuing to report good growth.

Alistair Jacks

Now: chairman, West Engineering Ltd.
Deal: MBO, aged 36, in April 1981 of BOS, computer software, raising £100,000.
Previously: sales director of CAP (UK).
Latest news: BOS was sold to Misys in 1988. West Engineering was an MBI financed in October 1991. The company is a Suffolk-based manufacturer of welded spiral tube.

Allen Jones

Now: managing director of A J's Family Restaurants Ltd.
Deal: start-up, aged 50, in April 1987, raising £2.2 million.
Previously: managing director of Happy Eater. Tried an MBO, but business sold to Trust House Forte.
Latest news: 'Struggle continues in extended recession. We now have 23 company-owned sites. We also granted a franchise to Granada PLC for use on seven trunk-road service areas. So the name of A .Js is now

"over the door" at a total of thirty locations from Edinburgh to Saltash. Profit eludes us, but we seem to contribute well to bankers and professionals!'

Allen is 'still in harness, happy but balder, supported by some very hard-working and caring staff'.

David Langston

Now: commercial director, Penny Plain Ltd, Newcastle upon Tyne.
Deal: start-up, aged 40, of Blue Ridge Care Ltd, disposable nappies, which is currently in receivership. Started in March 1984, raising approximately £2.2 million.
Previously: vice-president of Riegel Textile Corporation.

Tony Leach

Now: planning new venture for 1993.
Deal: start-up, aged 39, in February 1982, raising £125,000.
Previously: managing director of Daton Systems Ltd, software for government and local authority sector. Daton sold to AT & T Istel in July 1990.
Latest news: Tony left Daton Systems in October 1992.

John Leighfield

Now: president of AT & T Istel, computer systems.
Deal: MBO, aged 49, in June 1987, raising £35 million.
Previously: managing director of Istel, part of British Leyland.
Latest news: sold to AT & T in October 1989.

Roger McKechnie

Now: chairman of Derwent Valley Foods, manufacturing snacks under Phileas Fogg brand.
Deal: start-up, aged 42, in 1982, raising £500,000.
Previously: Tudor Crisps (division of Smiths).
Latest news: 1992 turnover £24 million. Roger is on to fitness campaign number 53!

Gerry Meredith Smith

Now: founder of Hi-Tech Rentals Ltd.

Deal: MBO, aged 41, in August 1987, of Mohawk Ltd, in the development, distribution and service of computerized printing systems. Raised £4 million. Company went into receivership in 1990 and subsequently sold to Bull.

Latest news: new company, Hi-Tech Rentals, started in late 1990. Successfully completed first year with turnover of £150,000. In 1992, turnover should be nearer £750,000.

Roy Mitchell

Now: retired from Carron.

Deal: MBO, aged 55, of Carron Phoenix, sink manufacturer, raising £1.2 million in October 1985.

Previously: managing director of Carron.

Latest news: Carron floated in 1988 and acquired by Franke of Switzerland. Roy retired in June 1990, after 'settling down' the company under Franke ownership. Currently Chairman of Saunders French & Co. Ltd.

Malcolm Parkinson

Now: chairman Imatronic Ltd.

Deal: start-up, The Retail Corporation (garden centres), aged 42, in August 1988, raising £10 million.

Previously: chief executive of Woolworth.

Latest news: The Retail Corporation now in administration: garden stores at Texas sold to Ladbroke's.

Malcolm is a trustee of National Garden Centre, is running a management company for artists and designers (mounting exhibitions in London, Washington, New York and Tokyo), and is a consultant to an international advertising agency group.

Bert Ramsden

Now: managing director of small group of companies overseas.
Deal: MBI, aged 47, of CEC-Time (inspection and testing equipment for offshore oil industry) in July 1989, raising £2 million. Was joint managing director. The company was sold from receivership in 1991.
Previously: managing director, OIS PLC.

Brindley Reynaud

Now: chairman of Clebern International and three other companies. Company founded in 1989.
Deal: start-up, aged 46, of Calidus Systems (software for distribution systems) in 1985.
Previously: director of Hoskyns.
Latest news: Calidus sold to Pi Holding PLC in August 1990.

Stephen Riley

Now: managing director of The Denby Pottery Co. Ltd.
Deal: MBO, aged 36, in July 1990, raising around £7 million.
Previously: managing director of The Denby Pottery Co. Ltd.
Latest news: turnover has increased from an annualized £9.7 million at the time of the buy-out to £13 million now. Business now has two subsidiaries, one in France and one in the US. Has invested heavily in factory to keep up productivity.

William Stogdon

Now: managing director of Fernox Manufacturing Ltd, central heating chemical treatments.
Deal: MBI, aged 35, in May 1984, raising £600,000.
Previously: business manager, BP Chemicals.
Latest news: Fernox sold to Cookson Group in July 1989. William says: 'Although no longer under original handcuffs, I am still MD of Fernox.'

Stuart Swinden

Now: managing director of EFM, design, manufacture and install educational environments, mainly for science and design and technology.

Deal: MBI, aged 51, in September 1989, raising £600,000.

Previously: managing director of Shandon Scientific Ltd, a subsidiary of Life Sciences International PLC.

Latest news: on acquisition, turnover was £3.1 million to June 1989. For year ended June 1992, turnover was £6.55 million with return on sales of over 5 per cent. Employees have risen from 75 in 1989 to 120 now (September 1992). Currently operating from 52,000 ft^2, compared to original 22,000 ft^2. Stuart is still in harness and planning to continue growth both organically and by acquisition.

Tina Tietjen

Now: joint managing director of Video Arts Ltd, producers and distributors of training videos.

Deal: MBO, aged 42, in December 1989, raising £43.75 million.

Previously: managing director Video Arts.

Latest news: company still trading privately.

Terry Weston

Now: owner of specialist civil engineering company known as Waterseal Ltd.

Deal: MBI, aged 48, of CEC-Time (inspection and testing equipment for offshore oil industry) in July 1989, raising £2 million. Left company in 1991 before company went into receivership.

Previously: joint managing director, CEC-Time.

Latest news: Waterseal employs three staff and ten operatives and provides a waterproofing and joint sealant service to the major civil contractors. Company is based in Durham and currently in the process of opening a Yorkshire office.

Peter Williams

Now: chairman of Vamp Group, computer systems to the health sector and medical database for research.
Deal: start-up in February 1984, at the age of 37, raising £300,000 in January 1985.
Previously: marketing director, Tycom Corporation.
Latest news: now established as a market leader in our niches, with revenues over £14 million and profitable, with 150 employees. Company still private. Now planning next stage of major growth.

James Wooster

Now: chairman of Martin Electric Ltd, manufacturers of resistance welding equipment.
Deal: MBI, aged 34, in April 1988, raising £70,000.
Previously: managing director of Machine Tools International.
Latest news: currently negotiating the sale of a stake to a large Japanese competitor. Has acquired other businesses as principal. General businesses are identified and introduced for a fee to other MBI teams.

Robert Wright

Now: heading up Connectair again, having repurchased business from administrator of ILG.
Deal: original start-up of Connectair in February 1984, aged 35. Sold Connectair to ILG, which went into receivership in 1991.
Previously: pilot, British Airways.
Latest news: raised finance from 3i, Grosvenor, Baronsmead, and Gresham to buy back original business from administrator.